Book Catalogs

Edited by

Robert E. Kingery

and

Maurice F. Tauber

The Scarecrow Press, Inc.

New York   1963

Introduction

The usefulness of book catalogs has been recognized by librarians, researchers, and general users of libraries as these catalogs have been made available. The industry of individuals or library staffs in compiling catalogs of book and other collections has been one of the commendable and outstanding activities in the general areas of publishing and library service. In Europe, book catalogs have had a longer history than in the United States, but actually the shift from the book catalog to the card catalog occurred at the beginning of the twentieth century, when the Library of Congress began its eventful printing and distributing of standardized unit cards. The first Harvard catalog, issued in 1723, was designed to provide information to prospective donors in London of the current holdings in Cambridge. In 1745, Yale's first book catalog was directed at assisting students in learning the contents of the library. Fifteen years later Princeton published its first book catalog to assist users. Seventeen additional catalogs were produced at Princeton before it went to the card catalog. Columbia University and the University of Pennsylvania similarly issued book catalogs periodically for the purpose of describing holdings. The Astor Library, the Boston Athenaeum, the Peabody Institute of Baltimore, and many other American libraries issued book catalogs as aids for those seeking information concerning specific authors and titles, as well as titles concerned with particular subjects.

The disadvantages of the book catalog, as revealed in the papers included in this compilation, have been obvious to those who have worked with both book and card catalogs. The disadvantages, of course, appeared to outweigh the advantages, and libraries moved over to card catalogs when the Library of Congress was able to set up a centralized and cooperative cataloging service which included sets of cards that could be intercalated quickly. The problem of keeping book catalogs up to date, without having too many supplements to examine, was not easily removed. Thus, the card catalog became the common instrument in America. In recent years, the introduction of economical catalog reproduction by various photographic and other devices has made librarians re-examine the theory and philosophy of the card catalog. Moreover, the revived interest in arrangements of the catalog away from the dictionary form has been related to the book catalog. Not the least of the reasons for a renewed interest in book catalogs has been the growing size of the card catalog, with its millions of cards in the larger libraries. Librarians and others have been concerned about the future of this card catalog in respect to both administration and maintenance as well as ease of use by patrons and staff. The large dictionary card catalog has grown in complexity as it has grown in size, and possible reduction of size through partial reproduction in book form has been considered.

The papers in this volume were assembled at the request of the Interdivisional Committee on Book Catalogs of the American Library Association. The Committee had observed the increase in the number of book catalogs in recent years, and was aware of the need to coordinate information concerning them. Even though book catalogs are not new, there are many unanswered questions about them that are being raised. The movement of large regional systems, or county systems, towards the use of book catalogs, the migration of portions of large card catalogs into book form, the making of book catalogs from card catalogs for special collections, the variety of techniques that are being introduced in the production of book catalogs, and the groping for standards for book catalogs are considered in the papers that follow. The observation may be made that there will be more book catalogs in the future, rather than fewer such records, and it is hoped that a consideration of the various aspects of them, as revealed in the literature and the new contributions to this volume, will be helpful. The reprinting of the items which have appeared in the various journals is being made with the permission of the authors and editors, and we are grateful to them for allowing us to use them here. The new papers were prepared at the request of the Interdivisional Committee on Book Catalogs. The authors or the present editors have made minor editorial changes and dropped some of the illustrations in some of the reprinted articles, but they are substantially in the form in which they were published originally. Although this approach results in some overlapping among some papers, the editors decided that cutting these portions would have required rewriting in many instances.

The compilers are grateful to several persons who have aided them in various ways in the preparation of the volume. These are Hubbard W. Ballou, Jean Hannigan, and Edgar W. Snell, Jr.

Robert E. Kingery
Maurice F. Tauber

Table of Contents

The Book Catalog and the Scholar -

A Reexamination of an Old Partnership*

By Jesse H. Shera

If librarians were to select a mentor from Classical mythology, he might well be Janus bifrons to remind them that in their professional philosophy, as well as in their book collections, the best of the past is brought together and preserved for the enrichment of the future. The revival of the library catalog in its earlier codex form gives reality to this symbolism, for the yellowed pages of the book catalog, honored by scholarly tradition, have been endowed with renewed usefulness through recent innovations in the technique of print.

Librarians were driven, according to Archibald MacLeish, to the card catalog "as a choice of evils;" a fortunate, though "logical result of the impossibility of unlimited use of paste and paper, " in the assembly of scrap-book catalogs. [1] Thus he believed that necessity was the mother of "one of the great advances of American librarianship, " a sentiment that reflects the conviction of most catalogers. MacLeish's emphasis upon the fortuitous is significant, for ever since the memorable Sunday morning in the Amherst College Chapel when the beauties of the decimal system and the vision of the new librarianship "flasht" upon the inward eye of Melvil Dewey,

* This paper was presented at the ALA-RTSD/RSD Book Catalogs Interdivisional Committee Program Meeting, July 10, 1961, Cleveland. Library Resources & Technical Services 6:210-216, Summer, 1962.

librarians have been guiding the destinies of their technical processes by Apocalyptic revelation.

The card catalog was not an American invention. Dorothy Norris has found reference to the species in the French Code of 1791,[2]
so the American development may properly be regarded as a rein-
vention. But whatever its origins, the catalog has always been the
librarian's defense against the scholar's contumely, and the 3 x 5
card the manna that has more than once nourished those children of
Biblos when they wandered in the thorny academic wilderness. If
MacLeish's reading of history is correct, certainly the card catalog
stands as one of mankind's greatest monuments to a virtue that was
born of necessity. Throughout the passing years it has come to
symbolize at once the universal key with which one may unlock the
totality of the library's intellectual store, and the scepter of domin-
ion over the limitless boundaries of scholarship toward which its
cards stretch out in neverending line like the progeny of Banquo.
Here, indeed, was the perfect bibliographic tool before which all
men could stand as equals.

The acceptance of the card catalog was not irrational, nor were
its most ardent advocates necessarily blinded by logical inference.
Its one and only virtue--currency, flexibility, responsiveness to
change--seemed quite rationally to compensate for its immobility,
complexity, destructability, and steadily-rising costs of maintenance.
That such a perfect thing could ever reach a point of diminishing returns, or carry within itself the seeds of its own destruction were
quite effectively concealed by the simplicity of its early symmetry.
A half century ago, who could have foreseen that an unprecedented

growth in the bulk and complexity of recorded knowledge would
place upon the card catalog an economic limit to its growth and be-
fuddle its arrangement with aberrant forms of corporate entry or
excessively elaborate subject analyses? On the contrary, in a day
when the book catalog seemed permanently bound, the pun is not un-
intentional, by the rigidities of nineteenth century typographic composition, the card catalog did, indeed, seem to approach the ideal of
the librarian's dream.

But for reasons which are largely psychological, the scholar has
never been entirely happy with the card catalog, even though he has
freely acknowledged its virtues. For centuries, the scholar and the
codex have been constant companions, and they have formed a kind
of silent partnership in the search for truth. The bibliography in
book form was, therefore, a simple and logical extension of this
union to which the efficiency of the card catalog seemed to do vio-
lence. Such great bibliographic monuments as the catalogs of the
British Museum, the Bibliothèque Nationale, the Surgeon General's
Library, the Astor Library and the Gesamtkatalog, to name but a
few, commanded, and for that matter still command, a respect that
one does not readily grant even to such a significant undertaking as
the National Union Catalog at the Library of Congress.

There are probably a variety of reasons for this emotional reaction, certainly not the least of which is the identity that these catalogs have achieved through their association with their compilers.
This is no mere catalog--who touches this touches a man. By contrast, a card catalog represents a continuing operation to which,
through the years, many hands have contributed yet upon which no

one has left the indelible mark of his own personality. Moreover,
the card file has always been the symbol of impersonality, identified largely with personnel records of one kind or another, in which
no one wants to be a mere cross-indexed annotation.   That this is
an irrational emotional reaction does not belie its potency.   Perhaps it derives from the very virtue of the card catalog--its flexibility, and hence its impermanence.   An entry in a book is there
forever, but a card can be withdrawn from a catalog and departing
leave behind it not even a foot print on the sands of time.

Unfortunately, little is known about the ways in which the individual scholar accumulates his store of bibliographic information.
But such studies as have been made suggest that the role of the
card catalog, especially as it relates to the subject analysis of recorded knowledge, is relatively minor as a bibliographic source for
the mature scholar.   Conversation with colleagues, foot notes in
professional writings, published bibliographies, indices, and abstracts supply the main avenues by way of which the scholar reaches
his goal.   There is good reason, then, why the research worker
feels a sense of incompatibility with the card catalog, for the bibliography in book form, whether it represents the contents of a specific library or the accumulated resources of the world of print, ap-
proximates the bibliographic form with which he is most intimately
familiar and in the use of which he is most confidently secure.   In
short, a book catalog "looks good like a bibliography should."
Whether in alphabetical or classified form, the book catalog spreads
its contents before the user with a transparent and obvious efficiency
that a tray of cards can never achieve.   One cannot scan a bank of

cards, in which each is given equal emphasis and none contributes to the differentiation between woods and trees.

Moreover, contrary to the opinions of those who have given us our professional cataloging rules, the scholar does not require, and can even be repelled by, an excess of bibliographic detail. The bibliographic citation with which he is most familiar is but the irreducible minimum, uncluttered by superfluities. The 3 x 5 card, however, provides ample space for such elaboration, and catalogers have not been slow to exploit it for their own esoteric ends. In the book catalog, however, a skillful use of typography, of indentation and subordination, and of lay-out can not only eliminate distracting detail, but also give dimension and reveal relationship.

At the Monticello conference of the Association of Research Libraries, William B. Hamilton, of Duke University, protested excessive attention to the refinements of classification. If it were eliminated, he argued, "we could put our thought and money, and the intelligence of our staffs, into more subject cataloging."[3] But at the same meeting, Joseph S. Fruton, of Yale, maintained with equal vigor for, the fundamental importance of organization, of classification, for "if we say that a library catalog is a finding list, then it should follow that all listings in it are themselves findable..."[4] The book catalog, by the effectiveness with which it displays its contents to the user, would certainly seem to offer the greatest hope of reconciliation of these divergent points of view. Both men, it is to be noted, were impatient with an embarrassment of bibliographic detail, and both agreed that they would be quite content "with sufficient information to identify the item."[5]

The library catalog represents, so far as the present writer
knows at least, the only major use of the card that presupposes
permanence. In business, in industry, even in the world of scholarship, the card symbolizes that which is transitory, impermanent,
subject to constant alteration and change. Until very recent years
librarians themselves regarded the bound volumes of the accession
record the most authoritative and nearly indestructable accounting of
the library's holdings. Today, however, librarians have entrusted
to one of the most impermanent of record forms their one and only
inventory of the totality of their bibliographic store. Such a change
may properly reflect a new concept of the library as a fluid, changing dynamic institution, and in many libraries, in public, college
and particularly in special libraries, this point of view is entirely
appropriate. But the world of scholarship is very heavily dependent
upon the archival function of the library, and there would seem to
be a certain inherent paradox in the ephemeral control of our intellectual heritage.

What then is the balance sheet of these two forms of the library
inventory? To the credit of the card catalog are two impressive
assets: complete flexibility and adaptability to centralization of cataloging procedures. Against these can be charged immobility, impermanence, high maintenance costs and manipulative cumbersome-
ness. The book catalog, on the other hand, suffers from inflexibil-
ity and unresponsiveness to change: in short, extreme susceptibility
to obsolescence. On the other hand, there may be credited to it,
mobility, ease of duplication, low maintenance cost, discouragement
of excessive bibliographic detail, and a format that facilitates use.

With respect to costs of production, the situation is unclear regarding both instruments. No one has yet developed an economical method for the reproduction of cards in limited quantities, and as a result their costs have risen as labor costs have ascended. The spread of cooperative cataloging should, however, mitigate this to a substantial degree. The costs of producing a book catalog have always been regarded as high, though in terms of cost per unit entry such costs may have been exaggerated. E. J. Crane was wont to argue that Chemical Abstracts was relatively cheap because its cost per word, to the buyer, was lower than that for many popular novels. This savors somewhat of the Madison Avenue slogan that, "pound for pound, a Buick is cheaper than butter." But the fact remains that, when one considers the relatively low costs of reproduction in multiple copies, the costs of production of the book catalog have probably been somewhat exaggerated. Moreover, new techniques of photographic reproduction and mechanized composition, through the use of the punched-tape typewriter (Flexowriter), have substantially lowered the production costs of the book catalog, and the future benefits of continued improvement in the technology available to the compositor and printer can at present be but dimly foreseen.

Even this cursory examination of their respective balance sheets reveals that neither bibliographic instrument enjoys a complete monopoly in assets and neither is bankrupt. Each is peculiarly adaptable to its own particular types of situation, and there is ample room for both in the world of scholarship. Only this is certain: that the book catalog is not an anachronism, a vestige of the library's paleolithic age. The bold step of the Library of Congress in returning to the book catalog not only greatly extended access to its bibliographic treasures to many libraries that could never have undertaken the maintenance of a depository set of cards and hence greatly widened its services, but also it directed attention anew to the virtues of the book catalog as a bibliographic device. The decision to incorporate the unique items in the National Union Catalog was a second major step in reaffirming the utility of this traditional bibliographic tool. Here, indeed, as MacLeish said of the original edition, was the beginning of a new chapter in American librarianship. New Serial Titles, begun in 1951 and expanded in coverage in 1953, pioneered in the use of tabulating card technique for the production of a major book catalog undertaking. At about this same time the public library at King County, Washington, and the New York State Library at Albany began to experiment with the same technique for the dissemination of the listings of their resources. The latter has issued listings in the social sciences, and a complete catalog is in preparation. The catalog of the Lamont Library at Harvard is a true reversion to the printed college library catalogs of the nineteenth century, and in it the entries are arranged by subject and identified by a minimum of bibliographic detail. That the procedure was sound is evident from the popularity of the volume.

The King County Library of Seattle, Washington, which has been credited with the initiation of the IBM techniques for the production of a book catalog, produces unbound and ephemeral compilations. The Los Angeles County Library also employs IBM equipment, but for an elaborate listing of both juvenile and adult materials, by subject, by author, and even by foreign language and literary form.   Monthly supplements and annual cumulations keep the listings of adult materials up-to-date.   Techniques similar to those employed in Los Angeles were adopted at the Columbia River Regional Library.   The National Library of Medicine Catalog, which, like New Serial Titles, may be regarded as a supplement to the National Union Catalog, has been reproduced from proportional spaced typewritten copy.   It not only provides complete bibliographic detail, but includes lengthy notes whenever they seem to be appropriate.   Author and subject listings are maintained in separate alphabets.   At the Long Island Lighting Co., of Hicksville, N. Y., punched card techniques are employed to produce a printed book catalog that is distributed to more than one hundred areas.   The major portion of the book is used for three main indexes: title, subject, and author in that order, but information is also included respecting periodicals, and serials, newspapers, films and film strips, clipping file, and miscellaneous.   Distribution of copies has greatly facilitated inter-library cooperation, encouraged inter-library loans, and generally promoted use of the collection.   The use of punched cards also makes possible the preparation of specialized bibliographies, and it is interesting to note that the book catalog has not replaced the card catalog.   The two forms are regarded as supplementing each other, and the latter, i.e., the card catalog, is still used for the recording of substantial amounts of bibliographic detail which, for practical reasons, is omitted from the book form. A Kodak Listomatic Camera, used in conjunction with punched cards, is employed at the Cardiovascular Literature Project at the National

Academy of Science.   This is not, strictly speaking, a library book catalog, but rather an indexing and abstracting service.   It is included here, however, because it illustrates a technique of reproduction that might well be applied to the publication of book catalogs. The libraries of the Monsanto Chemical Co. use punched-card techniques to maintain a union catalog of their holdings indicating author, brief title data, and, of course, location.   The Advanced Systems and Research Library maintained by International Business Machines Corporation at San Jose, California, maintains a comparable catalog showing the combined holdings of four autonomous company libraries on the plant site.   In an article in the November, 1960, issue of Special Libraries, Marjorie Griffin of the IBM Corporation has indicated that the use of punched-cards for the production of printed book catalogs is either currently in progress or under investigation also at the Lake County Public Library of Munster, Indiana; the Massachusetts Institute of Technology Library; The New York Public Library; Southern Illinois University Library at Carbondale; Squibb Institute for Medical Research, New Brunswick, N.J.; and the University of Wisconsin Library School.   However, since she interprets "book catalog" very broadly, to mean almost any current listing of titles, including even such services as the ASTIA Technical Abstracts Bulletin, and Chemical Titles of the Chemical Abstracts Service, her listing is to be viewed with some skepticism. Finally, one should mention the proposed subject and author catalog of National Reactor Testing Station of Phillips Petroleum, near Idaho Falls, Idaho.   This catalog, which will have monthly cumulated supplements, will, according to present plans, be produced from

Multilith mats imprinted by an IBM 704 tabulator.

Even this brief enumeration of activities indicates a substantial increase since 1950 in the prevalence of book catalogs and the new and constantly improving methods of reproduction suggest no diminution of this trend. At the present time, these new methods of reproduction can be identified as of three basic types: (1) reproduction of original text (typed or printed cards) by photo offset; (2) the use of punched card or tape equipment, of varying degrees of sophistication, to produce copy for Multilith, offset, sequential photography, or machine printing; and (3) the combining of microfilm with electrostatic printing. At the moment, the punched-tape typewriter, which has a print-out of 600 pages an hour, would appear to be especially promising. With certain types of equipment, print-out rates run as high as 900 lines per minute. But, there is, of course, no reason for believing that these innovations exhaust future possibilities for technologic improvement. The printer's art is today experiencing changes of a magnitude that no one can now predict, and that these innovations will further encourage the production of book catalogs would seem to be a justifiable assumption.

This revival of interest in the book catalog does not imply disillusion with the card form. Rather, it signifies a reexamination of the total problem of bibliographic organization, and a recognition that there is no universal, no one best, instrument that will meet all the needs of the scholar. At the same time that some librarians have been reconsidering the book catalog, others have been investigating a variety of mechanical and electronic devices for informational retrieval. Janus-like, the scholar is looking back to the past

as well as forward to the future for more effective means for the
organization of his materials.   The book catalog, the card catalog
and the electronic mechanism--each has its own unique characteristics that endow it with its peculiar utility for certain types of library and research situations.   This is in the best traditions of librarianship, a reaffirmation of the need for an unceasing search for
improvement, whether that search leads to a reassessment of the
past or to areas that are as yet unexplored.

References

1.   U.S. Library of Congress.   A Catalog of Books Represented by
     Library of Congress Printed Cards.   Ann Arbor, Edwards
     Brothers, 1942. V. 1, p. v. "Introduction."

2.   Norris, Dorothy M.   A History of Cataloguing and Cataloguing
     Methods.   London, Grafton, 1939. p. 195-196.

3.   Hamilton, William B. "What Scholars Expect of Library Cata-
     loging, I. " in Problems and Prospects of the Research Library,
     ed. by Edwin E. Williams. New Brunswick, N.J., Scarecrow
     Press, 1955. p. 70.

4.   Fruton, Joseph S.   "What Scholars Expect of Library Catalog-
     ing, II. " Ibid., p. 75.

5.   Ibid., p. 74.

Some American Twentieth Century Book Catalogs:

Their Purposes, Format, and Production Techniques [*]

By Richard H. Shoemaker

National Catalogs

If we are now in the beginning stages of a turning away from the card catalog toward the printed book catalog, the Catalog of Books Represented by Library of Congress Printed Cards is the monument about which we turn. It contains nearly 2,000,000 entries, including 192,000 cross references. The Association of Research Libraries is responsible for the production of this monumental tool, and credit must go to Harvie Branscomb and William Warner Bishop, among many others. The first catalog, which covers all LC cards issued up to July 31, 1942, has 167 volumes. It contains an introduction by Archibald MacLeish, then Librarian of Congress, and a preface by William Warner Bishop, at that time the Chairman of the Committee to see this book through the press. The introduction by MacLeish calls the card catalog the most wonderful invention of American librarians, and there seems to be no consciousness that this particular tool might mark a break away from the use of card catalogs.

It was evident to many at this time that the depository sets of cards distributed by LC were becoming less and less useful, taking up larger and larger floor areas, and requiring greater and greater

[*] Library Resources & Technical Services, 4:195-207, Summer, 1960.

expenditures of clerical help to keep the cards filed. About 2, 000 square feet of space was needed for the catalog drawers and continual filing and expansion cost about $1, 200 a year in 1942. This was probably the real reason for the development of the LC printed book catalog. It was to be primarily a bibliographical tool for reference librarians and scholars everywhere and to aid in the finding of books for interlibrary loan. In neither the preface nor the introduction is there any idea that it might be used in the Library of Congress itself as a sort of substitute author catalog. Of course not every card represents a book in the Library of Congress, but certainly the vast majority of entries represent books held there.

The printing of the set took place in war time, and during the three years in which it was in production many changes took place in the quality of the paper, the cost of printing and other factors; yet the latter volumes of the set are more legible than the earlier volumes as the techniques of such a huge printing job were mastered. In spite of the advance in the cost of labor, paper, and other factors in book production, the price of the 167 volumes was held to the originally-announced $750. 00.

There is one notable difficulty with the catalog: the photographic reduction is one half. This means that the small figures in the LC cards having to do with classification and with the serial number of the card itself, and many of the notes in small size type, particularly series notes, are reduced to such small size that they are barely legible. The reduction was so great that the definition was lost and the difference between a 3 and an 8 or other similar figures was lost in the printing.

The page capacity is 18 entries on a page size of 8" x 11". A great deal of each page is given over to white space since the LC cards were simply lined up in three columns of six cards each and photographed. All the waste space on the LC cards therefore takes up space in the book. The first supplement to this set covered the years 1942-47, and the method of photographing the cards remained the same so that there are still only 18 entries per page. By the time a second supplement was published covering 1948-52, a new method of compilation had been devised which saved a great deal of space. To save this space the Library of Congress printed a special edition of each of its cards taking out all the leading between lines and thereby compressing the entry into as few lines as possible. This card was printed only for laying up the forms to be photographed for the monthly edition and the final cumulation of the supplements to the original set. Other improvements were printing the classification numbers and the card serial numbers in ten point type rather than the small type that was used on the regular card. This made them reproduce at half size in a legible manner. By the use of photography of these condensed LC cards the capacity per page was increased to 34 or 36 titles, or about double that of the original set, and legibility was increased at the same time. After the second supplement, the name of the title was changed to The National Union Catalog since now not only LC printed cards but all unique cards or cards for books not held by LC and contributed to the National Union Catalog were printed. This part of the set shows a capacity up to 40 titles per page using the same one half reduction. Many of these entries are typed on a Varityper instead

of being made from specially printed cards. At the time The National Union Catalog from 1953-57 was published, the Library of
Congress was typing over all entries sent to it by other contributing libraries. This same policy is still being followed, apparently.

Mr. MacLeish in his introduction to the first basic set of LC
catalogs had this to say: "It is not excessive and certainly it is
not rhetorical to say that the appearance of this work marks the
end of one chapter of American librarianship. It is even truer to
say that it marks the beginning of another." Though he was applying this to the problem of bibliographical control in the nation in
general, he might just as well have been talking about the problem
of card catalogs of any large library. In the preface by Luther
Evans to the first supplement, a little history is given of the attempt to continue cumulated catalogs after the publication of the
first basic LC set. Again the ARL was the moving force, and it
was finally decided to publish a cumulative catalog beginning with
January 1947. It was then decided that the first major supplement
would cover all cards issued between August 1, 1942, and December 31, 1947, since there was some change in typography of LC
cards to be adopted on January 1, 1948.

The subject side of The National Union Catalog begins covering
the subject entries of all LC cards in 1950 and continues to this
time, with one basic set covering the years through 1954. Annual
cumulations appeared after that date, and the preparation of a second five-year cumulative catalog is now underway.

The National Library of Medicine Catalog, a List of Works Represented by National Library of Medicine Cards, 1958, and its predecessors are really supplements to The National Union Catalog. It differs in arrangement and format enough to be of special interest.

All of the entries seem to have been made on proportional spacing typewriters. Not only is full bibliographic information given, but frequently notes of some length as well. The page is divided into four columns and holds about 50 titles. The size is 8.5" x 11".

This Catalog is a joint operation of the Card Division and the Catalog Maintenance Division of the Library of Congress and the Catalog Division of the National Library of Medicine. It is a subject catalog as well as an author list, with both parts printed in the same annual volume, but not in dictionary arrangement. There are separate alphabets for authors and subjects.

Still another title that can be considered as a supplement to The National Union Catalog is New Serial Titles. Begun in 1951 as Serial Titles Newly Received at the Library of Congress, in 1953 it was expanded to include titles contributed by other cooperating libraries, thus becoming a sort of substitute for supplements to the Union List of Serials. It is issued monthly with annual cumulations. It is also issued in monthly subject lists, but these are not cumulated.

New Serial Titles is compiled by punch-card methods, so that we have two catalogs being compiled at the Library of Congress by the two major methods of producing printed book catalogs, for The National Union Catalog is produced by hand filing and photography.

Interesting comparisons should be possible here.

New Serial Titles has a page the same size as that of The National Union Catalog, 8.5" x 11", and which holds approximately 50 titles. The form of entry is about the same as the Union List of Serials, so that a good bit of space is lost in recording library holdings in a column, instead of compressing this information along a horizontal line.

The Lamont Catalogue

The Catalogue of the Lamont Library, Harvard College, published in 1953, harks back to the day when most college libraries published printed catalogs of their collections so that each student and faculty member might own a copy. During a large part of the Nineteenth Century, most college libraries had no card catalog, so that the printed catalog was the only index to the collection for both user and staff alike. The Lamont Catalogue is useful for Harvard, but essentially it is a list for the use of American college libraries: "The various requests [from 1949 to 1952 to borrow the Lamont card file] pointed up a common feature of interest in the Lamont list: its value as an actual, working list rather than an ideal, theoretical listing of books which ought to be in an undergraduate library." It serves as an acquisition check, a means for reviewing the strength of parts of a college library collection.

The Lamont Catalogue is a list of some 40,000 titles of books in the undergraduate library of Harvard College; it excludes periodicals and ephemeral material in the Lamont collection. The Catalogue is arranged in classified order (in 500 pages) with an author index (of 58 pages) and an index to the classification (of 4 pages).   The library is classified according to a local adaptation of Dewey.   In the Introduction, Philip J. McNiff, Librarian of Lamont at the time and in charge of the catalog preparation, states that it is a finding list and does not describe the items in bibliographical detail.   This, then, is an approach to the Richardson idea of the title-a-line catalog.   The information in each entry is minimal: the authors' names are abbreviated, authors' dates are not given, publishers are abbreviated, place of publication is not given, nor is collation.   But names of significant translators and editors, the edition statement, and the number of volumes are given.   The subject approach is entirely through the classification, aided by the key to it which is called the subject index.   The capacity is about 90 entries in two columns on an 8 x 10.5 inch page; and one line is skipped between each entry--41% of the space left blank for the sake of clarity.   About 25% of the entries require two lines and 6% require three lines instead of the ideal one, and about 12% of the total space is given to the printing of classification headings for each of the approximately 3300 divisions.   There are no cross references.

The method of compilation was based on the brief Lamont entries on standard catalog cards.   These cards were supplied the printer in batches comprising each subdivision of the classification. Each batch was held together by an elastic band; and each card for the entire Catalogue was serially numbered to ensure proper sequence if a batch should be dropped.   Entries for each column were then typed on a sheet with an IBM electromatic typewriter, the sheets were returned from the printer to the library staff which proofed and indicated corrections, the printer made revisions and mounted the two sheets on a large cardboard with running heads, these were proofed by the library staff, and the pages were then printed by photo-offset lithography with a reduction of 50%, giving six point type.

The Carnegie Corporation of New York made a grant of $9,000 to aid in the publication of this Catalogue; otherwise it probably could not be sold for such a reasonable price to the library world and to the students of Harvard College. In 1953, the cost of typing the 569 sheets, setting title page type, manufacture of 3,030 copies, binding of 1,912 copies, and printing of the dust jacket, was $9,312. The estimated library editorial costs incurred in typing the cards specially for this catalog and in other editorial work was roughly $10,000-15,000. The Harvard Library used some three dozen copies of the Catalogue, over a hundred copies were sold to students and faculty at a price of $4.00, and the Harvard University Press handled general distribution at $7.50 per copy. Receipts from sales have been:

1953/54 -	$2,518
1954/55 -	1,107
1955/56 -	585
1956/57 -	806
1957/58 -	909
1958/59 -	771

During 1958/59 an additional 434 copies were bound at a cost of $317.

The New York State Catalog

The New York State Library in 1956 published its Checklist of Books and Pamphlets in the Social Sciences. A Supplement cover-

ing additions to the Library from April 1955 through 1958 came out
in 1959.

In the Introduction of this work there is a description of the
reason for its publication.   Dr. Gosnell writes that in 1855 the
State Library of New York issued a complete catalog of its holdings
and from then on for half a century supplements were published.
One wonders why, with the rapid advance in the techniques of
printing, so useful a tool had not been made currently available.
The library decided to try it.   Their philosophy was to make it as
easy to find out what books the library has as it is to find telephone numbers.   The idea is that one lists a line of description of
the book, and instead of a telephone number, gives its call number.   This does follow Richardson's idea of his title-a-line catalog
of the Princeton University Library.   The book is said to be a
first attempt or a pilot project in controlling the rise of the flow
of publications.   "As a device to permit rapid and orderly assembly of titles, easy interfiling of additions, and simple production of
copy, we have chosen the punched card."   The punch-card machines were already available in the Education Department.   The
method of compilation was to punch the cards from the shelf list of
the library as the basic record.   The choice was to do social sciences first as that's where the greatest demand for interlibrary
loans came upon the library.   The Introduction states, and a letter
from Dr. Gosnell confirms, that it is still the case that there is
no machinery yet devised, to his knowledge, that will do the final
filing for such a catalog.   The cards are roughly arranged by the
machine and then finally filed by hand.   They are then put into a

tabulating machine which prints the entries on long sheets.

"Once the cards were punched, they were arranged roughly by machine, and were finally filed by hand. It has been a not unexpected disappointment that no machine yet invented can file library catalog cards properly. From these cards copy was typed. This copy has been reduced in size and printed by photo-offset." The original purpose of this catalog was partly to furnish the location of inter-library loan material, but the purpose is not solely that. Dr. Gosnell was fully aware of the fact that this was a venture in making known the resources of the State Library to anyone who would purchase the catalog. Cumulative supplements are published at fairly regular intervals. One was published in 1957, and this last 1959 publication covers all those titles acquired in this part of the library from April 1955 to December 1958. There are about 44,000 titles in the Checklist and 13,500 titles in the latest supplement. The Checklist and its supplements have a page size of 10 by 15 inches with about 312 entries per page. Very few titles require more than one line for their description. The author's name is not very full, the date of publication is given but neither the publisher nor the place, and the classification is given in full. In effect, this is a main entry finding list only, with very little bibliographical detail except for the complete call number. The alphabetical arrangement is used and there is, therefore, no subject or title approach unless the book has a title as a main entry. There is no way of distinguishing authors who have exactly the same name since there is no date differentiation. On the very first page of the catalog there is a John Adams writing on Everyman's Psychology right along in the list of the writings of John Adams, the President.   This is an inevitable happening when there is machine filing and when there is no distinguishing mark for two people who have the exact same name.

The rest of the State Library is now being put into punch-cards in preparation for publishing a catalog of the entire collection.   Dr. Gosnell reports that "One of the benefits is to simplify our inter-library loan procedures.   We issue hundreds of such loans every week.   Our form becomes the charge card in our circulation file.   When the borrowing library has our list, these cards come in with class marks already written in.   There is a great reduction in correspondence, too.   So far it has had no effect on our general card catalog."

The cost of producing Checklist in the Social Sciences, 1956, was reported by Dr. Gosnell to be as follows:

Total cost of editing and producing the cards alone--   43,785
   cards @ .15 $ 6,567.75
Total cost of producing this book--editorial, printing,
   binding, etc.   7,463.85
Total cost of editing and producing 1,500 copies $14,031.60
If cards are re-used at least ten times in succeeding
   editions, the cost of cards for this edition can be
   approximately   656.78
Making cost of this edition (with cards amortized)   8,120.63
Cost per copy on this basis   5.42

Concerning a comparison of punch-card compared to other compilation methods, Dr. Gosnell says, "If we were to start over again, I would give serious consideration to one of the photographic methods where we could use two or three lines, and still get a

very compact volume." He expects to be able to record the whole
library collection of some 350,000 titles in a one-volume catalog,
less bulky than the Union List of Serials, using the present method.

Los Angeles County Public Catalog

Probably the most elaborate printed book catalog currently being prepared is that of the Los Angeles County Public Library.
The third edition of the Adult Catalog which covers books in the library through 1957 contains thirty-seven volumes; eight author, six
title, four fiction subjects, and eighteen regular subjects, with one
volume listing all foreign books by twenty-two different language
divisions. This catalog of the adult collection is prepared annually,
and monthly supplements are sent out to all holders of the main
catalog. The page size is 13" tall by 8" across and the capacity
is approximately fifty-five titles per page in the author and title
list, with fewer in the subject list. There is also a children's
catalog which was in the sixth edition in 1958; it has one volume for
authors, another for titles, and two subject volumes.

This catalog is produced by punch-card methods and is one of
the earlier ones of this type, following the example of the King
County Public Library in Seattle, Washington, which is credited
with producing the first IBM book catalog. The King County Library produces throw-away catalogs unbound, but the Los Angeles
County Public Library produces a master card file from which
multilith masters are automatically prepared on an IBM 407 Tabulator, and stencils are then run to produce one hundred seventy
copies of the catalog. Some copies are retained in the central li-

brary.   The central library also has a complete dictionary card catalog which serves as the basis for the production of its book catalog.   There is no public use of the central library as it is simply an administrative headquarters.   These book catalogs are bound serviceably with paper board covers and are designed to last just one year.   The supplements are sent out in loose-leaf form, punched to fit into a binder.

The production methods used to compile this catalog and some of the departures from standard cataloging procedures as well as the effect on services are presented in a communication from the library, part of which follows.

Production methods:

One control card for each entry for the Book Catalogs is typed from the Catalog card giving full author, title, edition, series if any, publisher, date, number of volumes if more than one, a short annotation, subject headings and added entries.   The subject headings are coded from the subject heading code book; then the key punch cards are prepared in the 026 IBM print[er], one card for each line to appear in the Book Catalogs. The punched cards are sorted into sets for the author catalog, the title catalog, and the subject catalogs; and multilith masters are prepared once a month for the Supplements.   The Supplements are cumulative until time for the next edition when the cards are interfiled into the banks of cards for the catalogs.

Editions are re-run annually.   At the time we prepare to run a new edition, all last copy discards are withdrawn, changes and new entries interfiled, so that as of the date we run the edition it is up-to-date.

To prepare the pages for supplements and new editions, the punched cards are run through the 407 IBM tabulator which produces multilith masters.   The masters are multilithed, 170 copies of each page, and assembled into books which are commercially bound into volumes, using a cheap binding designed to last one year when the books will be superseded by the next edition.   The finished books and monthly cumulative supplements are distributed to our 110 branches, institutional branches, and bookmobiles so that each outlet has a complete up-to-date listing of our entire holdings and any patron at any branch has equal access to our holdings and can request any book listed.   A list of last copy discards and classification changes is also run monthly so that the branch librarian can delete or change entries in their catalogs.

Some points not brought out in the report are the fact that in the central library, the regional services divisions, the book selectors are said to use copies of the book catalog extensively in preference to using the dictionary card catalog.   Also some of the larger branches have four sets of the book catalogs.   Two sets are for use of the public and two used internally by the staff.   For example, a set of title catalogs is kept at the charging desk since so many requests for books are by title, and a set of the fiction catalog at the beginning of the fiction shelves.

In the author catalog of this set there is the presence of distinguishing dates for authors of the same name which is not true of the New York State Library Checklist.   In general, the cataloging seems to be even more meticulous and detailed than might be found in the usual card catalog.   As described in the changes in procedure, there is little left out and more added than one would expect to find in a new type of catalog.   It is trying to serve much more

than as a finding list.   The presence of annotations indicates
that this is no longer merely a list of books in the library and
their call numbers.   Reader's services has had a definite effect
upon the construction of the catalog.   Instead of being less elaborate, is this becoming more elaborate than the card catalog?

King County Catalog

The branch catalogs of the King County Libraries, Seattle,
Washington, serve a different purpose from those of the Los Angeles County Public Library.   These catalogs are unbound, uncut
throw-away lists, first distributed in 1951.   The branches of the
King County Public Library have continuously changing collections
of books sent to them from the central library.   With each ship-
ment comes an invoice listing the books sent and a catalog cumulated, apparently, to show all their holdings.   Rather than a multilithed copy produced by the use of IBM punch-cards, this one is
the actual printing from the IBM cards directly onto the paper which
is distributed.   It is in loose form with the IBM printing paper uncut so that it is one long strip.   Author, subject and title catalogs
are sent but they are not interfiled.

Phillips Petroleum Co. Catalog

The National Reactor Testing Station Technical Library, operated for the U. S. Atomic Energy Commission by the Atomic Energy
Division of Phillips Petroleum Company, and located 55 miles west
of Idaho Falls, is now in the midst of planning a book catalog produced by means of punch-cards.   The users of this library are
widely dispersed, some being 55 miles distant from the library, but
the only card catalogs are located in the main library and in a

branch one and one-half miles apart.

The library prepared a list, <u>Technical Journals at the National Reactor Testing Station</u>, in September 1959. It is a union list, giving holdings and locations of journals in four libraries. There are about fifteen titles per page, size 8" x 11". It is reproduced by Multilith, the mats having been printed on an IBM 407 tabulator. Hillis L. Griffin, Assistant Librarian, provided a copy of the publication together with a sample of a preliminary work paper listing, which shows the complete information on each entry, some of which is not printed in the finished list.

The plan at present is to produce a book catalog in three parts: author, title, and subject. Monthly cumulated supplements and a complete new edition each year will keep the catalog up to date. The data given in each entry will be author, title, complete call number, date of publication and location, if in a branch. The original plan was to list about 35 titles on a 50-line page, but recent experiments indicate that a photo-reduction process may be used with a two-column format to increase the page capacity.

The Library staff members do not think that the book catalog will greatly change cataloging policy, but they do anticipate a great change in the service to users. It is planned to distribute the catalog widely, beginning with an initial distribution of 25 to 30 copies, with the print run of later editions being determined by user demand. Since 80% to 90% of the circulation of the library is requested by telephone, and since the widely scattered users of the library now have to depend on a monthly, not cumulated, accession list, much time will probably be saved.

The accompanying flow chart shows the proposed method of producing the masters for the three-part book catalog.

Columbia River Catalog

The Columbia River Regional Library had both the King County Library and the Los Angeles County Library experiments in book catalogs to study before setting up its own. They chose to pattern theirs after the Los Angeles catalog. The first edition of their Catalog was in seven volumes: the adult catalog has an author volume, a title volume and two subject volumes, while the children's catalog consists of one volume each for authors, titles and subjects. As is true in Los Angeles County, each branch has a complete catalog of the holdings of the system. The pages are 8.5" x 11" and contain from 25-29 entries each in the subject catalog, the only one available for examination. A second edition of the Catalog will be produced early in 1960. Budgetary limitations have prevented the publication of periodic supplements; therefore, branch librarians must keep up-to-date through the use of monthly lists of new acquisitions.

Some of the reasons cited by Dorothy R. Cutler, Acting Director, for the adoption of a book catalog rather than a card catalog are: "They eliminate the necessity of investing in card catalog furniture; they save clerical time at headquarters such as typing cards, invoices, etc.; and, most important, they save the time of headquarters and branch librarians in adding and withdrawing catalog cards in the branches. Library personnel freed from these tasks by IBM-produced catalogs can perform other more vital library services."

NRTS TECHNICAL LIBRARY
IBM BOOK CATALOG
Flow Sheet

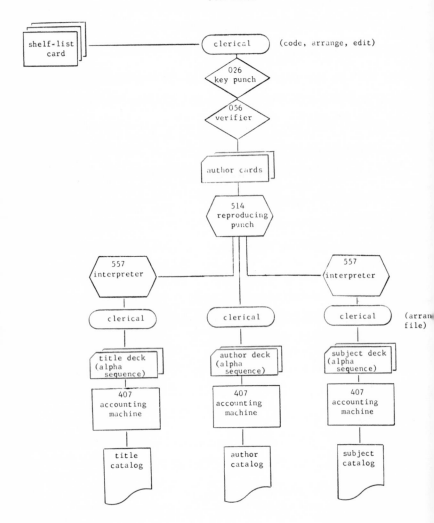

Miss Cutler gave a brief outline of the procedures for preparing the Catalog in an article in the Summer, 1958, issue of LRTS, as follows:

1. The official shelflist card is the source document from which the IBM cards are punched. It contains the subject headings assigned to each book and the code number for each subject.

2. Cards are punched by an 026 IBM Printing Punch, one card by author, one by title, and one for each subject assigned to the book.

3. Cards will be accumulated in alphabetical order by author, title, and subject.

4. When this process is complete, these cards will be shipped to the IBM Service Bureau Corporation in Seattle to be run through the 407 IBM Tabulator, which will print multilith masters.

5. Masters will be returned to the Columbia River Regional Library, Wenatchee, and pages of the book catalog will be duplicated on a Model 80 Multilith machine.

6. Pages will then be assembled and bound, and the catalogs distributed.

G.K. Hall Catalogs

G. K. Hall & Co. of Boston published in 1959 Subject Headings Authorized for General Use in the Dictionary Catalogs of The New York Public Library Reference Department, in five large volumes. The page size is ten inches wide by fourteen inches high containing twenty-one entries in three columns at two-thirds actual size. The book is made by microfilming the 3" x 5" cards on which the subject headings are recorded and then making electrostatic prints from the microfilm. These prints are then laid up in columns of

seven and rephotographed to make the offset plate. Such methods
of reproducing the whole of a 3" x 5" card in book catalogs inevitably leads to a great waste of space on each page and a consequent
high cost and bulk. It takes 5,000 pages to record only 100,000
entries in this subject heading list.

National Academy of Sciences Catalog

The Division of Medical Sciences of the National Academy of
Sciences has a research project, known as the Cardiovascular Literature Project, supported by a grant from the National Institutes
of Health. It is essentially a bibliographical attempt to make an
index-abstract of all information concerning the effects of chemical
agents on the cardiovascular system. A Kodak Listomatic Camera
in combination with punched cards is used for its compilation. Dr.
Isaac D. Welt, Director of the Project, has written an excellent
description of his use of these two devices, as follows:

> The Listomatic approach was chosen after careful con-
> sideration of all then available (in 1957) devices for
> the following reasons:--
>
>   1.   It enabled publication of index entries without
> the necessity of 'shingling' several hundred thousand
> entries at the last minute. Entries are typed up,
> proof-read and filed each working day. The speed of
> the camera, which can handle about 230 entries per
> minute, is more than sufficient to permit publication
> at the very earliest possible time following the tran-
> scription of the last index entry.
>
>   2.   Cumulations can easily be made by interfiling
> IBM cards.
>
>   3.   With the exception of the alphabet over-punches
> (11, 12, and 0) and positions 3 and 4 in column 52

(for use in telling the camera how many lines are to be photographed), the rest of the punch card is available for coding for the purposes of mechanized information retrieval.

Some groups, the Current List of Medical Literature among them, are utilizing the blank portion of the card for mechanical alphabetization. The size of our project and the complexity of the chemical nomenclature involved, however, preclude this use. Instead, we prefer to code chemical structure and biological activity in order to achieve avenues of data retrieval not permitted by the obvious limitations of our 'reciprocal' main subject heading-subheading approach. Thus, the same card, which serves as the 'manuscript' for publication of an index, does double duty as a unit of our mechanized information retrieval system.

The limitation of the camera field to 3 or 4 typewritten lines (we are using IBM Registry type) affects about 5-10 percent of our entries. In such cases, we prefer to use single-line entries on separate continuation cards. We utilize 6.6 inches of the card horizontally and photograph our entries at a reduction of about 40 percent.

When we began our data transcription, the only mechanism available which would permit us to type up our cards accurately enough (the distance of the first typewritten line to the top of the card is quite critical and must be accurate to within one-hundredth of an inch), was an Electrical Line Finder, manufactured by the Standard Register Company. When this accessory is used with an IBM typewriter (other machines may also be employed), a continuous card stock form with perforations along the sides is employed. The typist can go from one entry to the next

simply by pressing a button which moves up the form
the precise vertical distance of an IBM card.   The
first typewritten line is then accurately and precisely
positioned.

IBM cards are cut out of this continuous form by
means of a Card Form Die Cutter which can handle
100 cards per minute.   Incidentally, both this machine and the Listomatic Camera are not owned by
us.   We have an arrangement with Science Press,
Inc. of Lancaster, Pa., for the use of these machines
on a rental basis.

Recently, a card-holding platen has become available (IBM) which enables the typing of separate IBM
cards with the requisite degree of accuracy.

Cards are then gang-punched by means of an IBM
punch.   Position 3 in column 52 is punched to indicate two typewritten lines, and position 3 and 4 to
show three typewritten lines.   One-line entries do not
have to be punched.   Cards are then filed manually.

The Listomatic Camera will produce a paper negative
or positive which can be used for proof-reading purposes.

The final page is produced by conventional photo-
offset techniques.

It seems quite likely that such a photographic technique might
be both faster and cheaper than the present methods being used to
reproduce library catalogs by means of punched cards in which the
entry must be run through an IBM printer, either to produce the
catalog directly or to produce a Multilith master.

Summary

In summation, recent library book catalogs seem to have been
produced by the following six methods:

1.   Typing pages from card file for photo offset.

Example: a. 3000 copies of the Lamont catalog.
(1953)

2. Tabulating cards machine-printed on multilith masters.

Examples: a. 170 copies of the LA County Library (1956+)

b. Columbia River Regional Library (1959+)

c. Phillips Petroleum Co. Catalog (1960+)

3. Tabulating cards machine-printed as final copy.
Example: a. King County (1951)

4. Tabulating cards machine-printed to make copy for offset reproduction.

Example: a. New York State Library Checklist (1956+)

5. Tabulating cards printed by sequential camera.
Example: a. National Academy of Sciences'
Cardiovascular Literature

b. Index Medicus (1960)

6. Microfilm of 3" x 5" cards with offset printing, from masters prepared electrostatically.

Example: a. Avery Library (1959)

b. NYPL Slavonic (1960)

c. NYPL List of Subject Headings (1958)

References

Dewey, Harry. "Punched Card Catalogs--Theory and Technique." American Documentation, 10:36-50. January 1959.

MacQuarrie, Catherine. "IBM Book Catalog." Library Journal, 82:630-634. March 1, 1957.

Schwegmann, George A., Jr. "The Rationale, Planning and Technique of Publishing the National Union Catalog." American Documentation, 8:296-299. October 1957.

Alvord, Dorothy. "King County Public Library Does It with IBM."

PNLA Quarterly, 16:123-132.   April 1952.

Gull, C.D.   "The Cumulative Catalog Technique at the Library of
   Congress."   American Documentation, 2:131-141. August 1951.

Cutler, Dorothy.   "The Columbia River Regional Library Demonstration."   Library Resources and Technical Services, 2:181-182.
   Summer 1958.

Book Catalogs: Prospects in the Decade Ahead[*]

By David C. Weber

The paper that Frederick P. Keppel submitted to the ALA in 1939 serves to remind one of the hazards of forecasting. In his consideration of the library of nineteen years in the future (that is, of 1958), he then made this forecast for catalog cards:

> It is now the publisher's business to provide them for new books or other records. For old records we have them telephotoed from the Library of Congress or one of the other central catalogs. When it comes to using the cards, I blush to think for how many years we watched the so-called business machines juggle with payrolls and bank books before it occurred to us that they might be adapted to dealing with library cards with equal dexterity. Indexing has become an entirely new art. The modern index is no longer bound up in the volume, but remains on cards, and the modern version of the old Hollerith machine will sort out and photograph anything that the dial tells it, and, thank heavens, will then put all the cards back in their places.[1]

With this as caution against forecasting for nineteen years ahead, I should like to comment on the possible utility of book-form catalogs in the next ten years only. For this purpose one may use the trends of the past two decades to attempt a projection, as well as to review problems in the publication of recent library

* College and Research Libraries, 23:302-310, July, 1962. With corrections.

catalogs in book form.   This will permit me to describe some of
the hazards that we shall face in the years ahead and some ways
that we, as a professional association, may together make this a
period of fruitful experimentation. [2]

It may be said at the outset that this study results in renewed
confidence in the importance of card catalogs.   There does seem
to be a recent increase, however, in the number of book catalogs
issued on the initiative of the library; yet it may be too early to
call this a trend toward somewhat greater use of the book catalog
as replacement for the card catalog.   And the book catalog mani-
festly has the same advantages and disadvantages today as a hundred years ago.

Let me set the stage for our considerations by giving two
views of the present inadequacy of card catalogs.   In a recent lec-
ture at the Massachusetts Institute of Technology, Dr. John G. Kemeny reminded his audience of the increase of book production, the
increased ease of publication through photographic techniques, the
publishing activities that are now mushrooming in formerly unde-
veloped areas of the world, and the phenomenal rate of library
growth.   Dr. Kemeny has grown so concerned with this impossible
situation as to suggest that, by 1980, the United States government
and one hundred research libraries should cooperate to build an
automated "national research library" based on high reduction microfilm storage, long-distance telephone dialing for retrieval, and
local print-out of copies on regular microfilm or full-size sheets.
This proposal by the chairman of Dartmouth's department of mathematics and astronomy should not be taken lightly.

A second example may be found in the recent attempt of Harvard, Yale, and The New York Public Library to join forces to solve a common problem. This problem they describe thus:

> A crisis has been reached in the development of card catalogues for the largest research libraries of this country. These catalogues, which are mechanisms meant to serve scholars, are becoming more and more enormous and complex jungles of cards. It costs great sums to maintain them, unit costs increase steadily as they become more bulky, and they outgrow the space that is readily available for housing them. In spite of all the money and labor that is being invested in cataloguing...those who use the catalogues and those who make them are increasingly dissatisfied ...A bold approach on some new basis seems to be in order. [3]

These libraries saw three alternatives which might be developed singly or in combination with one another. First, the card catalog might prove to be preferable to anything else, and its undesirable features might have to be accepted as lesser evils. Second, a printed catalog--possibly a joint printed catalog--might be practical in spite of the high cost and numerous difficulties it would involve. Third, electronic solutions might be provided by new developments in technology. It may be reported that the three libraries held several meetings to consider the possibility of printing a joint catalog; however, agreement could not be reached.

The card catalog has served libraries well during the past century, but it cannot continue to serve research libraries adequately if cataloging techniques and catalog apparatus remain unchanged. These two examples may show that there is concern for the future

of card catalogs--at least in the larger research libraries.   And
the problems faced by these larger libraries are the ones that will
be faced by the medium-size libraries in another generation or two.

In order to see clearly the present condition of card catalogs,
it may be well to turn attention briefly to their development during
the past century.

Until this century, libraries made extensive use of printed catalogs in book form to answer the common question, "Is the book I
want in the library?"

Over a thousand such catalogs were published in the United
States between 1723 and 1875.   A library such as that of Amherst
College would sell one hundred copies of its book catalog within
four years of publication; and the Detroit Public Library would sell
six hundred copies within seven years and give away four hundred
more.

Then came the problem of larger and larger catalogs, resulting from greatly increased acquisitions; and the libraries of the
country changed to the card form, applying practices developed between 1847 and 1861.   This was no sudden and complete change of
library technique; and we are all aware that American libraries
keenly debated the two systems throughout the remainder of the century.   The involved arguments may be summarized by using Cutter's several points which he wrote down in 1876:

The advantages of a printed catalog are briefly:

That it is in less danger of partial or total destruction than a manuscript volume or drawers of cards.
That it can be consulted out of the library.

That it can be consulted in other libraries and it may always fairly be questioned by trustees how far the benefit to any other library is a justification for incurring the expense of printing.

That it is easier to read than the best manuscript volume and very much easier to consult. Here again everything depends on the hurry or impatience of those who consult the catalog. If that is so great that a very slight impediment will cause them to give up the search altogether or never undertake a search after having failed once, printing is necessary; but in college and county libraries, this can hardly be the case.

That several persons can consult multiple copies of it at once.

The disadvantages of a printed catalog are:

That it is costly and, if full and accurate, very costly.

That a mistake once made is made forever.

It is out of date before it is published. As it cannot contain the newest books, the very ones most sought for, fresh supplements are continually needed, each of which causes an additional loss of time and patience to consulters. The average man will not look in over four places for a book. A few very persevering or driven by a great need will go as far as five or six. It becomes necessary, therefore, if the catalog is to be of any use, to print consolidated supplements every five years, and that is expensive.[4]

The turn of the century saw discussions shift from this debate on form of catalog to concentration on rules for individual entries. This concern with the degree of bibliographic information is well summarized by Keyes D. Metcalf in his volume on library administration:

Librarians tended to line up in two camps. One
was made up of reference librarians and of catalogers
who were "perfectionists," represented by Miss Isi-
dore Mudge and Miss Minnie Sears. They believed
that unless very accurate and detailed cataloging rules
were followed, the catalog would sooner or later have
to be done over and that the extra cost of originally
doing it well would not only make better reference
work possible, but save money in the long run. The
other group was led by Dr. E. C. Richardson, then of
the Princeton University Library, who believed that a
"title-a-line" cataloging would make readily available
perhaps ninety-seven percent of all books and reduce
cataloging costs to such an extent that enough additional books could be purchased and cataloged as to more
than make up for the three percent lost through the
simplified methods.... The struggle still goes on. [5]

It may be said, however, that in the United States the period
from 1876 to 1941 was the era of the card catalog in complete
dominance. Perhaps this period of virtuosity ended with the recall
to duty clearly sounded in Andrew Osborn's "Crisis in Cataloging."
The integrity of the card catalog's meticulously detailed entries had
been strikingly challenged.

In 1942 the era of the marriage of the card catalog and the
book form catalog was ushered in with the great Catalog of Books-
Represented by Library of Congress Printed Cards. The word
"marriage" is used since in the present era it is not a case of
"either or." It is doubtful if the recent publication of any card
catalog in book form has resulted in the complete discarding of the
original card file. In these years, the question of format which
was tabled in 1901 has been reopened for further discussion. It is

still complicated by the continuing divergence of opinion as to the amount of necessary cataloging information.

The past twenty years have seen the publication of over sixty library catalogs of American educational institutions. (These are listed in the appendix at the end of this article; and it should be pointed out that in the last two years all but four were publishing ventures of G. K. Hall & Co.) These catalogs are occasionally substitutes for the cards, but generally are copies of the card catalog information. Some of them give book numbers; a few give multiple locations or joint listings. Through analysis of these catalogs, three basic motivations for publication seem discernible:

1. A library's internal concern with providing easier access for its clientele. This may result from one of four pressures:
   a. Complexity of use, since a book catalog provides simplicity of presentation and may include exceptional fullness in detail.
   b. Geographical dispersal of library units and availability of a single book collection in several locations.
   c. Fluidity of collections where the changing catalog record can be provided by mechanical reproduction of a central master file.
   d. Physical problems of card catalog space.
2. Local pride and an interest in scholarship generally, which usually results in a subsidized publication.
3. The interest in a particular catalog shown by scholars and libraries throughout the country, an interest which may make the catalog commercially practicable.

In its simplest terms, a publication is going to result either from the local library's saying, "I want it published to support my own responsibilities to my clientele," or from friends' encouraging and supporting special collections through endowment or gifts for current use, or from the national community of scholars' saying, "Your collections are so rich or your cataloging analysis so exceptional that we all need access to these records." The latter case results in a feasible commercial enterprise, while the former two require internal fiscal justification.

That these motivations often overlap is demonstrated by The New York Public Library's comment in introducing its catalog of French Revolutionary Pamphlets, A Check List of the Tallyrand & Other Collections:

> A printed check list rather than the customary cataloging on cards was decided upon for the following reasons: (1) The cost of recording a large but specialized collection would be considerably reduced, and at the same time material would be more easily accessible to students than if cards for each individual piece had been inserted in the public catalog. (2) The entries for the Tallyrand Collection would be kept together. (3) The use of the pamphlets by students would be facilitated. [6]

The three basic motivations are likely to retain their force in the future. Catalogs will be issued for current acquisitions, and they will be issued for older materials. Some will be limited in scope, and some will be comprehensive. Some will be issued by large libraries and many by small.

Since 1942 several techniques have been developed for the pro-

duction of these catalogs.   The study by Professor Richard Shoemaker of Rutgers University[7] and the analysis by George Piternick,
then of the University of California, [8] describe the methods that are
now available through technological developments.   Machines and
photographic applications that are in hand or are being developed
seem certain to revolutionize the production of small editions.

This, then, is the situation in 1961.   Let me now turn to the
future.   As a profession we have learned a good deal from the experience of the last twenty years.   However, there are difficulties
yet to be surmounted if we are to achieve anything close to ideal
standards for publishing book catalogs.   Some of the more important problems are the following six:

1.   The difficulty of choosing which of several catalogs it is most
desirable to publish.

> The scholar and the librarian would hope in theory
> that what money is available to a library could be
> spent to cover the entire range of knowledge, and that
> each thorough bibliographical index which is purchased
> would cover one clearly defined portion of knowledge.
> The several portions that are purchased by a library
> should form a composite whole, with as little dupli-
> cation and as few gaps as possible.   This is difficult
> to achieve.   In other words, the "ideal" catalog, to
> be worthy of publication and to be worthy of purchase
> by subscribing libraries, must thoroughly index a col-
> lection of notable distinction in its particular field.
> This field should be rather closely and carefully cir-
> cumscribed in order that it not impinge on catalogs
> that already have been published or will be published
> in related areas.
>   The Oriental field may be used as an example of

this point. Is The New York Public Library's Oriental catalog as significant for scholars as that of the Harvard Yenching Institute catalog, of which the first three volumes, from 1938 to 1940, have already been published? Or, in another field, one may ask whether the publication of The New York Public Library Slavonic Division catalog did damage to the possibility of publishing the Cyrillic Union Catalog at the Library of Congress. In this instance, there are reasons to publish both catalogs; for The New York Public Library Slavonic catalog lists some Slavic titles not in the Cyrillic Union Catalog, and it includes a large number of analytics and books in Western languages that are not in the Cyrillic Union Catalog. On the other hand, the Cyrillic Union Catalog includes about twice the five hundred thousand entries in The New York Public Library catalog, while a recent sample indicates that it contains cards for only about one-third of Russian language publications actually available in research libraries other than the Library of Congress. However there is a large, and theoretically wasteful, overlap between the two catalogs.

These examples may indicate the importance of publishers, scholars, and librarians working together to utilize to best advantage the newer techniques and the funds that are available. How can we find the ideal portions of knowledge having comprehensive collections carefully cataloged in depth? Obviously the quality of the collection is of major importance. I shall return later to this point.

2. The problems concerning the depth of indexing.

All libraries are faced with the dilemma that the cost of buying books is in competition with the expense of cataloging those books. Although cataloging perfectionism is a roadblock to adequate library serv-

ices, full catalog records are of clear value from a
national point of view. Consideration of the depth of
indexing increases the difficulty of the decision on
publication.

For an example, I may mention two collections in
the Oriental field, the catalogs of either one of which
might deserve publication. One is The New York Public Library's catalog of its Oriental collection, which
lists 65,000 volumes indexed on 352,000 cards. The
other is the collection of the London University School
of Oriental and African Studies, which has 400,000 volumes controlled by only 300,000 cards. One collection
is possibly given much more thorough cataloging treatment, and the larger collection covers a much wider
subject field.

It is a matter for scholarly decision, whether one
or another catalog is, or several catalogs are, indexed accurately enough, and in sufficient detail to
make it a widely useful bibliographic contribution.

This is not an easy problem to resolve.

3. Network complications--the problems of combined use of both
the book-form and card-form catalogs.

For most library situations, it seems probable that
the card catalog and book catalog will supplement each
other. Entries for part of the collection may be
printed, while cards will be used to list the remainder.
For the person coming to consult these records, the
logical steps in using two or more catalogs must be
made clear. Such an obvious pattern of use may be
difficult to achieve in simple fashion.

For example, picture, if you will, the largest
card catalog you have seen and consider that 80% has
been transferred to book form. You would then need
to devote almost as much space to the combination
card-and-book catalog under these new conditions because of the fact that the catalog needs to be adequate-

ly spread out so that many persons may have access
to the records at one time. You might, therefore,
have on one side of the "index room" the card file for
recent accessions. On the other side of the room you
might have a book catalog laid out on a counter, or
perhaps the catalog in duplicate on two rows of shelves
above a counter. There will be questions in the
reader's mind as he enters the room and wonders in
which catalog to look. The book catalog may be interleaved and annotated for additions or the supplementary materials may be in the card catalog await-
ing the next round of book publication. There may be
several author and several subject catalogs, some of
which may be union catalogs.

This will be quite a different type of bibliographical
facility from that we are accustomed to using, and
the network of bibliographical controls is bound to be
a bit more complicated than the single dictionary card
file. It will require careful thought to maintain as
simple a network as possible.

4. The major problem of supplements.

What is to be done with records for books acquired
after a catalog is published? Or, indeed, what happens as books are withdrawn or transferred to different locations? It is conceivable that publishing costs
will be reduced to such a level that catalogs may be
reprinted frequently with corrections and additions.
(However, such a program would probably require
the maintenance of a complete card file and thus eliminate any possibility of a sizable space saving which
would stem from discarding the card catalog entirely.
The Stanford Library would still have to maintain three
thousand trays of cards, and I am sure the library
staff would find it much more efficient to use the card
file than the book for most of its searching processes.)
If catalogs are now to be periodically reprinted, they

will probably have to be issued in some such format
as the telephone book, with inexpensive paper and the
cheapest of bindings.   And, since even inexpensive
reprinting is a costly job, some supplements will be
necessary.   May one accept a state of not cumulated
supplements in, say, twenty-year intervals?   Or fifty-
year intervals?

Deletions will also be a problem, and they will damage the basic set as well as its supplements.   Books
deleted may often be removed to a regional storage
library and the master copy of the catalog so annotated.   It also seems possible that the book form
catalog is ideally suited as the sole catalog for books
sent to storage, since those records would be seldom
altered; it may also have application for regional storage libraries.   However, what happens to The National
Union Catalog as transfers and withdrawals become
common?

It is too early to determine or propose the optimum
publication pattern.   Rather, libraries of the country
may have to live through a few decades of experience
with book catalogs before arriving at a generally satisfactory solution to the problem of continuations.   For
the present, one is led to assume a general pattern
not radically different from the examples of the past
twenty years, [9] and to suggest that the two best patterns are to issue supplements either frequently, and
cumulated, or to issue them infrequently.

5.   The challenge of combination.

There are three or four excellent collections in the
same field.   This is the sort of ideal which was ex-
plored by Harvard, Yale, and The New York Public
Library back in 1956, and, of course, it was achieved
in such union lists as Pollard and Redgrave and the
Union List of Serials.   Can it not be extended to subject fields?   There are three or four excellent collec-

tions of French Revolutionary pamphlets; it would be
a scholarly convenience to combine the records and
issue a catalog which would be definitive.   Hopefully,
the extra editorial expenses would be balanced by the
savings to be derived from libraries buying one catalog rather than three.   Of course, there are problems
with differing catalog rules, arrangement of information, filing order, and card legibility; but we can remind ourselves that in The National Union Catalog for
1952-55 the information is readily available in remark-
ably fine format.   More of such accomplishments are
to be encouraged.

6.   The physical format of the volume.

There is always the temptation for the publisher to
cut corners in typographic layout, in illustration, in
the quality of binding, the quality of paper, and so
forth.   Since catalogs are bibliographic tools of continuing value, high production standards should be
maintained.   It is easy, and sometimes necessary, to
let economic pressures dictate compromises in such
standards.   As one example, the new British Museum
catalog unfortunately has volumes weighing up to sev-
en pounds eight ounces when five and one half pounds
would have been a more satisfactory weight limit.

Since photography will enable libraries to print catalogs without retyping their cards, a sequential card
camera technique designed to handle 3 x 5 cards holds
more promise than does a machine requiring tabulating cards; yet here again there is danger of accepting
a product inferior in appearance.   Where completely
new catalog records are to be prepared, the tabulating card may offer substantial advantages over the 3
x 5 format because of the equipment presently available.   With tabulating cards there is a possible limitation of type faces, a point which substantially affects
the attractive appearance of a catalog and one which the

Los Angeles County Library has most satisfactorily
handled in its newest book catalog format.

The six problems here mentioned come in infinite variety. I
should like to comment on one particular aspect of commercialism
which may undermine achievement of an ideal publication. It was
earlier stated that the quality of the collection being indexed is of
major importance. This is obvious; but what if publication of a
catalog of a collection of second quality is commercially attractive?

May it be possible to offer sound guidance for the future publication of book catalogs? Such guidance should be designed to reduce unnecessary overlap, to concentrate on collections of first importance, and to select where possible those collections which have
received bibliographical control of a high order.[10] This is a difficult matter, but I would suggest an evaluative approach which the
library profession might pursue in collaboration with scholars. It
is the primary responsibility of the librarian to see that standards
are here achieved; commercial firms by their nature do not have
the time to go into this to the extent which is necessary.

There are several techniques for evaluating the relative
strengths of several collections covering the same field. As one
example, in 1942, the ALA published LeRoy Merritt's "index of
distinctiveness" to research library collections.[11] In the publication of book catalogs, of course, such a technique would need to be
applied to specific subject areas. I also refer to the study of Vaclav Mostecky which sketches five methods of checking the quality of
library collections and describes the check list method which was
selected for the Slavic study.[12] It is a good example of application

to one specific field.

I hasten to add that such comparisons of library strengths would have to be supplemented with information as to the quality of the bibliographical records, the amount of analytical detail, the physical condition of the catalog, and the extent to which the catalog records already appear in published union catalogs or in special catalogs for related subject areas. This panoply of information--surely never heretofore gathered for a commercial undertaking--would offer desirable guidance for publishing in the national interest some of America's great library card catalogs.

Considering all aspects of bibliographic control, there are major obstacles to a wholesale replacement of cards by books. This point is made even more strongly by Agnes Tysse. In commenting on the possibility of publishing the complete dictionary catalog, she states that without any doubt the card catalog must remain: "In view of the experience of such libraries as the Library of Congress and Princeton with their printed catalogs, it is questionable if printed book catalogs can ever fully supersede the flexible card catalog, that ingenious, if cumbersome and expensive, device so adaptable to additions and changes." However, she continues, "there is no question but that reference and other service librarians and divisional librarians would welcome printed book catalogs as additions to the complete, up-to-date central card catalog."[13] This duplicate reliance has been the pattern developed during the past twenty years. The next decade may see more independent use of book catalogs, in most instances supplemented by card files. The patterns will vary considerably.

Book catalogs have returned after a lengthy retirement.   Here is an important aspect of librarianship which will save library card catalogs from "breaking down" and growing to chaotic proportions. Although the "ideal" book catalog seems a myth, the book catalog is going to be the salvation of the card catalog.   Librarians, scholars, and publishers must strive for adequate bibliographical standards and suitable physical standards for these important catalogs on which the library world is certain to rely in the decade ahead.

References

1. Frederick P. Keppel.   "Looking Forward, a Fantasy." The Library of Tomorrow.   (Chicago: ALA, 1939). p. 5.

2. A shortened version of this article was read at a meeting of the ALA Book Catalogs Interdivisional Committee, Cleveland. July, 1961.

3. Annual Report for the Year 1955-56.   Cambridge, Mass.: Director, Harvard University Library, p. 6.

4. C. A. Cutter "Library Catalogues," Public Libraries in the United States of America... (Washington, U.S. Bureau of Education, 1876), Pt. 1, p. 552-54.

5. Studies in Library Administrative Problems.   (New Brunswick: Rutgers University Press, 1960), p. 60.

6. Horace E. Hayden, comp., French Revolutionary Pamphlets; A Check List of the Tallyrand & Other Collections. ([New York]: New York Public Library, 1945, p. [iii]).

7. Richard H. Shoemaker. Paper included in this volume.

8. George Piternick.   Paper included in this volume.

9. This is supported by the study of Mildred C. O'Connor, "Aspects of Frequency Factors and Patterns of Supplements." (MS, January 1960).

10. "Intellectual and Bibliographical Standards for Book Catalogs" was a study of Robert D. Stevens. (MS, January 1960).

11. LeRoy C. Merritt, "Resources of American Libraries: a
     quantitative picture." Robert B. Downs, ed., Union Catalogs
     in the United States. (Chicago: ALA, 1942), p. 58-96.
12. Vaclav Mostecky. "The Quality of the Russian Collections."
     Melville J. Ruggles and Vaclav Mostecky, Russian and East
     European Publications in the Libraries of the United States.
     (New York: Columbia University Press, 1960), p. 228-249.
13. Agnes N. Tysse. Paper included in this volume.

Card Catalogs Versus Printed Book Catalogs
and the Catalog User

By Agnes N. Tysse

The number of book catalogs currently being issued or planned and the variety of experimentation in their publication are evidence of the need felt by many administrators and librarians for finding more economical and effective means than card catalogs to represent a library's collections.

It is not the purpose of this paper to report on examples of such catalogs or the various methods by which they have been produced. These aspects have been covered in other papers in this volume. Our intention is to examine the feasibility of substituting book catalogs for card catalogs. Their format, in the light of the use to be made of them, the number of copies necessary and their location for easy consultation, the volume and kinds of use to be provided for, are all pertinent considerations.

That the printing of such catalogs is possible has been amply demonstrated in the last two decades. The Library of Congress, particularly, has pioneered in such publication. Their author and subject catalogs and the New Serial Titles have been real milestones - achievements of great significance in bibliographical development. Their experimentation in assembling, editing, and reproducing the entries, in determining the best size, paper, and format of the volumes, serve as patterns for other endeavors of this

55

kind.   Their author catalog has demonstrated in the experience of
many libraries that it was feasible for the printed book catalog to
supersede the bulk of the cards in the Depository Catalog.[1]
Whether a printed book catalog can successfully replace the public
dictionary card catalog in a large library is not so easy to determine, and about such a substitution there are many misgivings on
the part of users dependent upon its completeness and up-to-dateness.

   In order to explore the possibilities of such a substitution it
will perhaps be useful to examine the advantages and disadvantages
of printed book catalogs for the library user.

Advantages

1.   A printed book catalog allows for mobility.   One
     of its best features is that the use of it need not
     be confined to a single fixed area.

2.   It allows for multiple copies.   Catalogs can be
     located in all branch and divisional libraries, in
     various reading rooms and stack areas in very
     large libraries; and it would make possible the
     purchase of copies as bibliographical tools and
     finding lists in other libraries.

3.   It is visually superior; e.g.   The works of an
     individual author in a library are more readily
     seen and different editions compared on a printed
     page than in a card catalog, where only one entry
     can be examined at a time.

4.   It would make the compilation of bibliographies
     less difficult and time-consuming.   Photocopying
     of pages of entries under an author or subject is
     possible, certainly an advantage over the laborious
     hand copying necessitated by the use of the card
     catalog.

5. It condenses space and demands less physical ex-
ertion. The book catalog may concentrate in a
single easily manageable volume the entries occupying several heavy drawers in a card catalog.

6. It provides a resource tool for the scholar. The
catalog's location in other libraries would provide
scholars with an indication of the library's resources in their fields, and save the effort and
expense of visits to search card catalogs in other
institutions.

7. It would serve as a resource tool for a library
system. In city, regional, and state systems, a
printed catalog serves as an indication of resources
in the area. With a single central catalog, on
cards, for an entire system, divisional libraries
on a campus, branch libraries in a city, county
and regional libraries in a state system are at a
disadvantage in not knowing what the system has
available, and where. The New York State Library's Checklist of Books and Pamphlets in the
Social Sciences, the Los Angeles system catalogs,
the Louisiana State Union Catalog, are examples
of recent book catalogs attempting to make such
information more widely available.

Disadvantages

1. The expense and difficulty of editing and publishing could be very great, depending on the degree
of automation, the extent of the editing, and the
frequency with which successive editions appear.

2. A printed catalog would be out-of-date before it
left the printer's hands. It could not hope to keep
abreast of new accessions, or be a completely accurate index of holdings.

3. The printed catalog is inflexible. Changes in call
numbers and locations, indication of withdrawals

and transfers, of differences in publisher and place of publication, and insertion of new entries and cross references would not be possible. A loose-leaf arrangement does not stand up under heavy use given the catalog in many libraries. If write-ins were resorted to, the continual insertion of added information would result in messy copies, visually more and more difficult to use.

4. <u>More than one alphabet would have to be consulted.</u> The necessity for checking in more than one place for material in the library is a disadvantage every index user recognizes.

5. The <u>mobility</u> of the catalog could be a disadvantage as well as an advantage. If the printed catalog were to supersede the card catalog for the items included, the only access to them would be through the printed catalog. Unless multiple copies were available, a needed volume might have been carried off for photographing, for checking of items in the stacks, or even out of the library for leisurely perusal at the user's convenience.

6. <u>Condensation of space may also be a disadvantage.</u> If the printed catalog concentrates the contents of several card catalog drawers into a single volume, only one catalog user can be accommodated where before as many patrons as there were catalog drawers could be served at the same time. The catalog users, also, would be concentrated in a smaller area, and traffic might become congested at busy periods.

7. Printed book catalogs are <u>more susceptible to wear, tear, mutilation and theft.</u> It is true that the card catalog is also vulnerable, but not to the same degree. Books are often dragged into position by seizing on a single page; corners are turned to indicate where the user stopped; items are checked

with a pencil or pen; pages listing an author's
works are ripped out; titles are underlined; pages
loosen and are lost.

Books, at best, are very perishable. In an unpublished report
made by the Library Binding Institute in 1954, it was estimated
that for publishers' bindings in college and university libraries, the
average circulation was 24.6 times before the binding broke down;
in public libraries the average was 26.08. For a stouter library
binding, college and university libraries averaged 70.1 circulation
times, with 80.25 for public libraries. A printed volume containing T. S. Eliot, Ernest Hemingway or William Faulkner entries for
a college or university library community may well be handled
more than 70 times in the course of a single day.

A study undertaken at the University of Michigan Library in
February and March of 1958 for the Council of Library Resources,
and issued as a report on the Application of a Telereference System to Divisional Library Catalogs included a tabulation of the number of users of card catalogs during March 10 and 12. In the General Library, where the public catalog is a union catalog of the libraries in the University system, it was found that 2.3 people arrived each minute during busy periods. The average per minute
over a day's time was 1.025. On March 10 and 12 the tabulators
found that the peak period at the General Library occurred between
3 and 4 P.M., when 25 individuals arrived every 10 minutes. This
would mean that during the single hour between 3 and 4 P.M. the
number of persons using the catalog was 150. To obtain the number of users in an average day, the 14 hour day of 840 minutes,

multiplied by the average number of users per minute (i.e. 1.025 people) would suggest that an average of 861 individuals consult the catalog every day.   This figure gives an indication of the heavy use a printed catalog would have to be able to bear.   It often appears to reference librarians and readers' advisers that when printed indexes are advocated as substitutes for cards in the library's catalog, little thought is given to the enormous - and increasing - amount of use these volumes must be able to withstand.

It seemed pertinent to this study to inquire into what use has been made of book catalogs in those institutions where good printed catalogs existed, and where the demands were of a scholarly nature.

The best example is that offered by the Library of Congress. Robert D. Stevens, then Coordinator for the Development and Organization of the Collections in the Library of Congress, reported that 15 sets of the Catalog of Books Represented by Library of Congress Printed Cards were variously disposed.   Sets were housed in the Card Division, the Reference Alcove, the Law Reference Collection, Study Room Reference, the Loan Division, the Annex Catalog, the Law Library in the Capitol, the Main Reading Room Alcove, the Rare Book Division Reference Section, the Order Division, the Public Catalog, the Copyright Division, the office of the Chief Assistant Librarian, and in the Inter-Library Loan Office. Six sets of the subject catalog were distributed as follows: the Rare Book Division, the Main Reading Room Alcove, and four sets on the shelves.   At the same time, three card catalogs provide access to the collections: the Public Catalog in the Main Library,

the Official Catalog in the Annex Building, and a so-called Annex
Catalog on the fifth floor adjacent to the Jefferson Reading Room -
also a public catalog, but incomplete for entries before 1939.
"You will see from the list of assignments," Mr. Stevens wrote,
"that in theory the printed catalogs are widely used for acquisitions, cataloging and reference work. In practice, however, I
must report that the tendency is to use the card catalogs, primarily the Official or the Main Catalogs or even the National Union Catalog. The main reason is that search in the printed catalog can
never be regarded as final. In addition there is the problem of
reclassification and consequent change of call number." The Library of Congress does not have sets of its Catalog on the various
stack levels, mainly because the stacks are not generally open to
the public. Formerly they had "Deck Catalogs" (on cards) for the
works in the particular area in which these were located, but these
have not been kept up. In conclusion, he wrote: "I think that this
can all be summed up by saying that experience at LC so far has
not been such as to indicate that book catalogs are to the staff an
acceptable substitute for the dictionary card catalogs..."

Another printed catalog of a research collection which, though
now much out-of-date, is still a very useful identification and location tool for scholars and interlibrary loan librarians in other libraries, is Princeton University Library's Alphabetical Finding
List (1921). In reply to our question concerning the use now made
of the List in Princeton libraries, Frederick L. Arnold, Reference
Librarian, reported that the List never did take the place of the
card catalog. Multiple copies were distributed in the various de-

partmental libraries, "but are not now used at all." No copies
are placed on the various stack levels; the main library's copy is
in the bibliography collection.   As far as reference use in the library is concerned, the List is rarely consulted, except as in the
case of a reader wishing to look over the entire Civil War collection, for example.   In such cases it is easier for him to use the
List, Mr. Arnold says, than the shelf list.   The abbreviated entries are considered quite inadequate, and many inaccuracies exist.

In libraries where the object is not necessarily to give complete information, but simply to give an indication of the Library's
holdings and make its resources available, printed catalogs may be
the most inexpensive way of doing so.   Thus the New York State
Library's catalogs, abbreviated though they may be, no doubt provide a very useful source to libraries dependent on its aid to supplement their own collections.   Catalogs like the Los Angeles system catalogs keep the branches informed on what the system has
available.   In all such cases, however, some central card catalog
or supplement must keep the system's information up-to-date.

In large research libraries greater demands are made on the
catalog.   To be really effective, it must be tailored to the institution's needs.   Indeed, even the flexible card catalog cannot always
keep up with the current demand, and many difficult and involved
searches must be made by reference librarians for information
which has not yet appeared in it.

The idea that some central list, such as the National Union
Catalog, could be adapted as an economical means for serving as a
printed catalog for an individual library's collection, has been sug-

gested.   It would be difficult, indeed, to do this effectively from
the user's point of view.   Analytics and cross references needed in
one library may not be used by another.   Differences in call numbers would have to be indicated, or changed on the already cataloged books to conform to the printed catalog entries.   New books
might have to be held until the information appeared in the printed
catalog.   Uses of books may vary in libraries, and classification is
often determined by the particular subject emphases in the institutions acquiring them.   The book catalog would include much material the library did not possess, and the library, in turn, would certainly include some titles not in the union catalog.   The catalog
user who is now baffled by the intricacies of a card catalog would
be frustrated by attempts to determine which books in the catalog
the library actually possessed.

In this connection the University of California Library (Berkeley) which has a divided catalog, in 1951 conducted an investigation
to determine whether the Library of Congress Subject Catalog could
be substituted for the Library's own subject catalog.   CU News for
September 27, 1951, reported: "The results of this investigation
give partial support to the idea of substituting the LC Subject Catalog for our own subject cataloging.   A sample comparison of the
cards and LC's Subject Catalog for the letters A and B... shows
that 65 percent of locally manufactured subject entries produced in
1950 were found in the LC Subject Catalog for 1950.   On the other
hand, of the 2,789 (1950) imprints in letters A and B of the LC
Subject Catalog for 1950, only 16 percent were found in the CU
file.   Other parts of the investigation showed that as time goes on

more and more CU acquisitions appear in the LC Subject Catalog,
and theoretically it can be assumed that in the course of time substantially everything acquired by the University of California will
appear in the LC Subject Catalog. Nevertheless, this information
is embedded in the record of vastly larger LC acquisitions and the
probability of increasing numbers of abortive searches by users of
the LC Subject Catalog as a local substitute is certain. Consequently, it has been concluded that the substitution of the LC Subject Catalog (and for more recent publications the Cumulative Book
Index) for local subject cataloging is not feasible."

Some years ago the Library of Congress author catalog was
considered for marking as a union catalog for the holdings of libraries in the Ann Arbor-Detroit-Lansing area. Some of the earlier volumes were actually checked against holdings, but the project
fell by the wayside because of lack of funds and a use that did not
seem to justify the expenditure. When such checks are made, it is
astonishing how many entries in the local catalogs are not in the
Library of Congress catalog, and vice versa.

The heavy use made of the public card catalog in large research libraries will certainly mean heavy use of the printed book
catalogs, if these should be substituted. In order to get some idea
of what it would mean in terms of space and facilities, the University of Michigan Public Catalog is taken as an example for comparison with the printed catalogs of the Library of Congress and the
Slavonic Division of The New York Public Library.

There are approximately 3,500,000 cards occupying some 3757
catalog drawers in the University of Michigan catalog. If this dic-

tionary catalog were to be reproduced in the same fashion as LC's Catalog of Books Represented by Library of Congress Printed Cards (167 volumes) the cards would occupy approximately 304 volumes. (The LC catalog has about 640 pages per volume, with an estimated 18 entries per page, or about 11,520 entries per volume.) Each set of the Michigan printed catalog would occupy approximately 42.5 running feet of shelf space.

If the University of Michigan's dictionary catalog were to be reproduced in the manner in which G. K. Hall and Company reproduced The New York Public Library's Dictionary Catalogue of the Slavonic Collection it would occupy approximately 165 volumes. [The Slavonic Catalogue contains approximately 550,000 entries, occupying 26 volumes of some 900 pages each.] The 26 volumes occupy about 4.5 running feet of shelf space. A University of Michigan catalog reproduced in this fashion would occupy approximately 28 feet of shelf space. The size and weight of these volumes, however, is not conducive to long life if subjected to very heavy use.

Experience with various library catalogs used at Michigan has demonstrated that the Library of Congress catalogs - which get much the heaviest use of the printed catalogs - is of a size, weight, sewing and binding better adapted to heavy use than any of the others. The present amount of use of this catalog, however, would be negligible compared with the use of a printed catalog providing the only access to the greater part of the Library's own collections.

If one were to substitute a printed book catalog for the tradi-

tional card catalog, at least two sets of the printed catalog would
have to be provided at the supplemental card catalog (or central
catalog area) - one at standing height tables, with single shelving,
so that no great number of users need be concentrated at any one
spot; the other set double shelved at sitting height tables for
lengthier use. It must be borne in mind that in the University of
Michigan Library provision would have to be made for as
many as 150 users per hour, with an average time of 5.269 minutes per person. To be sure, if multiple copies were available in
the General Library and in departmental and divisional libraries, it
would undoubtedly have a bearing on the planning at the central
point.

In libraries where such copying facilities are readily available,
it may be necessary to have a third set for photoduplication purposes only, so that the volumes in the bibliography-supplemental
catalog area would not be absent when needed.

In very large libraries with book stacks covering many acres
and several floor levels, access to copies on the various levels (or
on every other level) would facilitate use and relieve some of the
present pressure on the central catalog. Especially where stacks
are open to the general public would the location of such catalogs
be advantageous.

The foregoing gives some idea of practical considerations, from
the use angle, of the substitution of printed book catalogs for card
catalogs. There is no question but that reference and other service and divisional librarians would welcome printed book catalogs
as additions to a complete, up-to-date central card catalog.

One alternative to the reproduction of the complete dictionary catalog might be the printing of the subject catalog only - an alternative with which, we think, most service librarians would (though reluctantly) compromise in the interests of economy. Another alternative would be the printing of catalogs of special collections (e.g. Howard University. The Moorland Foundation. A Catalogue of the African Collection in the Moorland Foundation (1958); New York. Public Library. Dictionary Catalogue of the Slavonic Collection (1960); Michigan. University. Library. Union List of Scientific and Technical Serials in the University of Michigan Library (1959)). Special collection catalogs like the British Museum (Natural History) Library catalog, with its analytics and contents for sets, careful detailing of editions, etc., provide wonderful and permanently useful bibliographic tools. These may, indeed, be the most economical means of giving access to special collections for which catalog cards have never been provided (e.g. Harvard's Kilgour Collection of Russian belles lettres). Such catalogs might well supersede card catalog entries in overloaded public catalogs where they now exist.

In view, however, of the experience of such libraries as the Library of Congress and Princeton, and the everyday experience of reference and other service librarians, printed book catalogs representing the entire library collection can never fully supersede the flexible card catalog, that ingenious, if cumbersome and expensive, device so much more adaptable to additions and changes.

References

1.   Gull, Dake.   "Substitutes for the card catalog" (In Taube's
     <u>Coordinate indexing,</u> 1953, p. 78).   Gull says that 87 libraries
     maintaining depository catalogs gave them up after 1947, when
     the L. C. catalog was printed.

Book Catalogs and Card Catalogs[*]

By M. Ruth MacDonald

The year is 1961 and we are less than forty years away from
the 21st century. We can expect that each succeeding year will
bring increased awareness of the proximity of the new century and
of the changes it will generate. Just as the 20th century has witnessed revolutionary changes not dreamed of in 1861, the 21st century can be expected to produce changes we can not now foresee.

What about libraries, and librarianship, in the 19th, 20th, and
21st centuries? We recall the revolutionary changes that came in
the last quarter of the 19th century and the first quarter of the 20th
century. They include a great expansion in the number and types
of libraries, in the growth of library collections, in concepts of
library services, in the development of library schools, and in the
techniques of our profession. In the last category, four major developments come to mind: classification systems, cataloging rules,
the dictionary card catalog, and printed catalog cards.

What changes have come during the second quarter of the 20th
century and the first years of the third quarter? These years
have witnessed tremendous growth in library collections and many
refinements and modifications of library purposes, services, and

* This paper was presented at the ALA-RTSD/RSD Book Catalogs Interdivisional Committee Program Meeting, July 10, 1961, Cleveland.

Library Resources and Technical Services, 6:217-222; Summer,
1962.

techniques, but no real changes.   Classification schemes have increased in number; cataloging rules have been revised; the number
of printed catalog cards has increased year after year; and dictionary card catalogs have grown to elephantine size.   We should modi-
fy this rather gloomy picture by citing the development of union
catalogs, depository centers, and the Farmington Plan, as evidence
of increased cooperation among librarians.

Looking back over the past 35 years it is difficult not to con-
clude that librarianship is a conservative profession.   It is a good
sign for the future that an increasing number of librarians are looking closely at the present situation and asserting that librarians
must act on new ideas and new procedures or stand a chance of being lost in the rush toward the 21st century.

Following this broad introduction, I shall now direct my attention to one segment of the problems that face large libraries: the
card catalog.   The dictionary card catalog, developed on the philosophy of encompassing an entire library collection in a single index,
has grown to monumental size.   As it has increased in bulk, it has
lost its ability to serve specialized needs.

It is now evident that the complete coverage attempted by the
dictionary catalog is impossible, and even undesirable, for the less-
sophisticated reader.   It is also evident that no one catalog can include enough information to satisfy all needs.   It has taken us a
long time to realize that the greater the number of elements we
crowd into one catalog, the less we can do with those elements.
The dictionary catalog, once our greatest hope, now threatens to destroy itself, and in so doing will wreak havoc on our library services.

We are faced with the realization that we must find and adopt different forms for the cataloging records if we are to curtail further losses in catalog efficiency. To foresee what is needed and then to remedy the situation will require careful observation, measurement, imagination, and probably a certain amount of trial and error. One thing is certain--the process of discovering a solution to our catalog problems must not be limited to a single pattern or method.

At this point I shall further limit my remarks to a discussion of one possible solution of the present dictionary catalog problem-- a pattern of book catalogs which might be supplemented by one or more limited card catalogs.

Let me digress long enough to point out how pertinent this discussion is to the current revision of cataloging rules. The revisions propose some changes which will have far-reaching results. A large library considering the effects of the revised rules on its catalog if implemented according to usual recataloging patterns, might decide to limit its acceptance of the new rules. It might not adopt all of them and it might have to find short-cuts in implementing those it does adopt. Compromising the application of the new rules will not provide a satisfactory solution.

It seems to me that library and catalog needs of the future support the adoption of the revised rules and further, that these needs dictate a shift to new catalog patterns. In fact, the new rules offer us the opportunity for a much-needed fresh beginning.

I believe this fresh beginning will mean a new pattern of book-and-card-catalogs for large libraries with research collections. I

believe this fresh beginning is inevitable, even without the stimulus
of the revised cataloging rules, and that we must begin now to prepare ourselves and our libraries for it.

It is a bit difficult to say how we should ready ourselves for
changes on which we are not yet agreed. Possibly the best first
step would be to cease to be satisfied with what we now have, with
the present purposes and patterns of our work, and with our individual knowledge. Instead of a personal and individual day-by-day
approach to our work it would be desirable to develop a unified approach that considers and relates present operations to future needs.
As individuals we would still get on with our immediate jobs, but
with an awareness of the future not now common among librarians.

While there does not seem to be any one way to ready our libraries for the needed changes, a common-sense approach is available. We can start by admitting that good as our libraries may be,
they can and must be made better if they are to measure up to
their greatest potential.

I would suggest that the work the catalogers have done during
the past several years in studying and revising cataloging rules is
a step in the right direction. The step has been too limited, however, because librarians other than catalogers have not participated
to any extent and because the work has been confined largely to one
element of cataloging. Similar work is needed on subject headings,
classification, on the form and content of library catalogs, and on
many topics outside the area of the technical services.

Let us return to a consideration of "a pattern of book catalogs
supplemented by one or more limited card catalogs."

My favorite approach to any catalog problem is an application of the "divide and conquer" technique. This is just another way of saying that a problem should be broken down into its component parts in order to identify where changes are needed and what changes should be made.

How might the "divide and conquer" procedure be applied in a practical way to the problems presented by a large dictionary catalog? I think the first and most important step would be to decide to close the present catalog and begin an entirely new one. The accumulations of the past would thus be separated from and sheared of their ability to influence the new catalog. The date selected for commencing the new catalog could be a publication date or a cataloging date. Whatever date is chosen should be set far enough in the future to allow ample time for planning, for preparing the staff, and for acquainting the public with the plans.

While the plans must include careful decisions on the form and arrangement of the new catalog, they do not need to include final decisions on the disposition of the old catalog. I have no doubt that the future will provide the technical know-how necessary to preserve in usable, space-saving form, the essential information presently contained in any large dictionary catalog.

Let us consider the case of a large university library with a correspondingly large dictionary catalog, a number of branch catalogs, a generous book fund, an active academic program, and a staff geared to current operations. Presumably its central catalog is a good one, although its size is an impediment of sorts, some of its subject headings and cross references are out of date, and some of its information duplicates information available elsewhere in the library.

This library makes full use of Library of Congress cataloging and participates in various cooperative cataloging efforts. It must, therefore, take into account what other large libraries are planning to do about implementing the revised cataloging rules before it decides on its own course of action. On the basis of its own future needs, and because of its cooperative interests and responsibilities, the library decides it will adopt the new cataloging rules as of a predetermined date. It also decides it will begin a new card catalog.

The new card catalog, either divided or arranged in dictionary form, will provide for some of the changes needed. The changes permitted, however, will not be sufficient to solve the problems of the future. These problems relate to catalog size and age, compounded by technical knowledge, subject and language proficiency, duplicate effort, staff shortages, time, and money. While a new card catalog would help, at least for a time, it would not be a lasting solution.

A combination of book catalogs and card catalog supplements on more or less traditional patterns might provide some relief for the university library's catalog problems. But "some relief" is not a solution.

It seems to me that combinations of book catalogs and card catalogs in new patterns are needed and are bound to develop. Let me outline briefly one pattern from the great variety of patterns we must consider as we search for the best patterns for the near future and for the more distant future.

This plan presupposes the existence of a national central cataloging office, properly staffed and equipped to service its subscriber libraries. We have such a center now, in part, in the Library of Congress.

The central cataloging plan would require the cooperation of publishers (commercial, educational, institutional, governmental, etc.). It would concern titles in their pre-publication form as well as in their published form. While the plan thus bears some resemblance to the recent Cataloging-in-Source experiment, it would avoid some of its difficulties because galley proofs could serve the plan's pre-publication needs.

Each new publication would be given a unique identification number. The number would become an inseparable part of the publication, being printed on an inside page and stamped on its cover. The number would become the title's publication-stock-order number, its library shelving and circulation number, and its catalog card number, if any.

For a discussion on such numbering I refer you to "A Proposal for a National Code Number System for Current Publications," by G. A. Harrer and Alex Ladenson (Library Resources & Technical Services, 6:4-12. Winter 1962).

On the basis of the galley proofs or the published titles supplied by publishers, brief or full cataloging records would be prepared. All name entries and their cross references could be properly established and subject headings would be regularly selected and assigned. The "briefness" in the description of titles cataloged

from galley proof would relate to such details as collation (1 v.
would be used instead of paging) and in the possible omission of
bibliographic notes.

The resulting cataloging records would appear in a frequently
issued and cumulated printed book catalog, issued in three or more
sections.   (For example, I suggest that three sections are essential: (1) author; (2) subject; (3) numerical.   There might well be
separate catalog series for different languages, for different types
of publications, etc., etc.).   All of the "brief" descriptions would
be superceded by full descriptions after the books are published.
Only the full descriptions would be published in the larger cumulations of the printed catalog.

The required sections of the printed book catalog in sufficient
copies would become the library's new catalog.   There would be a
supplementary numerical card catalog to supply information on local
ownership and on special locations.   Any such numerical card catalog would be a limited file because as each large cumulation of the
printed catalog is received, its numerical sections could easily be
marked.   If desired, the numerical cards then withdrawn could be
re-arranged and used as a basis for annotating the author section.

Cards for the numerical catalog and/or the shelflist could be
prepared from printed preliminary or final cataloging information,
because the essential data on identification number, names, and
subject headings would be complete in both listings.   If desired,
the central cataloging service could supply printed cards for the
usual records and for any special records, such as a catalog of local authors.

We must acknowledge that specialized local cataloging needs do exist. Because they are not all equally legitimate, each should be required to justify itself before it is permitted to interfere with any new plan for centralized cataloging. A centralized cataloging plan should provide enough advantages to outweigh the disadvantages that might result from the elimination of special local records designed to meet specialized local needs.

Titles published by the cooperating publishers after the plan becomes operable would be ordered by their identification numbers. Pre-order searching would be limited to a check of the publication identification number in the library's outstanding order file and in its ownership-location records.

Should the library subscribers prefer to continue for the present to use subject classification for all or a part of the new publications, this could be accomplished within the plan. The class number from an acceptable classification system could be printed as part of the identification number. The class number added above the identification number would turn the latter into the author and book number elements of today's call number. There could be no problem of duplicate call numbers. The card in the library's ownership-location records could still be arranged under the publication's identification number, and this number could still be used for order purposes.

Such a plan would bring large savings in personnel, time, money, and space requirements. It would curtail, and in some instances eliminate, present costs of subject classification, cataloging, call numbers, filing, catalog cabinets, and processing. Under such a plan there would be a greatly reduced need for librarian-catalogers, except in the central cataloging office. In the larger libraries a small staff would still be required to catalog books needed urgently, special collections, unique items, and old publications.

The convenience of multiple copies of the various sections of the printed catalog, and the availability of additional personnel no longer required in the technical service areas, should counterbalance any preference the public service staff may have for the present card catalog's well-known physical and bibliographical form.

One advantage of using a library collection through printed subject catalogs is the variety of approaches they afford. This is especially advantageous where distinctions between specialties are not clear-cut, yet their terminology remains distinctive. Another advantage is that as a need arises for a new subject approach, it can be supplied while the former approaches are still maintained.

Such a centralized cataloging plan would result in a uniform product and uniform records in cooperating libraries. This uniformity would help both the libraries and the users of libraries. I have no doubt that under such a system a more generous supply of entries will be technically and economically feasible. Under a centralized system there could be fully qualified experts in three major areas: cataloging, subject analysis, and languages, as well as experts in the various forms of material: documents, music, maps, serials, etc.

Under the centralized system suggested, a library could still have a card catalog, because the necessary cards could be reproduced from the book catalog, or obtained from the central office or through the book publisher or dealer.

The printed book catalog will no doubt include more entries than are available in any one library. I do not believe this is necessarily bad, for it will build into the locally-used catalog some of the advantages of union catalogs and subject bibliographies.

In using a library, the identification number will be a convenient way to list the books wanted from the shelves, and the library page (human or machine) would search the ownership-location records. An added advantage would be the use of the same number for a title in all libraries under the plan.

In case anyone thinks this plan is too modest and too unsophisticated--let me say that I agree. It is offered merely as a basis for further discussion on the immediate future of "Book Catalogs and Card Catalogs."

Is The Card Catalog Obsolete?*

By Margaret C. Brown

For half a century the card catalog has been unchallenged as
the accepted way in which to display the bibliographical record of
a library's collection. Despite the fact that the early catalogs in
this country were book catalogs, not card catalogs, the card catalog today is so taken for granted that a distinction is not always
made between form and content.

The actual information which appears on the cards--or what
should appear on the cards--has been the subject of considerable
debate, particularly in recent years. It is a topic which is still
serviceable and one which will doubtless occupy our attention more
rather than less in the years ahead. Recognizing that it makes
little difference in what form the catalog appears if the cataloging
itself is not done with care and competence, it is nevertheless the
form, rather than the content, of the catalog which is the subject
of comment here.

One of the most attractive features of the card catalog,
whether in dictionary or classed arrangement, has been the ease of
interfiling cards to maintain the currency of the catalog on a day-
to-day basis. When compared to catalogs on sheets or in book
form, the popular forms in the 19th century, the card catalog
possessed distinct advantages which the American librarian had no

*Pennsylvania Library Association Bulletin, 18:10-13, Feb., 1963.

difficulty in recognizing.

The prevalence of the card catalog over the years should not necessarily be considered evidence of the unwillingness of librarians to change methods and to try new techniques. It could be proof as well of the inherent flexibility and usefulness of the library catalog in card form. A good case could be made for the view that, in terms of our libraries' requirements during the first half of the present century, the card catalog served well.

The question which we should be asking now is whether the card catalog will serve as well in the next half century or even in the next decade. The catalog is one of the means--the principal one, it should not be forgotten--of making available to readers the resources of a library. As readers' requirements change, so service patterns change, and so perhaps catalogs should change. Has "adequate library service" been redefined in any significant way in the last ten or fifteen years? Does the present-day view of library service demand anything different, or anything more, of library catalogs?

Without going into an historical development of library service during recent decades, it may suffice to mention one or two aspects of modern library service which have been recognized and provided for in Pennsylvania's new Library Code. For example, there is a growing acceptance of the idea that a given library's service to its community, whether that community be a political unit, a college campus, or a business organization, requires access to resources outside its own immediate jurisdiction. The Library Code, a law which will make possible an integrated system of

library service in Pennsylvania, derives directly from the recognition of this interdependence of all libraries.

Library cooperation in its various manifestations is not a
new concept to librarians. The significant point is that it is no
longer a new concept to our readers. The increase in requests
for interlibrary loans and the up-surge in the non-resident's use
of libraries of all kinds reflect the reader's changing views toward
the availability of library materials. He recognizes that no single
library may have everything he wants, and in his search for what
he needs he is unhampered by any concern for political or campus
boundaries.

One reason no library can be expected to have all items
which its readers request lies in the great increase in the quantity
of published material available today over that of even two or
three years ago. Another is the increase in the cost of obtaining
and housing this material. It follows that cooperative buying--
up to now a policy honored more in the breach than in the observ-
ance, even by academic libraries--must find acceptance and recognition in book selection practices, as well as policies, of many
more libraries than at present. Again, the Pennsylvania law recognizes this development with the provision for four large resource
libraries in the Commonwealth to serve the specialized needs of all
its citizens. These Regional Library Resource Centers accept
responsibility for acquiring less used, but not necessarily less essential, items in designated subject areas.

How do these two developments, the growing need to provide
library service on a regional rather than a local basis and the

development of specialized regional collections, affect the demands made on the catalogs? The need for currency in the catalog, that is, for an up-to-date catalog which reflects the latest additions to the collection, has not changed. And the long-recognized need for wider adherence to accepted principles of cataloging grows more pressing as greater reliance is placed on cooperative cataloging and union catalogs. But, in addition, it has become increasingly important that each library have a means of learning quickly the contents of collections other than its own.

In Pennsylvania access to this information is necessary for at least two reasons: (1) to locate copies of books in neighboring libraries and thus strengthen the service within the district organization and (2) to insure the success of any plan of cooperative buying essential if the concept underlying the establishment of the four regional resource libraries is to be fully realized. It could be maintained that, to a degree, this information is already available. The National Union Catalog and the Union List of Serials, the two most essential tools for our national bibliographic health, indicate location of copies. However, these publications are not widely held by Pennsylvania's libraries and they are keyed more to the national than to the local picture. For the Philadelphia area there is a comparable bibliography on cards, the Union Library Catalogue of the Philadelphia Metropolitan Area, which as of January 1, 1963, will receive a record of all current additions of the four resource libraries in the Commonwealth. However, the resource libraries should not be called upon to furnish copies of titles held in district libraries.

If Pennsylvania is to have a truly integrated system of libraries, something more will be required. There would seem to be a need for catalogs of individual libraries and, when feasible, perhaps a union catalog of the holdings of a group of libraries. There might be union catalogs covering the holdings of a given geographical area, or catalogs covering a given subject field or restricted to a particular form, such as films.

These catalogs could be in card form, but, in terms of today's needs, the card catalog has two rather serious limitations. The card catalog can only be consulted in one place and a given entry can only be consulted by one person at a time. The catalog, in card form, is a cumbersome instrument, not easily duplicated nor made readily available in other locations. The Union Library Catalogue is a pearl beyond price, but, in its present form, it is not easily moved, as the staff is in a position to attest from recent first-hand experience. The only solution to congestion at a card catalog has been the design of the ranch-style catalog case as contrasted to the traditional upright catalog case. This is a solution which not all libraries have sufficient floor space to adopt.

Fortunately, along with changing concepts of library service, there have been some revolutionary developments in other fields such as the design of printing equipment and of data processing machines. Because of these advances, it now seems likely that book catalogs could be produced which would provide the same information as the card catalogs and also have one additional feature, namely, easy accessibility by readers at widely scattered geographical points.

Today a number of library catalogs are being produced in book form. Probably the best known and most important book catalog, since the book catalog was "rediscovered," is A Catalog of Books Represented by Library of Congress Printed Cards which ultimately became The National Union Catalog. Among the public libraries which have adopted the book catalog, the most notable are the King County Public Library in the state of Washington and the Los Angeles County Public Library. Recently it was announced that the University of California at Los Angeles would shortly begin the task of putting its catalog in book form. G.K. Hall & Company will publish this catalog as it has many other catalogs of special collections, by photographically reproducing the card catalog. There are numerous instances of special libraries using IBM equipment to produce book catalogs of their collections. One of the most spectacular bibliographies in book form, this one produced by the use of Eastman-Kodak Listomatic camera, is the Index Medicus published by the National Library of Medicine.

While there are at present several methods of making book catalogs, there undoubtedly will be still other means available very soon. The possibilities are likely to be so numerous that librarians will have to be cautioned against being dazzled by what is available and concentrate on what is needed. A good rule might be: don't settle for less than you need; and don't take more than you want. The method selected must satisfy requirements for currency and provide up-to-date information in the catalog. But, most of all, it must meet the needs of the particular library situation. If it is a bibliography that is wanted and it is a finding list that is offered,

the needs of the library or libraries are not being met. Probably
the greatest difficulty, in such a circumstance, will be to determine whether it is a finding list or a bibliography which is required!

Publishing a book catalog is not an inexpensive enterprise today, but undoubtedly it will be less costly in the near future. It
is not easy to say whether a book catalog is cheaper than a card
catalog, since most library systems have little reliable data on the
cost of the card catalog. Much has been written about the cost of
cataloging--usually in astonishment, awe, or disbelief--but it still
may turn out to be the bargain of the century. However, it is not
the cost of cataloging, but the cost of the catalog, which is being
discussed here. The suggestion that some catalogs might be produced better in book form than housed in a catalog cabinet is not
made in the interests of economy. It is necessary to state this,
since any suggestion made by a cataloger is suspected, especially
by reference librarians, of being motivated solely by reasons of
economy. Better service, measured in terms of improved catalogs
and easier access to library collections through these catalogs, is
the consideration.

Perhaps the first book catalog in Pennsylvania might be produced by a large library system which already has centralized processing. Ultimately, as methods are improved and costs are
reduced, other applications could be made. Those district libraries
with good catalogs could make their collections more accessible to
libraries within their districts by publishing their catalogs in book
form. If centralized processing becomes a reality in any of the
districts, it would be wise to consider a union catalog of district

holdings in book form.   Because the use of book catalogs need not be restricted to any one location, the distribution or sale of catalogs need not be restricted necessarily to libraries.   Schools and other educational institutions might wish to avail themselves of this means of locating desired material in the community or in the area.

Pennsylvania is fortunate in having the Library Code designed to meet the specific needs of the citizens of this Commonwealth. Pennsylvania is beginning a new stage of library development and embarking on a program which, when successfully under way, will be equal of that in any state in the Union.   At such a moment it seems entirely appropriate to study the best means available to improve bibliographical services so basic to good library service.

Shelf List As Union Catalog[*]

By Donald Coney
and George Piternick

In attempting to arrive at a reasonable plan of development the libraries of the seven University of California campuses have been exploring for some time means of providing the best possible intercampus access to their library collections. Since it appears certain that the student populations of the campuses will expand very rapidly, with corresponding increases of teachers, faculty interest in improved means of intercampus access is high.

One of the access devices frequently mentioned in faculty discussions is the well known union card catalog. This bibliographical device appears to have entrenched itself in the layman's concept of vital library apparatus. The union catalog, however, received its greatest development during the Depression as a by-product of massive white collar relief projects. Of the many union card catalogs launched during the thirties with W. P. A. and other governmental aid, only a relatively few are alive today, and most of these are sadly in arrears. It is doubtful that any conceivable increase in the intercampus use of library materials would justify the cost of a catalog of this type at each campus. There is another means, however, by which the intercampus availability of books can be advertised, at far lower cost. This is the printed catalog.

* College and Research Libraries, 22:193-194, May, 1961.

To obtain union catalog coverage it is not essential that the holdings listings of the member libraries be interfiled into a single catalog, desirable though that may be.   Basically, a group of separate printed catalogs, each containing the holdings of one of the campus libraries, constitutes a union catalog.   Need all the campuses be represented by their catalogs ?   Fully 85 per cent of the books held by University of California libraries are located either in Berkeley or Los Angeles, and it appears likely that catalogs of these two collections, available on all campuses, would take care of the great majority of all intercampus interlibrary transactions. (In 1959/60, 87 per cent of all intercampus interlibrary loans within the University of California were made from the Berkeley and Los Angeles campuses.)

The arrangement of such printed catalogs offers a variety of possibilities:

Author (main entry).   Although this arrangement is the most usual and obvious, it offers perhaps the least additional benefit to what facilities already exist in the way of intercampus leading aids. It is not difficult at present, through the services of the National Union Catalog and the communication facilities now existing (which include Teletype), to locate a book in one of the University of California libraries if a specific title is wanted.   A printed author catalog would perhaps facilitate the process somewhat, but it would be of no practical aid in cases where information on a given subject area were the desideratum.   It is felt that this need for subject aid is the major one facing faculty and research personnel on the smaller campuses.

Subject. Arrangement by subject in a printed catalog has many obvious advantages. Its disadvantages lie in its relatively greater bulk, and in the alphabetical arrangement of fairly specific subject headings which has the effect of obscuring hierarchical subject relationships.

Shelf list. A shelf list catalog of a library's holdings has one characteristic which would make it extremely useful in meeting the needs envisaged. A printed shelf list catalog is the closest possible equivalent to visiting the library represented and examining the books on its shelves. It is felt that this approach is the one most desired by the research personnel on the several campuses.

The idea of using a series of separately printed shelf lists in book form appears to be sufficiently unusual to provoke initial rejection. To the observation that classified arrangement makes such a list difficult to use can be opposed the fact that a public shelf list has been used successfully for many decades by students and faculty at the Berkeley campus of the University of California as a valued supplement to the author-title and subject catalogs. The users of this shelf list, employing the Library of Congress classification schedules as a key, apparently become accustomed to going to a particular location in the shelf list in much the same way as they learn to go to a particular location in the stacks for materials in their fields of interest. There are two interesting advantages to the use of the shelf list for this purpose which merit careful consideration. One, mentioned earlier, is that the shelf list is the least bulky of the several card records which can be duplicated in book form and, hence, the least expensive to manufacture. The other is that publication of a shelf list could proceed serially, each part being useful as published to a much higher degree than a segment of an alphabetically arranged list. This same advantage would permit the omission of some sections of the shelf list whose use might be judged to be insufficient to justify publication. To the objection that the shelf list may offer a less complete subject presentation of the library's holdings than the subject catalog, answer can be made that in relation to cost it may be quite enough, and that the subject catalog itself falls short of utter perfection.

This approach to a substitute for a conventional union catalog will receive further study at the University of California. The authors of this article would be interested in having comments on the ideas put forward.

Building Card Catalogs For Eventual Migration Into Book Form

By Robert E. Kingery

This paper assumes that the card catalog will eventually migrate into a book catalog by means of some photo-printing process, i.e., that copy will not be newly prepared for reproduction in book form. It also assumes that some reduction will be made in the size of individual entries in the photo-printing process. Hence, this paper is primarily concerned, although not exclusively, with the impact of the intention to migrate the public card catalog into book form on the format of unit cards and certain other matters related to the handling of individual card entries. It may be noted here that the early development of unit cards was as a basis for the creation of copy for eventual printing. Here, we have suddenly come full circle in this matter as we have in so many other library operations.

Card Stock and Dimensions. Other papers in this volume discuss card dimensions in relation to printing techniques. Here, we need only emphasize the importance of a standard dimension carefully maintained. The quality of the stock must be sufficient for the requirements of handling by human beings and by machines, but need not be better. For example if standard 3 x 5 cards will within five years be used as copy for a printed book catalog, then their permanence and durability should be geared to the five-year requirement.

93

Type Size. If migration to book form entails, and it usually does, some reduction in the size of entries, this should be taken into consideration in the choice of type size to be used on catalog cards. In existing examples, this reduction ranges from 25 per cent to 50 per cent. Obviously, elite type and IBM executive type of certain styles will not survive such reduction. The entries prepared by The New York Public Library for the Fichero Bibliografico Hispanoamericano undergo approximately 33 1/3 per cent reduction without loss of legibility. Of course, the use of larger type for the preparation of card copy will inevitably result in the increase of "continued" cards. This can be offset to a considerable extent by eliminating or reducing space between elements on the original cards. If a file is to be copied frequently, as for example by Listomatic, then a control file that is never used except for reproduction purposes may well be justified.

Leading. Just as migration to a book catalog usually entails some reduction in type size, it also results in the reduction of leading, or the white space between lines of typewriter-composed copy. If a reduction of 25 per cent to 50 per cent is intended, this ratio will also prevail on the leading. Accordingly, it may be necessary to compose the original card copy on typewriters equipped with special ratchets which increase white space, or leading, between typewritten lines. It is known that this can be done with IBM electrics. It may be possible on other makes of machines.

Colors. If eventual photo-printing is intended, then care

should be exercised in the introduction of any sort of color coding
into the catalog, whether this be done by the use of other than
black typewriting, color edging, or other approaches. Similarly,
stamped and written additions to unit cards should be in black to
provide the greatest possible contrast. The best contrast for eventual photo-printing is black to white.

Limitation of the Original. The quality of the original almost
always sets a ceiling on the possible quality of the reproduction.
While electrostatic reproduction sometimes may surprisingly improve on the quality of the original, it is important to remember
that there is an inevitable relationship between the quality of the
original and the reproduction. Typewriter ribbons must be changed
frequently, typewriter keys must be kept clean, and written-in
material should be thick and black. "Dim" cards must ordinarily be
retyped before photographing, although this is not always possible.

Everything on the Front. Under most techniques, it is essential that all important information be put originally on the fronts of
the cards. There are ways of bringing information to the fronts
of cards such as a separate photographing of backs with overlays to
the front, or the cutting and reassembly of cards. These are
largely hand operations and require skilled staff to carry out.

Catalog in Flux. The catalog of any growing, used library is
always in a state of flux. The continuing addition of new material
leads to the recataloging of some material already in the collection.
Customarily, libraries insert temporary or "charge" cards for
material in the process of recataloging. At the time of migration,
the number of temporary cards should be reduced to a minimum.

Where this cannot be completely accomplished, it is helpful to have at least the main entry in complete form.

Guiding and Indexing. One of the virtues of the printed catalog is the presentation of a number of related entries to the reader, simultaneously on one surface. In a large library, the book catalog offers opportunities to inform the user of the structure of a particular part of the catalog. This is often difficult to do within the physical limitations of the card catalog. This opportunity entails the equivalent of either a table of contents or an index, made available in the first volume or volume-by-volume or at the head of a major subject. Some of the catalogs of The New York Public Library, printed and distributed by G. K. Hall & Co., demonstrate various applications of indexes and tables of contents.

Many large card catalogs suffer from under-guiding. This may arise from lack of staff or in vast and heavily used catalogs from the fact the guide cards do not last long enough to justify their preparation. It should be noted that under-guiding adds considerably to the cost of filing into a catalog and to the time required by users and staff to consult it. Fortunately, when the decision is made to migrate the catalog, it is fairly simple to type drop-in cards showing the subdivisions. The subdivisions should be included in a table of contents with appropriate page references to facilitate the use of the book catalog. The drop-in cards should be typed on display-type typewriters.

Density. Some of the presently available methods of migration have been criticized because they do not reduce or close up white space on unit cards. It is easy and sometimes naive to point out

the white space consumes paper. However, it is possible to reduce
space-occupied by a printed catalog to the point where simultaneous access will require more than one set. There is also some
advantage in having each entry occupy a standard unit of space.
Where simultaneous use is low, it may be helpful to close up that
white space on the original card copy, e.g., to have no blank
lines between elements on the unit card, including the tracings.
Those who argue this confuse the book catalog with a bibliography.
They are substantially similar but eventually different.

Time to Redesign the Unit Card. Libraries building card
catalogs for migration into book form may well wish to consider
whether the present design of the unit card is satisfactory. Taking
a Library of Congress Card, is the wide left-hand margin necessary? Do we need space between the descriptive elements and
the collation line? Should not the whole card be printed without
space between various elements, e.g., in paragraph form. What
about the position of the call number? Should it be to the right and
all on one line?

Supplements. Any library embarking on a card-to-book program must give thought to the publication of supplements in due
course. It has at least three alternatives. It may date its cards
so that entries not included in the original book catalog may be
photographed later. It may set up a supplementary catalog for internal use and for reproduction. It may set up a control file for
reproduction only. Each library will need to work out what is
satisfactory to it.

Filing Rules and Transliteration Systems. Most book catalogs should include a summary of the filing rules followed, with examples. In multi-volumed catalogs, these may well be repeated in each volume. For non-Roman alphabet collections, the particular transliteration system followed should be included. This becomes increasingly important as some of the major catalogs now are used internationally.

Technology of the Book Catalog. Within recent years as documented by papers in this volume, the technology of the book catalog has taken tremendous strides. It is probably only the beginning.

Publication and Access. In most situations a library producing a book catalog is inviting wider access to its material. By the act of publication, it acquires several responsibilities.

It is assumed that most libraries which undertake to put into book form any part or the whole of the catalogs does become a library of record. There are some obvious exceptions. To become a library of record means to undertake to preserve listed material in some form (microcard, electrostatic reproduction, microfilm) for all time. The responsibility to preserve in some form does not include responsibility for informing holders of the catalog of change-in-form of individual items in its collections. In these days of microforms, it is quite possible for a library to discard an original copy, and to reproduce the content in any form that is useful to the reader.

Once a library has published in book form and for general distribution either its general catalog or the catalog of a special collection, it must give extremely serious attention to the responsibility for informing holders of the basic catalog of additions made to its collection. This may be done in a variety of ways, usually through supplements.

Once a library publicizes its resources through the publication and general distribution of a book catalog, it not only invites but must cope with requests for reproductions--photostat, microfilm, microcard and electrostats. However, no library should be expected to destroy its material for reproduction purposes. Where reproduction will damage the original, it should be understood that each library has the right of refusal.

Inter-library loan poses a problem. For libraries of record which publish major catalogs, the provision of electrostatic reproductions when requested probably relieves the library of any responsibility for agreeing to lend materials.

Ways To Prepare A "New Shaw" List*

By Hubbard Ballou

The first three assumptions upon which this inquiry is based are as follows: -

a. That a "New Shaw" would be published in book form, listing perhaps 50,000 titles, maybe annotated, maybe not.

b. That means would be found for keeping the list up to date ... additions and deletions ... perhaps 3,000 titles per annum ...

c. That the listing in both the basic volume and supplements would be "keyed" for various types of use.

These assumptions would indicate that though the finished list would be in book form, this volume would be based upon material collected, posted and stored as some sort of a card. Therefore, it is necessary to investigate means whereby entries on a card can be reproduced on the pages of a book. A brief outline of ways in which this has been done are as follows: -

A. By Whole Cards

    1) Photo-Offset of Arrayed Cards.

    2) Microfilm of Same + Xerox Copyflo + Offset.

B. By Parts of Cards

    1) Hot Type with Linotype Slugs.

    2) Photo-Offset of Shingled Cards.

    3) Sequential Camera + Offset.

*Prepared for the Council on Library Resources, Inc.

   4) IBM Machines + Photo-Offset.

In order to present a better picture of what is available, descriptions of each of these techniques follow:-

Whole Cards

A, 1) Photo-Offset of Arrayed Cards.

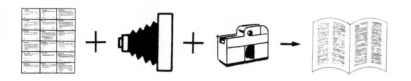

The most familiar example of this type of book catalog is to be found in the Catalog of Books Represented by Library of Congress Printed Cards. This monumental set of 167 volumes includes about 2,000,000 entries and began to come out in 1942. Each page consists of 18 Library of Congress catalog cards, 3 x 5 inches in size, arrayed in 3 columns of 6 cards each. This array was photographed at a reduction ratio of ca. 50 per cent (e.g. 1/2 size) and the resulting negative burned onto a photo-offset plate from which a page roughly 8 1/2 x 11 inches in size was printed. The illustration on page 103 is reduced to 80 per cent of its original size.

There has been a certain amount of objection to the lack of legibility resulting from this reduction in size, a feature especially noticeable in the sample page presented here, which exaggerates the loss of clarity by its two-generation reproduction from copy which is itself two generations from the original cards. Another weakness is the excess of white space on each entry. This results

in a large amount of paper which carries no information. For a
later supplement to this set, a variant method (actually belonging to
type B, 2: below) was used. After the Library of Congress cards
were printed in the standard form, the leading separating the various
sections of text was removed, and a condensed card was printed.
This resulted in a card with all of the information compressed into
the upper portion of the card. These cards were then shingled -
each card is laid on top of the card that it follows, so that it
covers up the white space at the bottom of the previous card. This
shingled array is photographed and printed. A reduction of about
50 per cent is still used, but an 8 1/2 x 11 page holding 33 or
more cards results. This can be seen in the sample page on page
104, from the <u>Author Catalog... 1948-52</u> (reduced to 80 per cent).

A, 2)   <u>Microfilm + Xerox + Offset.</u>

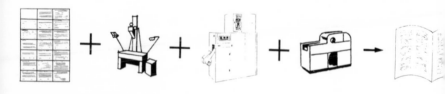

A variant on the previous method may be found in the catalogs
prepared by G. K. Hall of Boston. A sample page of the <u>Dictionary</u>
<u>Catalog of the Slavonic Collection of The New York Public Library,</u>
<u>Reference Department</u> shown on page 105.
Again we have an array of cards, in this case 3 x 5 inches, though
they have worked with other sizes. These 21 cards (3 columns of
7 cards each) are photographed with a planetary 35 mm microfilm

CATALOG OF PRINTED CARDS

aries Louis de Secondat, *baron de La Brède*
5.
aws. Translated from the French of M. de
de Montesquieu ... 7th ed. Edinburgh,
DCCCLXXVIII.

v. 2. State, The. 3. Law—Philosophy. 4. Juris-

JC179.M74 1778
[8Tbl-] 230.1

---

aries Louis de Secondat, *baron de La Brède*
5.
aws. Translated from the French of M. de
le Montesquieu. By Thomas Nugent ... 6th
r. and improved with considerable additions
ublin, W. Jones, 1792.

2. State, The. 3. Law—Philosophy. 4. Jurispru-
Thomas, 1700?-1772, tr. III. Title.

JC179.M74 1792
[8] 820.1

---

ries Louis de Secondat, *baron de La Brède*
5.
ws. Translated from the French of M. de
de Montesquieu. By Thomas Nugent ...
rev. and improved from the last Paris ed.
ndon, F. Wingrave [etc.] M.DCC.XCIII.

2. State, The. 3. Law—Philosophy. 4. Juris-
t, Thomas, 1700?-1772, tr. II. Title.

32—20874
[8Tcl]

---

aries Louis de Secondat, *baron de La Brède*
5.
ws. Translated from the French of the 5th
rinted at Worcester by Isaiah Thomas, jun.
ry Matthew Carey, Philadelphia; also by the
throughout the United States. July—1802.

hor's life and writings: v. 1, p. [v]-vii.

2. State, The. 3. Law—Philosophy. 4. Jurispru-

15—17880
[12g1]

---

ries Louis de Secondat, *baron de La Brède*
5.
ws. By M. de Secondat, baron de Montes-
te French by Thomas Nugent ... A new ed.,
compared with the best Paris ed. To which
noir of the life and writings of the author;
! the work by M. d'Alembert. In two vols
rinted for J. Collingwood [etc.] by T. C.

2. State, The. 3. Law—Philosophy. 4. Jurispru-
Le Rond d', 1717-1788.

JC179.M74 9—23888
[8ld1]

---

aries Louis de Secondat, *baron de La Brède*
5.
ws by M. de Secondat, baron de Montesquieu,
he French by Thomas Nugent, LL. D. A new
:. and compared with the best Paris ed., to
ed a memoir of the life and writings of the
alysis of the work by M. d'Alembert ... Cin-
& co., 1873.

2. State, The. 3. Law—Philosophy. 4. Juris-
ant, Thomas, 1700?-1772, tr. II. Alembert, Jean Le
III. Title.

15—17882
[4111]

Montesquieu, Charles Louis de Secondat, *baron de La Brède
et de*, 1689-1755.
The spirit of laws. By M. de Secondat, baron de Montesquieu. With d'Alembert's analysis of the work. Translated
from the French, by Thomas Nugent ... New ed., rev., with
additional notes, and a new memoir from the latest French editions, by J. V. Prichard ... London, G. Bell and sons, 1878.

2 v. front. (port.) 19ᶜᵐ. (*Half-title: Bohn's standard library*)

1. Political science. 2. State, The. 3. Law—Philosophy. 4. Jurispru-
dence. I. Alembert, Jean Le Rond d', 1717-1788. II. Nugent, Thomas,
1700?-1772, tr. III. Prichard, J. V.

15—18800 Revised
Library of Congress JC179.M74 1878
[r42j3]

Montesquieu, Charles Louis de Secondat, *baron de la Brède
et de*, 1689-1755.
The spirit of laws, by Baron de Montesquieu (Charles de Secondat) including d'Alembert's analysis of the work; tr. from
the French by Thomas Nugent, LL. D., with a special introduction by Hon. Frederic R. Coudert ... Rev. ed. ... New York,
The Colonial press [1899].

2 v. fronts. (v. 1, port.) plates, facsims. 24ᶜᵐ. (*Added t.-p.: The
world's great classics*)
Each plate accompanied by leaf with descriptive letterpress.

1. Political science. 2. State, The. 3. Law—Philosophy. 4. Jurispru-
dence. I. Nugent, Thomas, 1700?-1772, tr. II. Alembert, Jean le
Rond d', 1717-1788. III. Title.

0—516
Library of Congress JC179.M74 1899
——— Copy 2 PN6013.W8 vol. 14, 15 [s4ll2]

Montesquieu, Charles Louis de Secondat, *baron de la Brède
et de*, 1689-1755.
The spirit of the laws, by baron de Montesquieu, translated
by Thomas Nugent, revised by J. V. Prichard; with a critical
and biographical introduction by Oliver Wendell Holmes ...
[Aldine ed.] New York, D. Appleton and company, 1900.

2 v. fronts. (v. 1: port.) 8 pl., 2 col. facsim. 23½ᶜᵐ. (*Half-title:
The World's great books*). R. Johnson ... editor-in-chief)

1. Political science. 2. State, The. 3. Law—Philosophy. 4. Juris-
prudence. I. Nugent, Thomas, 1700?-1772. II. Prichard, J. V., ed.
III. Title.

0—5216
Library of Congress J-179.M74 1900
Copyright 1900 A 22157, 22158 [8lj2]

Montesquieu, Charles Louis de Secondat, *baron de La Brède
et de*, 1689-1755.
The spirit of laws, by Baron de Montesquieu (Charles de
Secondat) including d'Alembert's analysis of the work; translated from the French by Thomas Nugent, LL. D., with a special introduction by Hon. Frederic R. Coudert ... Rev. ed.
New York, The Colonial press [1900].
With v. 2 is bound: Bagehot, Walter. Physics and politics ... Rev.
ed. New York [1900].

1. Political science. 2. State, The. 3. Law—Philosophy. 4. Juris-
prudence. I. Nugent, Thomas, 1700?-1772, tr. II. Alembert, Jean Le
Rond d', 1717-1788.

4—16841
Library of Congress JC179.M74 1900 a
——— Copy 2 PN6013.W8 vol. 14-15
Copyright [30v2]

Montesquieu, Charles Louis de Secondat, *baron de La Brède*
et de, 1689-1755.
The spirit of laws, by M. de Secondat, baron de Montesquieu,
with D'Alembert's analysis of the work; tr. from the French
by Thomas Nugent, LL. D. New ed., rev. by J. V. Prichard ...
London, G. Bell and sons, 1902.

2 v. front. (port.) 19ᶜᵐ. (*Half-title: Bohn's standard library*)
Title varies slightly.

1. Political science. 2. State, The. 3. Law—Philosophy. 4. Jurispru-
dence. I. Alembert, Jean Le Rond d', 1717-1788. II. Nugent, Thomas,
1700?-1772, tr. III. Prichard, J. V., ed. IV. Title.

4—6462
Library of Congress JC179.M74 1902
[r001]

[Montesquieu, Charles Louis de Secondat, *baron de la
Brède et de*, 1689-1755.
Le temple de Gnide, par l'auteur des Lettres persanes.

(*In Bibliothèque de campagne. Nouv. ed. La Haye [etc.] 1749. 16½ᶜᵐ.
v. 10, p. [343]-439*)

I. Title.

CA 13-1042 Unrev'd
Library of Congress PQ1243.B5 1749 vol. 10

[Montesquieu, Charles Louis de Secondat, *baron de La Brède
et de*, 1689-1755.
Le temple de Gnide.

(*In Bibliothèque de campagne. Bruxelles, 1768. 17
ᶜᵐ*)

I. Title.

CA
Library of Congress PQ1243.B5 1785

[Montesquieu, Charles Louis de Secondat, *baron
et de*, 1689-1755.
Le temple de Gnide, nouv. ed. avec figures gra
Mire ... d'après les dessins de Ch. Eisen, la t
Drollet ... Paris, Chez Le Mire, graveur, 1772.

2 p. l. vii, 164 p. front., illus. (coat of arms) 9 pl.
Engraved t.-p. with ornamental border; italic type
Includes also Céphise et l'Amour (p. 99-164)

I. Eisen, Charles Dominique Joseph, 1720-1778, il
Noël, 1724-1801, engr. III. Title.

PQ2011.T4 1772
Library of Congress

Montesquieu, Charles Louis de Secondat,
Brède et de, 1689-1755.
Le temple de Gnide, par Montesquieu ...
de Didot jeune, l'an troisième [1794?]

3 p. l., v-xii, 153 p. front., 11 pl. 24ᶜᵐ.
Half-title: Le temple de Gnide, et Arsace et Isménie.

CONTENTS.—Préface du traducteur.—Le temple de
l'Amour.—Arsace et Isménie.

I. Title.

PQ2011.T4 1794
Library of Congress

Montesquieu, Charles Louis de Secondat,
Brède et de, 1689-1755.
The temple of Gnidus; a poem from the
of M. Secondat, baron de Montesquieu
Sayer, M. A. London, Printed for G. Wo
by F. Knight [etc.] 1765.

xv, [1], 84 p. 264 x 21ᶜᵐ.

I. Sayer, John, fl. 1759, tr. II. Title.

PQ2011.T4E7
Library of Congress

Montesquieu, Charles Louis de Secondat, ba
et de, 1689-1755.
A view of the English constitution. By th
Montesquieu. Being a translation of the sixt
eleventh book of his celebrated treatise, intit
loix. London, Sold by B. White, and H. Pay

2 p. l., 74 p. 21½ᶜᵐ. (*With (Maseres, Francis. An
ceedings) of the British, and other Protestant inhabitan
of Quebeck ... London, 1779*)

1. Gt. Brit. Constitution.

F1032.M38
Library of Congress [r339b1]

Montesquieu, Charles Louis de Secondat, b
et de, 1689-1755.
Voyages de Montesquieu, pub. par le
Montesquieu. Bordeaux, Impr. G. Gounou

2 v. facsim. 25½ᶜᵐ. (*Half-title: Collection bord*)

CONTENTS.—t. 1. Voyage en Autriche (Fragments)
t. 2. Voyage en Italie (suite) Voyage en Allemagne.
Mémoires sur les mines. Lettre sur Gênes. Floren
gothique. Réflexions sur les habitants de Rome. Re
Stanislas Lecszinski.

1. Europe—Descr. & trav. I. Montesquieu, Albert
de, ed.

PQ2011.A15 19
Library of Congress [r04l]

287

ele, 1907-
afen. Bergen, J. W. Eide, 1916.
illus. ports ; 26 cm
r. 1905 1945 · Personal narratives, Norwegian
39 1945 · Pictorial works.   ι. Title.
50 33584

M   de.
du climat sur les êtres vivants. La météoro-
ie. ¡Bruxelles? 1948,
diagrs. 24 cm   (Institut royal météorologique de
llandes, fasc 32)
graphies
statut and physical and sheets   2 Africa · Climate
ics · Brussels · Institut royal météorologique de Bel-
ies, fasc 32)
52 15384

M   de.
les orages au Tchad. ¡Bruxelles, 1946,
24 cm   (Institut royal météorologique de Belgique
¡24)
ional   Chad   2 Storms Chad.   (Series: Brus-
ral météorologique de Belgique. Miscellanées. fasc.
B3   551.57   51 18796

Agathe Ursula
Agathe Ursula (Backer) 1847 1907.

us Otto, 1876-   *ed.*
iron and steel. Cleveland, Penton Pub. Co.,
669.1   15 6360 rev*

10-
nde Beamtenhaftung der Reichspostbeamten
JI. Düsseldorf, Dissertations Verlag G. H.

rt am Main.
beichnis" ; p. ix-x.
an)   2 Postal service · Germany · Employees
49 55643*

Bálint, 1507-1576.

hee Elisabeth, 1925-
bewegung in der Politik nach dem Ersten
ihr Widerhall in der Presse von 1918 1933.
il.
4
rbon copy)
dunich.
leaves 1-ix.
ries 1918 1945.   2 European federation   ι. Title.
52 58686

ith M   1920-
ck, Verse. München, Drei Fichten Verlag

K6   50 30470

dns.
aftsfragen, die dich angehen! ¡Berlin, 1941,
(Tornisterschrift des Oberkommandos der Wehr
st 1941. Heft 36)
mbrauch innerhalb der Wahrmacht."
vii statue—Germany.   2 Germany. Heer · Pay, al-
ι. Title.   ιι. Series: Germany. Wehrmacht. Ober-
iterschriften, Heft 36.
A F 46 1306*
Library

y, ed.
rev hvad? Politikens litteraturhaandbog.
ditikens forlag, 1945 ¡i. e. 1946,
A 48 630 rev*

lly, ed.
rev hvad? 1945-1951. København, Politikens
4 52 7268

y, ed.
hvem, hvad, hvor. Politikens musiklexi-
vn, Politikens forlag, 1950.   A 51 2718

Backheuser, Everardo, 1879-
Breve noticia sôbre a geologia do Distrito Federal e seus
sambaquis.   Ed. rev. e com acréscimos dos trabalhos "Os
sambaquis do Distrito Federal" e "A geologia do Distrito
Federal" publicados no Boletim geografico n.° 32 de Novem-
bro de 1945 e n.° 35 de Fevereiro de 1946. Rio de Janeiro,
Serviço Gráfico do Instituto Brasileiro de Geografia e Esta-
tística, 1946.
80 p   illus., fold map   24 cm
1 Geology · Brazil · Rio de Janeiro   2 Rio de Janeiro   Antiq
QE235.B3   52 16462

Backheuser, Everardo, 1879-
Manual de pedagogia moderna (teórica e prática) para
uso das escolas normais e institutos de educação. 3. ed.,
atualizada e remodelada, de "Técnica da pedagogia
moderna." Pôrto Alegre, Livraria do Globo ¡1942,
408 p   illus., ports   19 cm   (Coleção "Vida e educação," v. 4)
1 Teaching
LB1025.B126   1942   50 47123

Backhoff, A   E   T
Korta ofver kanal vägen mellan Stockholm och Göteborg,
med teckningar ofver de märkligare ställena samt text på
svenska och tyska språken ¡Stockholm, Norstedt, 1873,
40 p   6 fold col maps   17 cm
Text also in English and French
1 Gota Canal   2 Sweden · Descr & trav
DL617.B18   50 43445

Backhouse, Anna (Gurney) 1820 1848.
Brief memoirs of Anna Backhouse, by one who knew her
well, loved her much, and was often instructed by her.
¡n. p., 185 ì¡
201 p.   19 cm
Pub in 1852 under title A brief sketch of the life of Anna Backhouse
CT788.B12A3   49 38573*

Backhouse, Anna (Gurney) 1820-1848.
A brief sketch of the life of Anna Backhouse, by one who
knew her well, loved her much and was often instructed by
her. Burlington, N. J., J. Rodgers, 1852.
201 p   19 cm
CT788.B12A3   48 42358*

Backhouse, Hugo.
Among the gauchos. London, New York, Jarrolds ¡1950,
208 p   illus., port. 22 cm
1 Pampas   2 Gaucho   ι. Title
F2926.B27   918.2   51 4630

Backhouse, W   H
Religion and adolescent character; the secondary school
and the Christian church. London, Lutterworth Press
¡1947,
16, 158 p   22 cm
Bibliography   p ¡155,   154
1 Religious education of adolescents   ι. Title
BV1609.B3   377.1   48 14907*

Backlund, Helge Alfred Oskar, 1915
Swedish Enchytraeida. Lund, C. W. K. Gleerup ¡1946
v.   illus.   25 cm   (Lunds universitets årsskrift¡. n. f., avd 2,
bd 42, nr. 13)
Kungl. Fysiografiska sällskapets handlingar. n. f., bd 57, nr 13
"References" pt 1, p ¡23,
1 Enchytraeidae   2 Botany · Sweden   (Series: Lund · Uni
versitet. Acta Universitatis lundensis. n s · Lunds universitets års-
skrift. n. f., avd. 2, bd. 42, nr. 13. Series: Fysiografiska sällskapet i
Lund. Acta. Handlingar, n. f., bd. 57, nr 13)
¡AS284.L262   bd. 42, nr. 13,   A 48 5034*
Chicago   Univ   Libr

Backlund, Helge Alfred Oskar, 1915-
Wrack fauna of Sweden and Finland, ecology and chorol-
ogy. Lund, Entomologiska sällskapet i Lund, 1945.
296, ¡1, p. illus. plates   26 cm.   (Opuscula entomologica. Supple-
mentum 5)
Bibliography   p ¡281,   287,
1 Invertebrates   2 Zoology · Ecology.   3 Zoology · Sweden
4 Zoology · Finland   5 Algae   ι. Title   (Series)
QL267.LB3   591.9485   50 56431

Backlund, Helge Götrik, 1878-
Probleme der arktischen Plateaubasalte. Berlin-Zehlen-
dorf, Gebr. Borntraeger, 1942.
18 p   26 cm.   (Veröffentlichungen des Deutschen Wissenschaft-
lichen Instituts zu Kopenhagen. Reihe 1 · Arktis, Nr. 3)
"Schrifttnenachweis" p 16–18
1 Basalt   2 Geology · Arctic regions   ι. Title.   (Series:
Copenhagen. Deutsches Wissenschaftliches Institut. Veröffentlichungen, Reihe 1, Nr 3)
AS281.D4725   Reihe 1, Nr. 3   50 51666

Backlund, Jonas Oscar, 1875-
Our questioning age; does Christianity have the answers?
Chicago, Moody Press ¡1950,
128 p.   18 cm.   (Colportage library, 196)
1 Apologetics · 20th cent.   ι. Title.
BT1106.B25   239   50 7579

Backman, Albin Lennart, 1880
Ceratophyllum submersum in Nordeurop
Postglazialzeit. Helsingforsiae, 1943.
28 p   illus. maps   26 cm   (Acta botanica fenni
"Literatur" p. 36, 38
1 Ceratophyllum.   2 Paleobotany · Scandinavia
QH7.S76   vol 31
John Crerar Library

Backman, Albin Lennart, 1880-
Najas flexilis in Europa während der Qu
zingforsiae, 1948.
44 p   illus. maps   26 cm   (Acta botanica Fennic
"Berichtigungen" slip inserted.
Bibliography p 39–44
1 Paleobotany   Quaternary.   2 Paleobotany —
flexilis.   (Series)
QH7.S76   vol. 43
Ohio State Univ   Libr

Backman, Albin Lennart, 1880-
Najas marina in Finnland während der
Helsingforsiae, 1941.
28 p   maps ¡1 fold,   26 cm   (Acta botanica F
"Literaturverzeichnis" p ¡36, 38
1 Najas marina   2 Paleobotany · Finland   (
QH7.S76   vol 39
John Crerar Library

Backman, Albin Lennart, 1880-
Najas tumor ill in Europa einst und jet
sine, 195)
3¡ p   illus   26 cm   (Acta botanica Fennica, 45)
Bibliography p 29–32.
1 Najas tumor   2 Paleobotany · Europe   (Se
¡QH7.S76   vol. 48,
Ohio State Univ   Libr

Backman, Allan E   ed.
see National Better Business Bureau, in
Do's and don'ts in advertising copy ... N
HF5831.N28   659.1

Backman, Charles Pierre, 1892-
London under Big Ben; strövtåg och skis
Wahlström & Widstrand ¡1950,
199 p   illus   21 cm
1 London · Soc · life & cust
New York   Public Libr

Backman, Charles Pierre, 1892-   *joint au*
see Ottoson, Lars Henrik. Här är Londo
A. Bonnier ¡1948,
DA679.O8

Backman, Eugène Louis, 1883-
Jungfru Maria Nyckelpiga. Stockholm
311 p   illus., music   23 cm
Bibliography p 304 311
1 Mary, Virgin, in literature.   2 Mary, Virgi
birds ι in religion, folk lore, etc.)   ι. Title.
BT609.B27

Backman, Gaston Viktor, 1883-
Wachstum und organische Zeit. Mit 7
Text. Leipzig, J. A. Barth, 1943.
vi, 195 p   diagrs   24 cm.   (Bios, Abhandlunge
Biologie und ihrer Geschichte, sowie zur Philosop
Naturwissenschaften, Bd. 15)
"Schrifttum" p ¡185, 196.
1 Growth   ι. Title   (Series: Bios, Abha
rischen Biologie und ihrer Geschichte, Bd. 15)
QH831.B23   574.0151

Backman, Gaston Viktor, 1883-
Zeit der spontanen Motilität und Gebärac
und beim Menschen, von Gaston Backman u
Hjortsjö. Lund, C. W. K. Gleerup ¡1946,
22 p   25 cm   (Lunds universitets årsskrift, ¡
nr. 14)
Kungl. Fysiografiska sällskapets handlingar, n
"Schrifttum" p 21 22.
1 Fetus   ι. Hjortsjö, Carl Herman, 1914-
Title.   (Series: Lund. Universitet. Acta Universit
n s · Lunds universitets årsskrift. n. f., avd. 2, bd
Fysiografiska sällskapet i Lund   Acta ... Hand
nr 14)
¡AS284.L82   bd. 57, nr. 14,
Chicago. Univ. Libr.

Backman, Jules, 1910-
Bituminous coal wages, profits, and pr
pared for Southern Coal Producers Assoc
before Presidential Coal Board. ¡n. p., 195
iii, 123 p.   diagrs.   24 cm
Bibliographical footnotes.
1 Wages · U S.   2 Labor productivity · U.   1
U S.   4 Coal mines and mining · U S.   5 Sout
Association.   ιι. Title.
HD4966.M65U415   338.2794

ZN

Ѵ d. с. d b .

Write on ally words underlined **(Orientalia)**

ch, Ukrainian and class work.

ts. "L'Église orthodoxe panukrainienne" Adresse au Patriarche de Constantinople. orthodoxe panukrainien" (octobre 1921 duction, traduction et notes. Roma: ale, 1923, 54 p. 8°. (Orientalia

Herbigny, S. L.

Ukrainian—Hist. 2 Eastern Patriarch. 3 Herbigny, Michel

October 11, 1927

° QGA p.v.189

лини і українські оповчення у Вітчизняній вна, Указна ЦК КП(б)У, 1943. 19 р.

SLAVONIC DIV.

2 Ukraine—Hist. March 21, 1944

° QO

m polskiego wybrane. [Wyd. 1] iggarnia, 1967. 189 p. illus., maps.

°QK

ободотно, за озбирене и оуне-нная обяза, и оъ омадоиная нр белекя. и. оъ крвтия укавання: тооть и. оъ Раздврони квавин-ичонорь-зиниять Богомиаь Пг-амж, 1941-42 v. illus.

ва oaaaqy, hoi ny, 'u'i'onl--

SLAVONIC DIV

° QK

из спомените и белешкте на едини пу-146 p. 18cm.

Хербет.

SLAVONIC

September 9, 1943

° QO

:mieślnicze. Zarys przeszłości. Toruń: ński, 1933. 256 p. incl. tables. m.

MZEF

Herbstman, Aleksandr Osipovich.

... De schaakstudie der nieuw-Russische grootmeesters, met een voorwoord van Dr. A. A. Aljechin; vertaling uit het Russisch van Mr. G. C. A. Oskam... Lochem: N. v. uitg.-mij. "De Tijdstroom", 1937, 188 p. illus. 25cm.

9IAISA. 1. Chess—Russia.   2. Chess—Problems. 1. Oskam, G. C. A. N Y P L.   December 2, 1937

°QDK

Herbstman, Aleksandr Osipovich.

...Театр Бальзака. Предисловие Конст. Державина. Ленинград, [etc.] Гос. издат. "Искусство," 1938. 150 p. front., plates, ports. 23½cm.

At head of title: А. Гербстман.

971767A. 1. Balzac, Honoré de,   1799–1850.   November 20, 1938 N.Y.P.L.

Herbststerne   NGL

MUNIER, MARIS (WROBLEWSKI), 1882–

Unter dem wechselnden Mond; Werden, Wachsen und Welken eines kurländischen Geschlechts. Heilbronn, E. Salzer, 1965-66 [1927–28] 6 v. 20cm.

CONTENTS.—Buch 1. Märzhoffen.—Buch 2. Sommernogen. — Buch 3. Sonnenwende.—Buch 4. Herbststerne.—Buch 5. Winternot.—Buch 6. Osterwinde.

1. Courland—Hist.—Fiction.   5. Russo-Japanese war, 1904–1905—Fiction. I. Title.   II. Title: Märzhoffen.   III. Title: Sommernogen.   IV. Title: Sonnenwende.   V. Title: Herbststerne.   VI. Title: Winternot.   VII. Title: Osterwinde.

NN R X 4, 57 p/o OCs PC1, I1, I2, I3, I4, I5, I6, IIs, III1, IV5, V5, VI,   I6, II1, III2, IV2, V3, VI, VII SL4 VII [LC I3, X1x]

XWN

Poland. Statutes.

Statuta regni Poloniæ in ordinem alphabeti digesta: a Joanne Herburto de Fulstin... Dantisci: Apud Ægidium Iazonum, 1693. 497 (really 505) p. 4°.

Coat of arms (bookplate?), mounted on t.-p.

47ANBA. 1. No subject. 1. Her-   burt, Jan, 1508–1566, editor. N.Y.P.L.   April 2, 1931

Herburt, Stanisław Hejbowica-.
See
Hejbowica-Herburt, Stanisław, d. 1901.

N.Y.P.L.   September 11, 1926

Herbg. 1   translation

Onip, M.   ° Q p.v.323

...Dođi, idi za mnom; evanđeoska slika u 2 čina, preveo J. Herceg, uredio i upute dodao V. Rahadan. [U Zabrebu: Nadbis-kupska tiskara, 19—] 30 p. illus. 19cm. (Društvena pozornica. Svezak 3.)

Herceg, Rudolf.

Nemojmo zaboraviti; Zagreb: Jugoslovenska štu (ports.) 8°.

Cover-title.

Herceg, Rudolf.

...Teško je čovjeku u 68 p. 12°.

1. Education, Croatia. N.Y.P.L.

Herceg, —

Jakovljević, Ilija, 1898—
...Hercegovke; pripo Jakovljević, slikama uresio Hrv. književ. društvo sv. J port.) 19cm. [Jeroni

"O plaru ove knjige," p. 64.

660255A. 1. Fiction, Croatian. N.Y.P.L.

Hercher, Bernard.

...Учебник элементарног менного издания (обработ свой... вып. 1   Москва 23cm.   (Учебники в учеб

At head of title: Б. Герхер "Научно-педагогическог вета дополнено для школ II Пос. 1, 2d ed.

1. Geometry—Textbooks, 1924, 1906— II. N.Y.P.L.

Herčík, Emanuel.
...Folktoys...
illus.,175 col. pl.

Title and text i "Translated by E. "Bibliography," p

1. Toys—Czecho-Slo Slovakian.
NN

Herčík, Ferdinand, 1905–
...Jak pečuje Sovětsk Vydavatelství Rovnost, [Rovnosti. sv. 6.)

camera. The subsequent negative film is printed by a Haloid-
Xerox Copyflo enlarger onto offset matrix stock. The resulting
plates are printed by offset on sheets 10 x 14 inches in size and
bound into volumes. The end result is an entry which is again
about 50 per cent of the original, though it has gone through considerably greater reduction (ca. 8 per cent) in the microfilming.

There is still the same problem of white space, although one
library welcomes the additional number of volumes that it causes,
as it makes it possible to serve more readers. There is a noticeably greater loss in legibility over the previous process. Little
can be done to correct these faults, as the cards cannot be reprinted in condensed form, nor are new cards available. A great
deal of the illegibility is due to the poor quality of the originals.
In many cases the entries are more legible (though reduced) than
the original cards, though it may be hard to credit this from the
second generation illustration shown here, which has been further
reduced to about 72 per cent.

Parts of Cards

B, 1)   Hot Type with Linotype Slugs.

The many H.W. Wilson publications that have been of such
value to librarians are examples of this type of book catalog. The
printing techniques are not new, and are of no interest to this
study. It is the subsequent storage step that is unique and which
leads us into the techniques that follow. After the first edition is
printed, the linotype slugs are unlocked and stored for future printing. Each slug (line) can be filed, interfiled and manipulated in
much the same manner as a catalog card. New entries can be in-

serted and obsolete items discarded.   They can be locked up in a
new page form whenever a new edition is required.

Aesthetically, this is probably the best method of producing a
book catalog.   However, the slugs of type metal are relatively
expensive, and are both bulky and oppressively heavy to store.   The
H. W. Wilson Company has developed this technique so that they
get the most out of it, but it would not be recommended for a new
venture starting from scratch.

B, 2)   Photo-offset of Shingled Cards.

This method combines features to be found in A, 1 and B, 1.   Instead of a lintotype slug, we have a light-weight card with a line
of text typed (or printed) along its upper edge.   Sometimes more
than one line appears here.   The cards are shingled in the manner
described above, so that only the line of text shows above and
behind the card that follows.   This column of shingled cards may
be photographed alone, or additional columns may be arranged be-
side it and all photographed together.   Reduction ratios are chosen
to yield a negative with legible type sizes resulting.   Subject headings in variant type sizes, as well as page heads and folios, may
be shingled up at the same time.   The resulting negatives are
used to prepare offset plates which are run off in the usual manner.

There are two major techniques for holding the shingled cards
during the make-up and camera stages.   The oldest version uses
double-surface pressure-sensitive tape (e.g. Scotch tape).   The
cards are aligned on bands of the adhesive tape for make-up, and
the completed board is often placed in a vacuum frame for photographing.   The cards below the top card are held by adhesion of a

small area at the bottom of the card.   This system was used for the cards illustrated on page 103.

The other version uses a mounting board with plastic flaps (guides) set between wooden reglets at regular line-distances apart. The cards are slipped beneath these flaps which hold them in position during the camera stage.   Registry of cards is based on the lower edge of the card.   This board is more expensive to install but leads to faster make-up.   This system is used by R. R. Bowker Company in the preparation of a number of their publications.

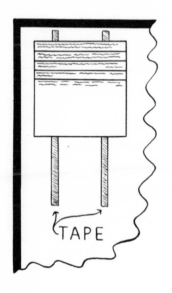

TAPE

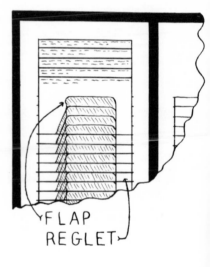

FLAP
REGLET

A variant form of this technique may be found in the Panel
Board based on the Kardex file. Remington Rand supplies "Flex-o-
print" strips that may be typed along their upper edge and then
locked in the board for photographing. This is used for the preparation of lists and directories, but does not appear to have applications to our study.

B, 3) Sequential Camera + Offset.

This technique is a natural extension of the previous one. In
this case the same type of entry is made on the card and the
shingling is done as the cards are fed rapidly through the camera
as shown on the following page. The camera photographs the
selected area of the card (where the entry appears) and then moves
a new line of film up in readiness to receive the image of the entry on the next card. Spacing between sections is produced with
blank cards. Paging may be done by counting lines (or cards

which have the same number of lines) with an automatic counter
and inserting blank cards, or by cutting and stripping up the negatives. The camera may be loaded with sensitized paper (cheaper
than film) for running proof for checking or dummying-up. There
are three models available at this time.

a) Foto-List

This camera was introduced by the Vari-typer Corporation at
the 1958 Business Show, though it was developed before this. It
photographs a single line of text, that must be placed on the special
cards designed for it. What makes these cards special is a round
hole at the middle of the left edge, and a square hole at the middle
of the right. These holes are used by the Vari-typer Line Com-
poser typewriter, and the camera. These cards are the standard
EAM size (3 1/4 x 7 3/8 in.) and may be subsequently punched
and sorted by IBM equipment. Cards feed through the camera at a
rate of 120/minute. The card feeds from side to side, from a
deck of 3000 or less. The camera can photograph from 100 per
cent (same size) down to 50 per cent, and uses orthochromatic film.

This equipment was developed by Eastman Kodak for Dunn and
Bradstreet and placed on the open market about the same time as
the other. It can photograph one, two or three lines of type (or
multiples on more than one card) and does this in response to signals triggered by punches in the card. The cards may be standard
IBM or Foto-list cards. Cards are fed through the camera at 230/
minute, and a strobe light flashes on and off to make the exposure.
Cards feed from above. Reduction ratios of 100 per cent to 45 per

cent are possible, and the film is panchromatic. This is necessary because of the strobe lighting, and results in negatives that
do not have the crisp contrast of the orthochromatic.

   b) Compos-o-Line.

This model was designed for Navy use, and the first commercial introduction was at the 1959 Business Show. It will photograph
varying widths (heights?) on cards ranging from 3 x 5 to 5 x 9
inches. The present models will shoot only one width, unless the
machine is stopped and a new width set on it. A future model is
being designed to vary widths within certain limits. Cards feed at
120/minute, using a Pitney Bowes Tickometer, feeding from above.
Reduction rations are 200 per cent to 50 per cent, and the film is
orthochromatic.

There have been at least two other cameras of this type in
development, but they are not available now. The first was a model
under consideration by Ernest Taubes of Photo Devices. It was
never completed. The other is the basis of a patent (U.S.P.
2,849,916) assigned to IBM. It uses IBM tab cards with perfora-

Comparison Of Sequential Cameras

Feature	Foto-List	Listomatic	Compos-O-Line
Card Speed	120/minute	230/minute	120/minute
Card Size	EAM or 3.25 x 10	EAM (3.25 x 7 3/8)	3x5 to 5x9
Max. Reduction	50 per cent	45 per cent	50 per cent
Max. Enlargement	100 per cent (unity)	100 per cent	200 per cent
Viewing Area	3 pt. to 36 pt.	0.630' x 7 3/8" max.	3 pt. to 3.5 in.
Film Feed	4 pt. to 18 or 36 pt.	3 pt. to 48 pt.	3 pt. to 36 pt.
Max. Film Width	9.75 in.	8 in.	9.75 in.
Min. Film Width	3.75 in.	35 mm.	2.5 in.
Max. Film Length	100 ft.	400 ft.	200 ft.
Max. Paper Length	100 ft.	400 ft.	400 ft.
Mask Film ?	Yes	No	Yes
Remove Magazine?	Yes	No	Yes
Film Sensitivity	Orthochromatic	Panchromatic	Ortho.
Lights	Hg.-vapour	Stroboscopic	Incandescent
Shutter	Double Guillotine	No	Dbl. Guill.
Hand Operation ?	Yes	No	Yes
Electric Require.	Standard	Standard	Standard
Weight	ca. 1000 lbs.	600- lbs.	750 lbs.
Size	ca. 6L x 2.5W x 4.5H ft.	ca. 3 x 2 x 3 ft.	60 x 24 x 52 in.
Cost	$18,850	$20,500	$13,700
Rental ?	Yes	Yes	Yes
Comments	One line card	1, 2 or 3 line card	Variable area card
	Special card	EAM card	Variable card

tions along the right and left edges, and claims that it will work
with cards holding "... randomly spaced printing thereon ..." However, it is not available for public use at present, and there is no
indication when (if ever) it may be.

B, 4)   IBM Machines + Offset.

This is the most mechanical of any of the techniques described
(though it requires the human hand at one point).   IBM cards are
prepared from standard library cards, using a Key Punch to place
the information on the card.   Cards prepared from this master
card (for specialized groupings) are run through the Interpreter in
order that their information may appear in a form (conventional
alphabetic) understandable to the human beings who will have to do
the close filing that the machine cannot do as quickly or economically.   After the file is arranged correctly, the cards are sent
through the Accounting Machine which prepares a typed list from
the cards.   This list is then photographed and offset plates made
for printing the volume.   Again we have the single-line-per-card
process that we found in some of the other systems.

The following illustration is of a page from the New York
State Library's Checklist of Books and Pamphlets in the Social
Sciences.   As the original 10 3/8 x 15.25 inch page has been
reduced about 75 per cent for this illustration, it does not give as
favorable an impression for legibility as does the original. Another
catalog, also prepared in 1956 by the same system, is the Los
Angeles County Public Library's Children's Catalog.   It is note-
worthy in that it includes annotations on many of the entries.

The Problem

Now that we have quickly scanned the various methods available for preparing book catalogs from cards, let us look a little more closely at the Shaw List and the Lamont Catalog, to see (by analogy) what we may be faced with.

Shaw List

This list, sponsored by a grant from the Carnegie Corporation, came out in a preliminary edition in 1930. It was a checking list; and three copies were sent to about 250 colleges, two to be checked and returned and one to be kept. When returns were received from 100 colleges, the author called upon experts from 50 institutions for collaboration. The list was first tested on Swarthmore. Work began in 1929 and was completed in 1931 as:-

> SHAW, CHARLES B.
> A List of Books for College Libraries ...
> Chicago, A.L.A., 1931.   810 pp.

A sample page follows with the typography reproduced full-size. The list contains ca. 14,000 titles, arranged in 24 major subject divisions. These are as follows (with the number of pages for each): Astronomy (7), Botany (9), Chemistry (11), Classics (35), Economics (39), Education (29), English (99), Fine Arts (33), General (49), Geography (9), Geology (5), German (17), History (101), Mathematics (19), Music (19), Philosophy (23), Physical Education (9), Physics (7), Political Science (31), Psychology (15), Religion (23), Romance Languages (43), Sociology and Anthropology (27) and Zoology (13). They follow an alphabetic arrangement based on college curricula rather than conventional library classifications. These 24 divisions are further broken down into 500 ± sub-divisions. The entries are arranged in two columns per page, ca. 45 characters per line and ca. 58 lines per column. Most of the entries are three or four lines each, though many run to two or three times this. There are no annotations.

In 1940 a continuation list carrying the original from 1931 to 1938 was published. This was a supplement and not a revision. It follows the same subject divisions and runs to 284 pages. For some entries there is noted a source for a review of the title.

Lamont Catalogue

This listing was also prepared under the sponsorship of the Carnegie Corporation. The Lamont Library opened in January 1949 with 100,000 volumes (39,000 entries). The information presented is abbreviated, and it is meant to be a finding list. It is reported that it was prepared by the shingling method, described previously.

> HARVARD COLLEGE, LAMONT LIBRARY
> Catalogue of the Lamont Library ...
> Prepared by Philip J. McNiff ...
> Cambridge, Harvard, 1953.   562pp.

A sample page follows reduced 90 per cent from the original. The 39,000 entries are arranged by a modified Dewey classification (e.g. Music is 770). There are ten major subject divisions. They are as follows (with number of pages for each): General Works (17), Philosophy and Psychology (25), Religion (20), Government and Economics (60), Social Relations and Education (28), Science (40), Applied Science (19), Art and Music (35), Language and

Literature (164) and History (92). The major divisions are broken down into sub-divisions and sub-sub-divisions. This results in about 2,500 divisions in all. The entries are arranged in two columns per page, ca. 70 characters per line and ca. 112 lines per column. Most of the entries are two lines, though there are a few that are three lines. There are no annotations.

Economics Library Selections

It began publication in March 1954 and comes out four times a year. It is classified by subject within the major classification of economics. Each entry includes a bibliographic citation and a short annotation. In most cases the annotation is longer than the citation. Each entry is keyed as follows: A - recommended for libraries with an annual budget below $250. B - budgets $250-500. C - budgets $500-1000. D- budgets $1000-1500. E - less important acquisitions. Each entry in a lower keyed class is also recommended for all higher classes. There are very few foreign books and no government publications. This publication is usually cited as:

JOHNS HOPKINS UNIV., DEPT. OF POLITICAL ECONOMY
Economics Library Selections

A Hypothetical New Shaw

A rough average drawn from the Shaw List gives us twenty entries per page. If a volume of this same loose typography is desired, it would take a 2500 page opus to handle it without annotations. With annotations, we should probably expect almost twice this bulk, unless the notes were shorter or printed even smaller than in Economics Library Selections. The Lamont List averages 80 entries to a page. A New Shaw in this abbreviated form would run to 625 pages, quite a respectable volume even so. Let us examine the New Shaw as it would appear if produced by some of the various techniques discussed earlier.

A, 1) L. C. Catalog. Since it would be too much to expect to get special L. C. cards printed for this list, except perhaps in the case of new titles, it would be necessary to prepare it like the older volumes (e.g. no condensing). Without annotations, it would run to just under 2800 pages. This would result in a volume over four times as big as the Library of Congress Catalog (640 pages/ volume). Annotations would require a second card, doubling the size. Keying would have to be by a visible mark, though this could be a marginal notch in the bottom of the card, to help in needle sorting keyed cards. Keeping the list up to date would be relatively simple. Annual supplements of 166 pages could be print- ed and the cards filed into the master list. It would be a relatively expensive process to supply purchasers with portions of the up- dated master list to order. As this technique was not considered practical, no costs were investigated.

A, 2) G. K. Hall. The preparation of the New Shaw by this method would follow the above in most features. The basic list, without annotations, would be a volume of just under 2400 pages. The addition of annotations (unless cards with annotations included were specially prepared) would double the size. The Slavonic Catalog averages about 1000 pages a volume. This is about as much as a reader can be expected to handle (though the Manhattan

Telephone Directory is just under 1800 pages). The same techniques for keying and up-dating would be possible. Annual supplements of 143 pages would be required. Since new cards would be used, rather than the beat-up variety found in working catalogs, the results would be more legible than is possible with the other G.K. Hall projects. Mr. Hall has suggested that the basic volume be loose-leaf, and supplementary pages be added at the ends of the sections.

The company has developed a formula for figuring out the costs for this technique. For editions of less than 250 copies, the following formula may be used: -

>   75 cents a page (21 cards) - Camera and Copyflo.
>   + 1 cent a page a copy   - Printing.
>   + 25 per cent of the above - Presumably their profit
>   margin
>   + Binding costs.

When an edition in excess of 250 copies is required, the costs would be somewhat less than the formula.

This would bring an edition of the basic list to about $48.00 a copy if under 250 were printed, and less than that if over. The supplement volume would come to about $6.00 or less. With annotations we would get a cost of $94.00 a copy, and about $8.50 for the supplement. Mr. Hall is very much interested in this project as it ties in with some other projects that he is considering. He was quite pessimistic about the size of editions to be printed. He reported that if we estimated a market of 2000 purchasers (the number of junior colleges, colleges and universities), we should more than halve that for our edition.

B, 1) H. W. Wilson. This technique was not considered a practical one for this project.

B, 2) Shingling. A possibility that came to mind was using standard Library of Congress cards in a shingling operation. The first objection was in the excessive white space above the author's name. Then it was noted that the white space was not uniform as shown below:

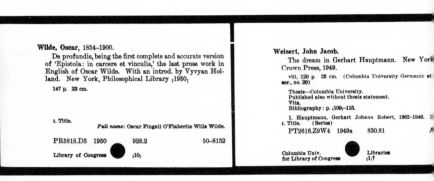

This would require trimming all the cards down to the entry. These trimmed cards would be most difficult to shingle by the flap method, and might cause trouble with the tape method.

This indicated the advisability of using cards typed from copy (presumably Library of Congress cards) and annotation cards. It would add a composition cost to the cost of the Library of Congress cards. A check with a local typewriting composition house came up with the very rough estimate of about 20 cents per card for an average (sic.) 3-line bibliographical citation. Annotations, if on

the same card, would add to this; but not double the amount. If a
different type-face was desired for the annotations (to save space,
as well as add to readability), it would be better to type the annotations, on separate cards, which would bring the cost up to ca.
40 cents an entry.   Shingling and photographing would add something under 3 cents per item.   This would be a pre-printing cost
of ca. $11,500 or less.   Printing and binding would be additional
and would depend upon many variables for which specific requirements would be necessary.   It is hard to use an analogy when one
has only an indefinite hypothetical case to work from.

In the case of <u>Books in Print,</u> Bowker quotes a price of $8.00
a page for typing, shingling and photography; but that is when
working with a file that has already been prepared, so that the
only typing needed is for additions.   It also uses an abbreviated
citation, and a condensed page.   This figure would not be applicable
to the New Shaw.

B, 3)   <u>Sequential Camera.</u>   For this method, a newly typed
card would be necessary.   For the Foto-list it would require a card
per line.   This would minimize correction charges but add to the
storage expense.   With the Listomatic it would be possible to use
one, two or three-line cards, or multiples of these.   For the
Compos-o-line it would be necessary to establish a fixed size of
entry (e.g. 3-line), which would involve wasted white space on
shorter entries.   Annotations would double the number of cards.
The Listomatic is the fastest and most versatile camera but not as
suitable for paper proofs.   The other two use ortho film which
results in a negative requiring less care in printing the offset plate.

With all three it is possible to key-punch the cards for sorting
and selecting. This would lead to many applications of the New
Shaw list where selections of specific subject matter were desired.
It would also make it possible to merge the New Shaw material into a larger file (e.g. a centrally located file) from which many
publications could be printed.

Composition costs would closely approximate those quoted for
the shingling method, i.e. ca. 20 cents for a 3-line card (Listomatic and Compos-o-line), double that for annotations. Preparation of the negative by Listomatic would run to a little over 3 cents
an entry. The other cameras would be about the same. Foto-
list would require three cards, raising the composition and storage
costs. Printing would be the same as for the shingling method.
The costs would be somewhat higher than for shingling (e.g. more
than $11,500) but would involve less time between composition and
printing. There would be no expense for shingling boards (this is
cancelled by camera time-charges) and the cards would probably
be damaged less in the sequential camera method.

B, 4) IBM. The New York State Checklist includes some
45,000 titles, and was published in an edition of 1500 copies. In
1956 it cost $14,031 (about $9.35 a copy), and subsequent re-
issuing was expected to lower the original capitalization for cards.
These figures would be somewhat higher today, but they include
total costs of editing and publication. Expanding these to account
for a 50,000 title publication would still be much lower than for the
other systems described. The chief sacrifice would be in the very
greatly abbreviated citations and the less than satisfactory typog-

raphy involved.

Recommendations

The G. K. Hall method involves the smallest amount of work.
It requires the editorial selection of Library of Congress cards.
For 50,000 titles the pre-printing costs would be about $2,250 as
against the interpolated N.Y. State pre-printing costs of ca.
$7,500. Shingling would be under $11,500 and Listomatic would
be over $11,500. Against this we have a catalog prepared by
shingling and Listomatic that would be more than a finding list. It
would also be a good deal easier to use. Listomatic would add the
mechanized sorting and selecting also present in the IBM method.
I think that I would settle for Listomatic.

Incidentally, everyone that I talked to commented that the
editorial costs would greatly outweigh the publishing costs. They
also felt, though some were too polite to say so outright, that we
were approaching the problem by the back door.

References

Davy, Joseph. "New Procedures Speed up Production of 'Paper
    bound Books in Print,'" Publishers Weekly. 177:75-77, 2
    May 1960. (Briefly describes Bowker's use of Listomatic.)
Day, Melvin S. and Lebow, Irving. "New Indexing Pattern for
    Nuclear Science Abstracts," American Documentation. 11:120-
    127, April 1960.
    (Considers Listomatic plus IBM sorting.)
Dewey, Harry. "Punched Card Catalogs - Theory and Techniques,"
    American Documentation. 10:36-50, January 1959.
    (A good description of the IBM method.)
Gull, C. D. "The Cumulative Catalog Technique at the Library of
    Congress," American Documentation. 2:131-141, August 1951.
    (A good description of the Library of Congress Catalog tech-

nique.)

Melcher, Daniel. "New Composing Technique Speeds Production of the New Bowker 'Books in Print' Index," <u>Publishers Weekly.</u> 154:1038-1043, 11 September 1948.

(Describes the tape method of shingling.)

Shoemaker, Richard H. "Some American Twentieth Century Book Catalogs." Included in this volume.

(A good general view. A librarian's approach.)

Spence, A.N. "A Line, a Page, a Publication ..." <u>Filmsort Facts.</u> 2, 5:3-14, August 1959.

(A good description of the Navy's use of sequential cameras and Filmsort cards for publication.)

Weaver, Vance. "Preparation of the Index to the Journal of Chemical Physics." To be published in a future issue of <u>American Documentation.</u>

(A very good study of the Listomatic technique.)

Techniques Of The Modern Printed Catalog And Its Supplements

By George Piternick

An examination of printed library catalogs which have appeared within the last two decades and which may be held to be characteristic examples of a trend toward reinstitution of the printed library catalog as a useful library device, reveals a variety of composition techniques. Richard H. Shoemaker's "Some American Twentieth Century Book Catalogs" * illustrates this diversity. Notwithstanding this variety, however, the catalogs fall into three basic types: the traditional type, featuring letterpress or offset composition of entries de nove; catalogs manufactured through reproduction of cards actually used or potentially usable in conventional card catalogs; and printed catalogs produced by reproduction of cards manufactured for the special purpose of printed book catalog compilation. Within these categories, especially the latter two, subgroups may be recognized.

The traditional method of printed catalog production, featuring letterpress composition of pages, is now rarely used. No recent counterpart, technically speaking, of the Index-Catalogue of the Library of the Surgeon General's Office is currently being started. The high costs of letterpress composition make such projects infeasible today. Printed catalogs of discrete collections of rare or special materials do appear in this format, e.g., the catalog of

* Paper included in this volume.

the Arents Tobacco Collection at The New York Public Library,
but its use for more general, dynamic, collections is pretty
definitely a thing of the past.

Development of methods whereby entry cards, already produced for use in card catalogs, could be utilized for book catalogs
without recomposition marked a great step forward in printed catalog production.   The Catalog of Books Represented by Library of
Congress Printed Cards, published during the early forties, is the
great pioneer effort in this area.   Library of Congress catalog
cards were arranged in three columns of six cards each and reproduced photographically onto offset plates.   More recently, the
supplements to this catalog, and its descendant, The National Union
Catalog, utilize special cards from which all superfluous leading
has been removed, greatly reducing space wasted in the catalogs.
This permits the columns of cards to be "shingled", resulting in
many more entries per page.

Some recent catalogs, such as the Catalog of the Avery Memorial Architectural Library of Columbia University, the U. S. Department of Agriculture's Plant Science Catalog; Botany Subject
Index, and others, have exploited more economical devices in utilizir
catalog cards.   The cards are again arranged in columns, but the
resulting page is microfilmed.   The microfilm exposures resulting
are then magnified to the suitable enlargement and copied onto offset paper masters by Xerography.   This method, although it continues the space wastage characteristic of the first Library of
Congress catalog, is comparatively inexpensive, and has found
favor in those applications where only a relatively small number

of copies is desired, and where beauty and extreme clarity of impression are not essential.

Another technical innovation has been utilized in yet another way--that of doing the original cataloging upon cards especially designed for use in the production of printed catalogs as a substitute for card catalogs. The technique utilized here is that of electronic printout from punched cards onto offset masters, exemplified by the printed catalogs of the King County (Washington) Public Library, the New York State Library Checklist of Books and Pamphlets in the Social Sciences, New Serial Titles, and others.

Punched card printout equipment is quite limited typographically, however; all letters are in upper case, no accent marks are available, and marks of punctuation are severely limited in number. The method is also somewhat wasteful of space. The use of automatic cameras, such as the Eastman "Listomatic," permits extremely rapid photographic copying of text from punched cards and production of offset masters therefrom. The text can be produced by special typewriter or Varityper, and thus attractive and versatile typography can be achieved. No manual shingling is used in these devices, and the use of cards punched for filing and coding but bearing text produced by other, better, instruments confers the advantages of both methods, with a bonus of better space utilization and format. The book catalogs of the Los Angeles County Public Library, previously produced by electronic printout, are now being done in this manner. It appears that the product will be more attractive, less bulky, and somewhat cheaper to produce.

Preparation of Supplements

The acceptance of the card catalog as the access medium par
excellence to the resources of libraries was almost unanimous in
the United States in the late nineteenth century. Not the least
important consideration in determining this acceptance was the fact
that card catalogs can be easily kept up to date by daily accretion,
whereas printed catalogs are out of date even at the time of appearance. Printed catalogs can be kept more or less current only
by the issuance of either revised editions or supplements. In
either case there are periods of time, sometimes lengthy, during
which materials in a library are not displayed in its printed catalog. Moreover, issuance of supplements introduces a multiplicity
of alphabets through which searching is necessary, a drawback
which can make printed catalogs comparatively inefficient for some
purposes. Cumulative supplements are, of course, a device for
minimizing this difficulty, but they do not remove it entirely.

These objections to printed library catalogs cannot be shrugged
off--they are as valid, in principle, today as they were in 1875,
whatever benefits printed catalogs may confer in increasing total
access to libraries. The necessity of being able to produce cumulative supplements or revised editions rapidly and inexpensively is
crucial to the success of printed catalogs for most purposes. An
examination of the methods employed in producing supplements
to book catalogs manufactured according to modern methods may
be examined briefly.

Traditional methods of printed catalog production using letterpress composition are at a distinct disadvantage insofar as the

production of cumulative supplements is concerned. The reasons are fairly obvious. The setting of entries in type and their ultimate inclusion on plates provide no easy method for subsequent intercalation of other entries. Simple supplements, to be sure, can be produced; but a sensible amount of time would normally intervene before an accumulation of entries sufficient to warrant the production of a supplement was at hand.

Catalogs produced by photographic reproduction of more or less conventional catalog cards permit supplementation somewhat more readily, as exemplified by the production of The National Union Catalog: Authors. A given period's accretion of new cards are filed separately, shingled and photographed in format, and unshingled and reconstituted as a card catalog. This is done initially on a monthly basis; monthly supplements are combined into quarterly cumulative catalogs; these are broken down and reconstituted into annual supplements; and these in turn distributed and reconstituted into quinquennial supplements. The amount of filing, shingling, and refiling is considerable. It must be remembered that the cards used here are special catalog cards, and are used for the purpose of the printed catalog alone; any considerable consultation of these cards for other purposes would be very unhandy.

No basic difference in preparing supplements to printed catalogs would be encountered in those cases where the reproduction technique is that of microfilming shingled pages and using Xerography to produce offset masters. It does not appear, however, that supplements, at least cumulative supplements, are intended in any of the catalogs so far produced by these techniques. Because all card catalogs put into printed form by these techniques have been active catalogs, used in their card form, an additional difficulty of unavailability during reproduction and periodic multiplicity of alphabets during the production of supplements would be encountered.

The great advantage in the publication of supplementary volumes conferred by punched-card methods of preparation, whether by direct printout or in combination with photographic composition, is that of avoiding the necessity for shingling and unshingling. The process of composition, whether by direct printout or by automatic photography, is extremely rapid, and the catalogs need not be out of use for any significant period of time. Moreover, the coded information on the cards permits a portion of the work of ordering or alphabetizing to be done by machine.

This necessarily brief outline of printed catalog techniques and types of supplementation permits little in the way of summary. An attempt has been made to describe briefly the various techniques used. Choice of a method for any specific project must be determined by a complex of considerations, of which technical facility is only one.

Bibliographic And Cataloging Standards
For Book Catalogs

By Robert D. Stevens

It is apparent from a reading of Richard Shoemaker's "Some American Twentieth Century Book Catalogs"* that widely varying bibliographic and cataloging standards have been followed in their compilation. It is apparent also that in many cases standards have been devised with a view to meeting minimum needs at minimum cost or as an accommodation to machine techniques. Unfortunately such standards are sometimes so inadequate that the reader is effectively prevented from locating a book. There is a strong temptation to dismiss criteria simply by stating that the matter is readily settled by the application of a rule based on local pragmatism. There is some justification for saying that in a particular local situation the objective should be to produce a book catalog that will meet the needs of local readers at minimum expense in manpower and money. Such a practice carried to its extreme leads to the same sort of anarchy which existed in the card and book catalogs of American libraries before 1876 or to the same fumbling that is found even today in libraries where processing control over a collection is put into the hands of amateurs.

The real strength of American librarianship today derives from the standardization introduced by men like Dewey and Cutter during

*Paper included in this volume.

the last quarter of the 19th century and at the beginning of the
20th century. It is this standardization of equipment and techniques
which permits nationwide systems for the production and distribution of catalog cards, which makes professional mobility possible,
and which provides the basis for cataloging data of sufficiently
high quality so that a variety of parts from a host of sources all
over the United States and Canada can be fashioned into an integrated tool such as the National Union Catalog. Those librarians
who fashion card or book catalogs purely in terms of local needs
or in terms of the requirements of punched card or tape driven
machines which may not as yet have sufficient capacity to meet the
requirements of librarianship are doing a grave disservice to themselves, to their fellow staff members, to their readers, and to the
nation. Book catalogs, which are grounded in and intricately related to local card catalogs, must be judged in a much broader
framework than that of purely local requirement and bibliographic
and cataloging standards, for the compilation of book catalogs on
every level must be such as to permit eventual integration of the
parts produced in different places and situations into a larger whole
on either a regional or national level.

There may be certain situations where the resources of a
local public library may not appear to contribute to the research
resources of its region or to the nation and where it is easy to
be skeptical of the need for feeding information about commonly
held works into a larger pool of information. However, experience
in the Northwest has indicated that even the smallest library may
contribute to a common pool of resources set up to insure the

preservation of at least one copy of each title unique to the region. It is to be hoped that more such regional centers for the screening of discards will be established. Against such an eventuality, cataloging controls of some uniformity must be developed simply as the mechanism for identifying unique volumes unless libraries are willing to fall back on the clumsy and expensive expedient of shipping all discards to a central point for checking against a catalog record in place of the more convenient and cheaper method of sending catalog cards or lists for checking. Another consideration to be kept always in mind in resisting the temptation to admit that differing rules of cataloging or other standards can be utilized to meet local needs whether in a special library situation or in a popular local library is the need to protect the public who can now, for the most part, move from one library to another without making a difficult adjustment to a completely different system of cataloging. Just as this relatively easy move from one card catalog to another is now possible so should a future move from one book catalog to another or from the card catalog of one's own library to the book catalog of other institutions be possible. A reader who is accustomed to using the catalog of the Takoma Park Public Library with its collection of some 30,000 volumes and a catalog of 70,000 or so cards will not immediately be at home in the intricacies of the Library of Congress Public Catalog of more than 10,000,000 cards, but the citizen of Takoma Park is considerably better off in this new situation than a scholar who was trained in Germany and is accustomed to using catalogs based on the Prussian Rules.

The remainder of this paper examines briefly some of the
extreme views that have been put forth in this century concerning
the level of standards which is needed for book catalogs, describes
some of the standards that have been applied in the compilation of
book catalogs, discusses the effect on users caused by the use of
standards or the lack of them, and sets forth the minimum bibliographic and catalog standards which the evidence shows must be
followed in order to produce a useful end product. In an attempt
to minimize bias, the examination and evaluation of book catalogs
has been supplemented by recourse to critical reviews of book catalogs and to handbooks and guides designed to train librarians in the
use of book catalogs and bibliographies. The number of truly
critical reviews and of critical examinations in handbooks is unfortunately small but a few of these were found to provide some
guidance.

The extreme view that adequate catalogs of library holdings
both in card and book form can be compiled satisfactorily by
relatively unskilled workers restricted to the use of greatly abbreviated entries is perhaps best represented by Ernest Cushing
Richardson. At various places in his writings he advocates the
virtues of "title a line cataloging," a concept he developed as an
outgrowth of studies of the mechanical means of reproducing book
catalogs available in his day. These means were based on the use
of type bars and possibilities of revising and updating printed catalogs by interfiling new single line entries among the existing bars
of type. But even in the production of card catalogs themselves,
Richardson, in the interest of economy, advocated a lowering of

the standards then in existence. As he puts it:

> The chief trouble with full cataloging is that it costs
> through the nose. When a protest was made against a
> cost of five dollars a title for cataloging books which
> had themselves cost on an average of two dollars apiece
> it was said 'what of it- if this cost is necessary why
> not?' The answer is of course the Yankee answer, the
> question, 'Necessary for what?' One earnest cataloger
> urged that, 'we are taught that every card should be a
> work of art' - have every possible perfection that is
> perhaps except usefulness. The purpose of the catalog-
> ing entry is not to minister to the asthetic pleasure of
> the reader but to minister to finding needs. If that need
> can be served for five cents as well as five dollars,
> four dollars and ninety five cents have been spent for
> other than primary library purposes. The Library of
> Congress Union Catalog of printed books freshly cataloged
> several hundred thousand titles at the cost of a little over
> three cents per title, ninety nine percent plus accurate
> for finding purposes. Bibliographica cataloging is strictly
> not the business of libraries at all. It is the responsi-
> bility of bibliographers and bibliographical societies. It
> belongs to science and learning not to the primary serv-
> ice of books. The business of the library is to furnish
> finding cataloging. [1]

In support of his proposals for abbreviated cataloging, Richardson quotes John Cotton Dana to the effect that 'any book ever
printed can be sufficiently described for identification in eighty
letters."[2] Just how Dana would have described a work whose
corporate author heading is far more than eighty characters long
is not stated and we can only assume that Dana would depend on
elements other than corporate authorship as a means of identifying
such titles. We are at any rate no longer tied to the limitations

of the type bar in reproducing book catalogs and the need for extreme brevity of entry is no longer so great as it was once despite
the current vogue for use of methods of reproduction tied to IBM
cards or Listomatic cameras and the like. More recent developments in the area of automatic electrostatic printing and in cameras
which will automatically adjust to the photographing of entries of
varying numbers of lines promise one or more technical break
throughs which will free us from present devices which limit us to
the use of severely abbreviated entries.

At the other extreme, that of the highest standards for description and damn the cost, stands Fredson Bowers, who may be regarded as a current representative of the bibliographic as opposed
to the cataloging or finding list school. According to Bowers:

> A book cannot be described correctly (except by
> accident) unless the method of its printing has first been
> determined by analysis. Moreover, the determination of
> the true primary (or substantive) editions of a text,
> and then of the details of the transmission of this text
> through various editions and impressions - a necessary
> prelude to the establishment of the most correct form of
> this text - is an operation inseparable from analytical
> bibliography.

Analytical bibliography, as explained in an earlier paragraph in
Bowers' article, involves a knowledge of printing processes and
the analysis of the book as a physical object in order to distinguish
between editions and further between the variant copies within a
particular edition. Nowhere in his article does Bowers say point-
blank that library catalogs should be built upon the niceties of
analytical bibliography but a careful reading of his article forces

one to the conclusion that under ideal conditions, research libraries
at least would be able to afford the astronomical costs of a detailed bibliographical control of the sort advocated by Bowers.

If we are to approach the matter from a practical viewpoint,
admitting for the moment that the ideal card or book catalog
envisioned by Bowers is not likely to be forthcoming in the near
future, some analysis of what practicing librarians have had to say
about existing book catalogs may prove a helpful starting point.
Some American comments on the British Museum Catalogue of
Printed Books are helpful because the authors of these comments,
thoroughly grounded as they are in American librarianship, approach
another system of cataloging with a basis for comparison and at
the same time a naivete which leads to the posing of questions
which might not otherwise be formulated. In Carter and Bonk's
work on building library collections there is a section on the catalogs and bibliographies useful in acquisitions work. They have the
following warning against the British Museum Catalog:

> The major difficulty in using the British Museum
> Catalog arises from the fact that the first series used
> rules of entry which do not coincide with American li-
> brary usage. If any author - take as an example a
> woman - has published anonymously, under three
> pseudonyms, under three different married names, as
> well as under her maiden name, all these works will be
> gathered together by American catalogers under the latest
> form of her name, with cross-references from alterna-
> tive forms. American cataloging has long been convinced
> of the usefulness of the uniform author entry, whether for
> persons or corporate bodies. The British Museum Cata-
> log, on the other hand, prefers to take the book in hand

as the ultimate source of main entry, rather than any information gathered from sources extraneous to the book. From the American point of view, the application of this rule can lead to a dismaying scattering of an author's work. Various titles by a given author, or even various editions of the same titles, may have been published under the author's real name, under a pseudonym, and anonymously. Entry in the British Museum Catalog would be made in three different places and sometimes without cross-references to tie the various entries together. [4]

A second major difference arises in the treatment of anonymous titles. In standard American use, the entry for anonymous titles is the first word of the title not an article. British Museum practice centers around catchwords, i.e., content revealed by the title, and there is a sequence of preferences for choice of catch-word. Any book naming or adequately describing a person, place, or object is catalogued under that name. If the book lacks such a person, place or object, the first noun in the title is chosen as entry . . . This rule, of course, requires that the cataloger recognize the different parts of speech, which some might consider a most unreasonable requirement. [5]

A third major difference according to Duncan is in the distinction drawn between pseudonymous and anonymous. In addition there is the tendency to use form entries such as "congresses, periodical publications", etc. rather freely. Winchell, on the other hand, sees virtues in the catalogue which should be brought to the attention of the user, namely "(1) the large amount of analytical material included (analysis of sets, etc.); and (2) the many cross references from names of editors, translators, or other personal names connected with the title."[6]

When it comes to a discussion of the Library of Congress Catalog, the two authors cited above, perhaps overwhelmed at the enormity of the task of criticism, fall back on a description of the scope and the pattern of cumulation with caveat that there are a number of separate alphabets to be searched in order to make certain that one has not missed a work sought for, or worse still, has not found the latest version of the pertinent Library of Congress card.

Some more or less critical reviews of The Library of Congress Catalog offer a few more clues which may point in the direction of desirable standards. Two catalogers have written fairly recently and critically of the published National Union Catalog, both with the point of view that the Catalog is not as useful as it might be in aiding the catalogers of the country in the task of cataloging the works in their own libraries. Marian Harmon, Catalog Librarian at the University of Illinois Library, complains that The National Union Catalog excludes outside reports of serials and that the brief entries in New Serial Titles are not as helpful as they might be. Her more specific criticisms of the Catalog have to do with the use of transliteration, with the perhaps needless editing of what should be a uniform cataloging product received from outside libraries, and with the difficulty of consulting so many alphabets in searching for a particular work. She has the following to say on these points:

> I feel compelled to register a strong protest against
> the decision to prefer transliteration to transcription in

character. It is difficult enough to recognize personal,
corporate, and geographical names in the translitera-
tions long established for author entries; but to extend
transliteration to the entire title and imprint is to impose
a real hardship on users of the catalog. It takes about
twice as long, even for those familiar with the Library
of Congress system of transliteration, to comprehend
Cyrillic titles in transliteration as it does to read them
in character. For those familiar with another system
of transliteration, or with no system at all, reading is
much more difficult . . . It would seem that cooperation in the matter of entry and form of reports is not
too much to expect of libraries in view of the benefits
they derive from the use of the printed catalog. Theoretically it should be possible to incorporate the original
reports just as though they were Library of Congress
printed cards . . . A published catalog with periodically
issued supplements becomes less and less wieldy as
time goes on. Assuming the present frequency, by
October, 1970 it will be necessary to search through
eleven alphabets to ascertain whether a particular title
is listed. (If the retrospective <u>National Union Catalog</u>
will have been published by that time, this would mean
another alphabet, making a total of twelve.) [7]

Robert Slocum, Associate Catalog Librarian at Cornell, in one
brief sentence raised a number of questions: "Time and again cooperating libraries ignore or purposely limit some feature of
description (size, full title, biographical dates, tracings, part of
the imprint, etc.) and employ subjects quite different from those
of the Library of Congress subject headings list or quite irrelevant
subjects." [8]

Finally, to cite briefly from one more critical review because

it presents strongly a point not mentioned above, there is the following from a review of the Louisiana Union Catalog published in
1959:

> Each title is represented only by the main entry,
> a practice which works relatively well with personal
> names but leads to loss of control in union lists rich in
> titles with corporate authorship. A few cross references
> are provided, however, from variations in forms of
> entry and there are some <u>see also</u> references. [9]

To summarize: The authors cited above have indicated a
need for standards to be applied to book catalogs as follows:

1.   It is desirable to follow uniform rules of entry.

2.   Some authority for entry beyond the book in hand is
     needed.

3.   Provision should be made for cross-references.

4.   In title entries the use of catch-words leads to difficulty
     and in so far as possible it is well to transcribe the
     title in the order given.

5.   Form entries such as "periodicals, annuals, etc." are
     to be avoided and author, corporate, or title entries to
     be used where possible.

6.   Transcription of non-Roman alphabets is to be preferred
     to transliteration.

7.   The single alphabet is preferable to multiple alphabets.

8.   Description should be given fully including size, full
     title and full imprint.

9.   Standard subject headings should be employed.

10. An adequate number of added entries is a desirable

feature.

All of this leaves as much unsaid about areas where standards need to be applied in the production of book catalogs. There can be no question but what the primary need for standards is in the area of entry. Here we are fortunate in having a well established body of rules, well known to and followed by a large number of institutions and familiar through usage to a wide public. There is no question in the mind of the author but what the ALA Cataloging Rules for Author and Title Entries should be a basic tool for use in compiling any book catalog.

When it comes to the body of the entry, there is some room for difference of opinion. The Rules for Descriptive Cataloging in the Library of Congress provide a basic guide, but some departures from these rules or the adoption of more brief descriptions than called for seems possible and may perhaps be economically desirable The present editorial staff of The National Union Catalog find no particular difficulties with abbreviated titles, but there are occasionally questions because collation is not given as fully as it might be, or the place of imprint for the same work is given differently by several libraries. Granted the aim of distinguishing between editions and at the same time bringing together all reports of the same edition, it would seem desirable to follow fairly closely the standards for collation and recording of imprint as given in the Rules for Descriptive Cataloging.

In the matter of establishing entry, it seems logical to accept the Library of Congress Catalog and its parts as the standard and to adhere to the no conflict rule that the name of an author as given on the

title page may be used without further search if the same name
has not been preempted by another author recorded in the printed
catalog.

In the matter of transliteration, again we have standards
approved by the American Library Association and incorporated
into the ALA Cataloging Rules. During the interim between new
editions of the Rules newly adopted, rules for transliteration are
published in the Cataloging Service Bulletin. The practice of using
transcription of non-Roman Alphabets in preference to transliteration is advocated provided always that somewhere on the original
copy, even if it does not show in the final printed catalog, there
is sufficient information given in transliteration for use of those
who must arrange the entries in proper order and are not thoroughly familiar with all of the scripts used.

In arrangement of entries there are also available standards
which can be followed. The Filing Rules for the Dictionary Catalogs of the Library of Congress provide a possible guide for large
complex catalogs but the ALA rules, which differ not in philosophy
but only in minor detail, would serve just as well in many instances.

Guidance on provision of added entries and cross references
is to be found in the ALA Cataloging Rules. These rules, however, are aimed at a dictionary catalog situation and book catalogs
tend somehow to be either author or subject catalogs rather than
dictionary catalogs. The editors of The National Union Catalog
claim to use "common sense" in providing added entries or cross
references beyond those called for in the rules. Obviously more

precise standards could be formulated if it were thought necessary
or desirable.

Standards for pattern of cumulation are difficult to formulate
and at any rate are a question more properly the topic of another
discussion. It should perhaps be standard, however, for book
catalogs in which entries are arranged chronologically by year of
publication to provide an index which would serve as a guide to
the user who has no precise idea of the date of publication.

Finally, in the matter of subject headings there is available
as a standard Subject Headings Used in the Dictionary Catalogs of
the Library of Congress. In this particular area the lack of a
practical guide leads to non-uniform application of headings.

Johannes Dewton has recently pointed out that some of the
standards stated above are a snare and a delusion since they do
not cover absolutely all possibilities or leave room as his examples show all too well, for errors in cataloging. One would be
discouraged indeed about the prospects for standardization, if one
took Dewton's views at face value. But the proof of the pudding is
in The National Union Catalog itself, which owes its uniformity
and usefulness to large degree to the uniform standards applied to
cataloging all over the country and to a somewhat smaller degree
to the incredible skill and imagination of Dewton and others in
imposing standards on the relatively small percentage of faulty
entries received from contributing libraries.

Summary

The extremes of title-a-line and bibliographic standards for
book catalogs are rejected in favor of the more traditional library

cataloging techniques. A review of some criticisms of book catalogs and of the catalogs themselves indicates the need for standards
in the areas of entry, description, transliteration, authority for
entry, subject headings, added entries, cross references and arrangement of entries. Certain basic tools of the cataloger's trade
provide the necessary standards for these areas. Local need may
suggest slight modification of existing standards but caution in
departure from these standards is urged in the interest of future
cooperatively compiled book catalogs.

References

1. Richardson, Ernest Cushing. A Union World Catalog of Manu-
    script Books; Preliminary Studies in Method. Volume VI.
    Summary of Method, New York, Wilson, 1937, p. 30.

2. Ibid, p. 78.

3. Bowers, Fredson. "The Function of Bibliography," Library
    Trends, 7:498, April, 1959.

4. Duncan, Mary Carter and Bonk, Wallace J. Building Library
    Collections, New York, Scarecrow Press, 1959, p. 157.

5. Ibid., p. 158.

6. Winchell, Constance M. Guide to Reference Books, Chicago,
    A.L.A., 1951. p. 9-10.

7. Harman, Marian. "The National Union Catalog: A Review,"
    Library Resources and Technical Services, 2:211-214.
    Summer, 1958.

8. Slocum, Robert B. "The Printed National Union Catalog;
    Notes and Suggestions," Library Resources and Technical
    Services, 3:59-60, Winter, 1959.

9. Dewton, Johannes L. "Louisiana Bibliography," Library of
    Congress Information Bulletin, 18:645, October 19, 1959.

Preferred Practices

in the

Publication of Book Catalogs*

By the Book Catalogs Committee, American Library Association

The following criteria are designed to guide the publication of a book catalog of a library (or of a special collection within a library) so that it may best serve the interests of the scholarly world. The Book Catalogs Committee of the American Library Association prepared the statement in the belief that it will be a helpful guide to librarians considering publication of their catalog and may also help publishers to determine the best possible product in intellectual, aesthetic, economic and practical terms.

The criteria cover specific problems involving scope, bibliographical arrangement, physical presentation, and general convenience of use. They relate to published catalogs whether they are limited to authors, subjects or titles, or are a combination of approaches. The criteria are designed to convey a sense of the practical ideal. However, for any particular catalog, one or more of these points may not be suitable of application; circumstances will alter the reasonable criteria in individual cases. Relationships of a proposed catalog to existing national catalogs are not here considered. The recommended practices are not intended to apply to library catalogs produced solely for local internal use.

*ALA Bulletin, 56:836-837, October, 1962.

While some of these preferred practices may be technically
difficult or financially impracticable at the present time, it is
expected that feasibility will shortly result through experimentation
and technological development.

A. General Criteria

1. To be worthy of publication, and to be worthy of purchase by
   subscribing libraries, the book catalog must index a collection
   of notable distinction in its particular field. This field should
   be rather closely and carefully circumscribed in order that it
   not vaguely impinge on catalogs in related areas that have been
   published.

2. The selection of the catalog for publication and its editorial
   refinement should be accomplished with the advice of a group
   of both scholars and librarians competent in the particular
   subject area being considered.

3. An introduction to the volume should identify closely related
   catalogs and justify publication of an additional catalog. It
   should also clearly present the plan of publication, the inclusiveness of the cataloged collection, the rules followed in
   catalog entries, and related information.

4. Premature announcement of publication should be avoided;
   however, advance notice is desirable for expensive sets to permit libraries to make budget provision.

5. Libraries publishing their catalogs should make arrangements
   to provide photocopy service for materials outside of copyright or material not otherwise under restriction.

B. <u>Bibliographical Criteria</u>

1. The index records should have been prepared by readily under-
    standable and consistently applied rules, preferably following
    the American Library Association rules for entry. The ex-
    tremes of 'title-a-line' form of entry and full bibliographic
    description are usually to be rejected in favor of recent A-
    merican library cataloging practice; however, considerable
    latitude is desirable as indicated by the complexity of the
    collection and its relation to other collections.

2. If transliteration of non-Roman alphabets is felt necessary,
    it should conform to the system approved by the American Li-
    brary Association, where one exists, or a system followed in
    the best scholarly circles. In all cases where there is trans-
    literation, the transliteration table should be included in the
    prefatory matter.

3. Standard forms of subject headings should be employed, with
    terms being appropriate to the content of the collection. Where
    a more suitable list of headings does not exist, use of the
    Library of Congress list should be considered.

4. Standard filing rules such as those of the American Library
    Association or the Library of Congress should be generally
    followed; however, special arrangements may be indicated by
    the complexity of the collection. The filing rules that are
    used should be summarized in the prefatory matter. Cross
    references should be liberally included.

5. 'Information cards' or other signs should always be included
    to explain a peculiar arrangement of entries in complex

portions of the file. And a table of contents in each volume is desirable to indicate the organization of the records when the arrangement is complex.

6. Indexes to the catalog are necessary to provide a different approach than that of the main order when normal intellectual approaches so indicate. Thus, subject or classified arrangement may be desirable as a basic approach, but should then normally be supplemented by an author index.

7. If two or three collections are roughly of equal strength in the subject covered, are equally well indexed, and are in a significant degree complementary to one another, then the several catalogs should be jointly published if at all feasible.

8. Records for acquisitions cataloged subsequent to publication of the initial sequence should be published as frequently as logic and financial support allow, hopefully at annual intervals with cumulations each ten years.

9. All withdrawals should be noted in the next supplement or edition and cataloging errors of major importance should be corrected.

C. Physical Criteria

1. The clarity of catalog record information in a catalog prepared by photographic methods should approach closely the clarity of newly set type. No important information should be reduced below 8 point type.

2. The grade of paper used should be heavy enough so that the end leaves will not become curled after heavy use, and the quality of paper should be permanent/durable and relatively

opaque.

3. Unless it is planned to republish the basic set frequently in order to incorporate additions and changes, the binding should be of the highest quality, sewn and in full buckram, and with sufficient set in the adhesive that the volume will remain tight but open reasonably flat. In other words, the materials and methods of binding should exceed the standards set in the Library Binding Institute <u>Minimum Specifications for Class 'A' Library Binding.</u>

4. The size and weight of each volume should be convenient for heavy use by students and scholars and should not in any case weigh over five and one half pounds.

5. The alphabetical or other basis of division between volumes should be clearly featured on the spine of each volume, and each volume should be numbered.

6. Supplements should generally be bound in volumes of the same size and general characteristics as the basic set; however, they should have some readily apparent difference in order to help distinguish the several sequences.

February, 1962.

Printed Book Catalogs[*]

By Marjorie Griffin

Librarians today face a challenge. They must publicize the increasing mass of literature which flows into their libraries. Some librarians are accepting this challenge by departing radically from conventional procedures. Paradoxically, necessity is leading them to revert to a practice used first in France in 1643 - the compilation of the book catalog. The French catalog was hand-written. With the passage of time, librarians replaced hand copying with the typewriter, and today we are replacing the typewriter with electronic machines for the compilation of book catalogs.

The book catalogs we will discuss now are of many different types. Some are loose-leaf, some bound, but all forms are basically listings of library holdings arranged in various sequences, and providing a diversity of bibliographic data.

These catalogs are printed by many different methods. This discussion will include not only punched card techniques, but also punched paper tape and a photographic process. But regardless of the method of printing or format, a book catalog has many advantages not common to a standard card catalog:

1. It is compact, and therefore a space saver, and readily carried from table to table.
2. Borrowers find it easy to use because they are accustomed to looking in dictionaries and directories.

*Revue de la documentation, 28: 8-17, 1961.

3. It is quick to use: the eye can scan a page of text faster than it can look at separate cards.

4. All the available information on a subject, or all the books by one author, can be seen at a glance.

5. It saves the librarian's time: there is no typing of repetitive data, as in cataloging, and no filing of duplicate cards, since once the data is punched on a card it can be duplicated and rearranged mechanically.

6. Multiple copies of the book catalog can be prepared easily by machine, and therefore distribution to other geographic locations is economical in time and cost.

7. A general distribution to departmental offices, and other company libraries, and to each engineer's desk, results in greater use of the library holdings.

8. Subject bibliographies can be tabulated readily by printing appropriate sections of the punched cards in the subject deck.

Different libraries have different needs, and the catalog must be designed to answer these. The flexibility of a machine-produced book catalog gives the librarian leeway to design a tailor-made system to meet these needs. After recognition of these unique values of a book catalog, the librarian must analyze the primary functions of the catalog in the library.

1. Is it a finding list, a printed guide to information for locating a book in the library resources by author, title, or subject?

2. Is it expected to give complete details regarding publisher, date, editions and annotations?

3. Is it to be used chiefly in a library, or at every office desk, or in the workroom for the convenience of a cataloger?

4. Is it to be a master catalog to replace the card catalog, or will the card catalog still be the source of the full data?

5. Must the author entry be complete or will initials suffice?

6. Will abbreviated titles be acceptable, permitting one line entry, and thus keeping the book catalog small and the

machine work faster and simpler?

7. Will the processing be done in a central unit or will each unit forward its information to one library? There is greater uniformity in entry when there is central cataloging.

The answers to these questions define the objectives and determine the function of a printed book catalog. And it is only after specific objectives have been outlined that a catalog can be developed for the operations and services of a specific library.

In addition, before designing a system for the production of a book catalog, there must be, for the uninitiated, some understanding of the various problems of "machines", and their basic operating principles.

Machines are like children; they need a mother to guide them. They must be told explicitly what to do, and we must not expect more from them than they can give, or more than they have been instructed to give. Machines operate on logical principles, and the instructor must recognize and be able to dictate every step of the operation. The planner must recognize certain limitations characteristic of specific machines and accept them; he must decide upon and use consistently rules of entry and regulations for symbols, abbreviations, and punctuation.

Two means of input for the machine are available to the librarian: punched cards and punched paper tape. There are 80 columns in an IBM card, and each column has 12 positions into which holes can be punched. It is these holes which have significance when the card flows through the machine.

Paper tape has holes punched in channels comparable to the columns on a card. The holes in both the cards and the tape provide similar information, and are read mechanically, and printed lists are made from them. Information once punched in cards or tape can be used again without repunching, and provides flexibility in reproducing and printing complete or selected data.

If there is no machine installation, then the librarian must investigate different processes and review the literature to appraise actual systems, for to plan a library system as an additional application of machines already in use in a company requires one approach, but to plan to purchase machines specifically suited to fulfilling library objectives for the printed book catalog requires another.

The evaluation of long-established systems provides a background and opens new channels of thinking to substantiate a decision to prepare a printed book catalog. However, one must be alert to the inevitable frustrations attendant upon any major conversion process, be it from manual-to-manual system or manual-to-machine.

> "But, my dear," said the Hatter, "Was there progress?"
> "Well," said Alice earnestly, "There was change."

There will be times when you will agree with Alice.

Two pioneer libraries in this sort of experimentation warrant special mention; both have now been established for seven years, so they can no longer be considered experimental. The King County Public Library System in Washington produced in 1951 its first printed book catalog as an expedient way of circumventing the county problem of changing branch catalogs every month. This loose-leaf book, called "A Throw-Away Catalog for Changing Book

Collections," is an invoice listing arranged with an author, title and subject approach, and today fulfills the purpose for which it was established.

In 1952, the Los Angeles County Library started a system for distributing a master book catalog of all the county library books to every branch. Today, they have an efficient, streamlined procedure, publishing a book catalog for 117 branches. This printed book catalog is much more than a checklist; it provides analytics and annotations. It gives more bibliographic data than any other printed catalog, but does not give complete information. The less-needed information may be found at the central card catalog in the main library.

The efficiency of the machine operation and the success in making available to every branch all the books in the system have brought to the Los Angeles County Library merited publicity. This system is the pattern for other printed book catalogs both in this country and abroad.

The following survey of systems in operation progresses from the simple in procedures and machine installation to the complex, from the unsophisticated to the sophisticated. All are relatively recent and consequently subject to the modification that is a part of every experimental period.

The U.S. Naval Postgraduate School at Monterey in California successfully prints its current list of periodicals on a Flexowriter. A listing in alphabetical order, typed on the Flexowriter, is punched simultaneously on a paper tape. The tape is retyped automatically on masters and then multiple copies are run by photo offset. Up-

dating this periodical listing is facilitated by a special feature of
the Flexowriter which can punch a new tape as an old one is
printed: if there are changes in dates of holdings or inclusions
of new titles, the operator types the new information at the correct place, which is simultaneously punched on the new tape, and
actually makes a revised edition of the former tape. The advantages: (1) Upper and lower case letters will appear in the finished
type (most machines have only capitals available); (2) Erasing of
errors is easily accomplished; and (3) Updating is simplified.

A new method to speed up the production of listings involves
the Listomatic camera, a photo composing machine that photograph
listings from typed IBM cards and produces a continuous roll of
negatives at a reduction of about 40 per cent. Each IBM card is
a complete entry, and can contain only three lines of typewritten
information. The cards are sorted manually, and column 52 in
the card is then gang-punched and this control punch used to position the typewritten cards for the machine. The final printing is
by photo offset. The Cardiovascular Literature Project of the National Academy of Sciences uses this system.

The New York State Library issued in 1956 a <u>Checklist in the</u>
<u>Social Sciences,</u> an author and title catalog produced on the IBM
Cardatype 856, a machine in their Education Department. The
purpose was to make this listing akin to a telephone directory
with the call number in place of phone number; therefore it consists of one-line entries. Initials of authors and abbreviations for
titles are considered sufficient. The cards are punched and sorted
into proper order. Since an alphabetic sorting takes twice as long

as numeric sort, the cards are roughly sorted by the first few letters and then manually sorted for complete alphabetizing. Then
listings are automatically typed from the cards; the copy is reduced in size and printed by photo offset. The application of this
available machine, although a slower printer than current models,
and not equipped with lower case letters, provided a very satisfactory printed catalog for making resources more available, and
for lessening the interlibrary loan problem of knowing whether the
wanted book was in the system.

The foregoing have been examples of relatively simple systems
performing adequately the purposes for which they were installed.

More sophisticated systems using more machines, and giving
more information, utilize the IBM 026 keypunch, IBM 056 verifier,
the IBM 083 sorter, IBM 089 collator, and IBM 407 tabulator. The
following special library systems differ in their objectives and,
consequently, in their resultant catalogs. The systems reveal
initiative and resourcefulness in the attempt to communicate to the
user the resources of the library.

The National Reactor Testing Station Technical Library near Idaho
Falls has a master list of periodicals for six libraries with entry
checked according to the Union List of Serials. A portion of this list
is shown in illustration on the following page. It can be compared
with the list of periodicals produced by a Flexowriter shown on the
following page. Title cards were punched from a typed, proof-
read alphabetical listing. Information included titles, a serial
numeric code, and a sequence code. The overflow trailer card
contains holding information of volumes, year of first volume held

NATIONAL REACTOR TESTING STATION
TECHNICAL LIBRARY

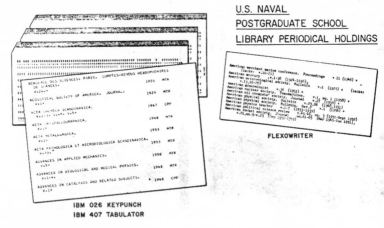

U.S. NAVAL
POSTGRADUATE SCHOOL
LIBRARY PERIODICAL HOLDINGS

FLEXOWRITER

IBM 026 KEYPUNCH
IBM 407 TABULATOR

by the library, a three-letter designation of location of periodical, and the branch code. A working paper is run for editing before the final printing is done on Multilith mat stock using the IBM 407, and reproduced by Multilith equipment on both sides of the page.

This is a satisfactory mechanized operation. After a general distribution to all personnel, it was found that the use of the periodical holdings was greater. The title deck was designed, as well, for future application to accounting, ordering and routing pro cedures. The NRTS Library is presently developing an IBM punched card printed book catalog.

The Long Island Lighting Company of Hicksville, New York, has devised an informative catalog for notifying personnel in any company location of the holdings in the library at the company headquarters. An IBM keypunch, sorter and 407 accounting machi are used to compile the list of library resources. The book col lection can be approached by author, title, or broad subject. Li brary periodicals and serials, and newspapers, films and film strips are listed.   There is also a subject classification of a clip-

ping file, and a miscellaneous section points to holdings not already

listed, such as almanacs, dictionaries, catalogs of colleges, annual

indexes to periodicals.   There are two lines of abbreviations in the

catalog to guide the user.

In the following illustration each page is divided into six col-

umns with a title, author, abbreviated publisher, date, abbreviated

broad subject and a call number.   On the IBM card the 80 avail-

able columns have been allotted thus: the title, 46 columns; the

author, 20 columns; publisher and subject abbreviations have 3

columns each; the date requires 2, and the call number, 4 columns.

LONG ISLAND LIGHTING COMPANY
LIBRARY PRINTED CATALOG

FINANCE & ECONOMICS

SUBJECT INDEX - FE

TITLE	AUTHOR	PUB	DATE	SUB	CALL #
ADMINISTERED PRICING ECONOMIC AND LEGAL ISSUES	ADELMAN M A ET AL	CFB	58	FE	4372
ADVERSE EFFECTS OF EXPANDING GOVERNMENT	NATIONS BUSUNESS*	NB	57	FE	4291
ALUMINUM CARTEL	MARLIO LOUIS	BRK	47	FE	4357
AMER ECONOMIC DEVELOPMENT	KROOS HERMAN E	PH	55	FE	1701
AMER HOUSING PROBLEMS AND PROSPECTS	COLEAN MILES L ET AL	TCF	44	FE	4354
AMERICAS CAPACITY TO CONSUME	LEVEN MAURUCE ET AL	BRK	34	FE	4345
AMERICAS CAPACITY TO PRODUCE	NOURSE EDWIN G	BRK	34	FE	4346
ANATOMY OF DEPRECIATION	NASH LUTHER R	PUR	47	FE	1783
ANN REP 1955	FORD FOUNDATION	FRD	55	FE	3978
ANN REP 1956	FORD FOUNDATION	FRD	56	FE	3979
ANN REP 1957	FORD FOUNDATION	FRD		FE	3980
ANN REP 1958	FORD FOUNDATION	FRD		FE	3981
ANN REP OF STOCKHOLDERS ACTIV AT CORP MEETINGS	AMER STOCKHOLDERS	GJL	55	FE	3025
ANN REP OF STOCKHOLDERS ACTIV AT CORP MEETINGS	AMER STOCKHOLDERS	GJL	57	FE	3026
ANN REP OF SUPT OF INS VOL 1 STOCK AND MLIC	NEW YORK STATE	WMS	50	FE	4046
ANTI RECESSION POLICY FOR 1958	COMM FOR ECONOMIC DEV	CED	58	FE	977

PAGE 133

The title section begins with the title in the first page column, with the author, publisher, date, subject, call number in this sequence. For the author section, the author is placed in the first page column with the title following, and the remainder in the same sequence. The subject section is primarily a bibliography in title alphabetic order of books under the broad subject. There are seven subject listings and one miscellaneous.

This is an inclusive catalog. Its very compactness should make it welcome in every engineer's office and to the administrative staff.

The Monsanto Union Catalog is a checklist of books in ten libraries compiled simply for the purpose of identifying a title and its location; therefore only the first author, the title, and the date of publication were chosen for entry. Each library catalogs its own books: each library submits an IBM key punch data sheet, with title, author and date indicated in the appropriate spaces, to the processing library shown on the following page.

To simplify card handling, information was compressed into one card, with 72 columns for author, title and date, and 2 for the library symbol (TC = Texas City, SP = Springfield, etc.). Instruction sheets for abbreviations, symbols and punctuation are issued to each library. The listing is updated annually. This enterprising library network produces a union list of serials and a unique pamphlet index as well.

MONSANTO CHEMICAL COMPANY.
KEY PUNCH DATA SHEET SUBMITTED BY EACH LIBRARY
FOR ALL TITLES ADDED DURING THE YEAR.

KEYPUNCH DATA

Author	Title / Year	Code
SKEIST IRVING	EPOXY RESINS 1958	SL
MOORE THOMAS	VITAMIN A 1957	SL
PETERS J P ETC	QUANTITATIVE CLINICAL CHEMISTRY V1 1946	SL
TODD JAMES C	CLINICAL DIAGNOSIS BY LAB METH 11ED 1948	SL
US DEPT AG	LAND YEARBOOK OF AGRICULTURE 1958	SL
COLEMAN T J	SOME CHARACTERISTICS OF PACKED RECT COLMN 1934	SL
INST MECH ENG	PROC CONF ON LUBRICATION + WEAR 1957	SL
SPIKER S K	INDEXING YOUR BOOK 1954	SL
SOKOLNIKOFF I S E+C	MATH OF PHYSICS + MODERN ENGINEERING 1958	SL
LITTLE ARTHUR D PUB	ATOMS FOR PEACE USA 1958	SL
LIMKE WM F	SEIDELLS SOLUBILITIES V1 4ED 1958	SL
DE SOLA RALPH	ABBREVIATIONS DICTIONARY 1958	SL
CHEM SOC LONDON	SYMPOSIA 1958	SL
DRUCKER PETER F	AMERICAS NEXT TWENTY YEARS 1957	SL
SOC CHIM FRANCE	FILE CENTENAIRE DE FOUNDATION 1957	SL
PRIGOGINE I ED	ADVANCES IN CHEM PHYSICS V1 1958	SL
HARWOOD J J ED	EFFECTS RADIATION ON MATERIALS 1958	SL
HARKINS W D	PHYS CHEM OF SURFACE FILMS 1952	SL
ALLEN ROY M	PHOTOMICROGRAPHY 2ED 1958	SL
MARANVILLE L F	STUDY OF STRONG ACIDS BY RAMAN-SPEC METH 1949	SL

At IBM in San Jose we have developed a master catalog of books for four libraries on the plant site. Since each library belongs to an autonomous division, each librarian does her own ordering and cataloging. However, the spirit of cooperation is strong, and each librarian submits her shelf list cards for new titles each month to the oldest library, the Advanced Systems and Research Library, for processing. In the processing library, a master shelf list card is punched for each entry with the location letter code. The fixed fields are shown as follows:

IBM SAN JOSE ADVANCED SYSTEMS & RESEARCH LIBRARY.
PUNCHED SHELF LIST CARD

These master shelf list cards are reproduced on an IBM 514,
making one card for the author deck and one for the title deck.
The new cards are interpreted (the punched information is printed
along the top of the card for visual use), sorted into their respective order, and then filed in the main author or title decks, in
readiness for the monthly printing on an IBM 407. We send six
author, title and subject catalogs each month to other IBM San
Jose locations.

The installation of the subject catalog needed thoughtful planning. First the subject headings in the standard card catalog were
counted and a numeric code computed mathematically on the IBM
650. Each subject heading was assigned a code number, leaving
ample digits between the numbers for interpolation of new subject
headings. Subject headings and their numbers were then keypunched on IBM cards and printed on the IBM 407. This formed
our Subject Heading Dictionary, which is updated monthly. As

the 3 X 5 shelf list cards arrive in our library, the subject headings are assigned a code number from the subject dictionary, and
new subjects are identified for the key puncher to make a new
subject card for the subject code dictionary, and one for the subject catalog.

As shown in the flow chart on the next page, the key puncher
reproduces on an IBM 514 the punched master shelf list sorted
into two decks, an author and a title, and gang punches an identity
punch for each deck.   The author cards contain all data except
the title, and the title cards, all data except the author.   The key
puncher then reproduces on the keypunch, author and title cards
for each subject printed on 3 X 5 shelf list cards.   The key puncher then merges the two decks in call number order so that author
card precedes title card for each book, and punches from the
original 3 X 5 shelf list card the subject code number into columns 66-71.   The cards are then sorted by subject code number
and manually filed in the subject catalog.   Under each subject, the
cards are filed by call number because it is quicker to sort by
number than by author.   We are planning to change this and arrange by Cutter number.

The recognition of the merits of mechanization in producing
"finding lists" has recently brought large-scale computers into use
for compiling these guides.   Librarians using ASTIA are grateful
for the more current announcemēnts of the reports which have appeared since ASTIA undertook the prodigious task of mechanization.
Currently, reports are listed in the Technical Abstract Bulletin

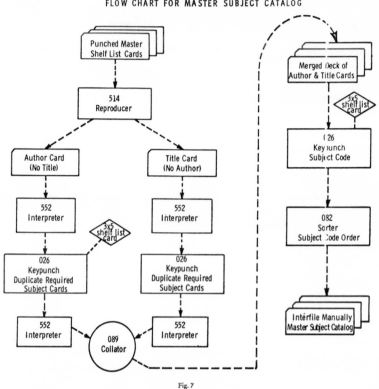

Fig. 7

60 days after receipt, and the aim is to reduce the delay to 25 days.

Since April 1, 1960, the Remington Rand Synchrotape typewriter has been used at ASTIA to type document abstracts, the Univac Solid State Computer 90 used to arrange the material automatically into the format in which it is published. This computer use for more rapid handling is another achievement in the processing of a book catalog.

The challenge to arouse interest in the library resources, and guide the seeker to specific information has been very recently met with still another computer system. Chemical Abstracts has for some time been concerned with the late entries of articles - there has been at least a four-month delay before announcement in the semi-monthly issues. To counterbalance this deficiency, without sacrificing the indexing in depth, Chemical Abstracts has issued its first Chemical Titles, a permutation index of approximately 3000 titles in current chemical journals.

Author, title, and publication source are keypunched on an IBM card, and then converted to magnetic tape: from here the IBM 704 selects significant words in the title and arranges them in alphabetic order by key word, with the number of times the title appears determined by the number of key words it contains. The eye can quickly scan the titles that are grouped under descriptive terms which form a vertical column down the page. An identification code guides the user to a bibliographical section.

We can project our thinking from these increasingly sophisticated systems to tomorrow, when inevitably, there will be greater standardization of information processing in major regional or national centers; when all documents will be initially recorded in machinable form; and when the very flexibility of machine systems will simplify the transfer of information.

Today we have a diversity of printed catalogs serving small and large audiences, planned to meet a variety of objectives, and printed by a variety of methods. These applications are proof that there are ways of eliminating the repetitive tasks of cataloging, that there are ways of reducing the manual filing of cards, and that the printed book catalog with its primary purpose to make materials readily accessible. But its compactness, its ease and speed in use and economy in time and cost for reproducing multiple copies and facility in specific author and subject bibliographies, is a partial answer to the perpetual library responsibility for the dissemination of information.

References

Alvord, Dorothy. "King County Public Library does it with IBM," PNLA Quarterly, 16:123-132, April, 1952.

Armed Services Technical Information Agency. Automation of ASTIA..a preliminary report, December 1959, AD 22700.

Casey, R. A.. Punched cards, their applications to science and industry, 2d ed. New York, Reinhold, 1958.

Dewey, Harry. "Punched card catalog, theory and technique," American Documentation, 10:36-50, Jan., 1959.

Dubester, H.J. "Catalog - a finding list?" College and Research Libraries, 18:107-111, Mar., 1957.

Jackson, J.B.S. "Loose leaf printed catalogue," Library Association Record, 57:470-473, Dec., 1955.

Lubetzky, S. "Function of the catalog," College and Research Libraries, 17:213-215, May, 1956.

Luckett, G. R. "Partial library automation with the flexowriter automatic writing machine," Library Resources and Technical Services, 1:207-210, Fall, 1957.

MacQuarrie, Catherine. "IBM book catalog," Library Journal, 82:630-634, Mar., 1957.

Seaton, J.R. "Book catalogues, their varieties and uses," Library Review, 16, no. 128:513-14, Winter, 1958.

Singer, T.E.R. Information and communication practice in industry, New York, Reinhold, 1958.

Warheit, I.A. "Machines and systems for the modern library," Special Libraries, 48:357-363, Oct., 1957.

Some Libraries Using Printed Book Catalogs

1. Armed Services Technical Information Services, Arlington Hall Station, Arlington 12, Virginia

2. Columbia River Regional Library, 124 Benton Street, Wenatchee, Washington

3. IBM Advanced Systems and Research Library, Monterey and Cottle Roads, San Jose 14, California

4. King County Public Library, 1100 East Union, Seattle 22, Washington

5. Lake County Public Library, 1050 Ridge Road, Munster, Indiana

6. Library of Congress, Serials Division, Washington, D.C.

7. Long Island Lighting Company, 175 Old Country Road, Hicksville, New York

8. Los Angeles County Library, 322 South Broadway, Los Angeles 53, California

9. Massachusetts Institute of Technology Libraries, Cambridge 39, Massachusetts

10. Monsanto Chemical Company, Organic Research Library, 1700 South Second Street, St. Louis 4, Missouri

11. National Academy of Sciences, Division of Medical Sciences, Cardiovascular Literature Project, Washington, D.C.

12. National Reactor Testing Station, Technical Library, Phillips

Petroleum Company, Idaho Falls, Idaho

13. New York Public Library, Fifth Avenue, New York, New York

14. New York State Library, The University of the State of New York, Albany, New York

15. Southern Illinois University Library, Carbondale, Illinois

16. Squibb Institute for Medical Research, New Brunswick, New Jersey

17. United States Naval Postgraduate School Library, Monterey, California

18. University of Wisconsin Library School, Madison, Wisconsin

Some machines used in the preparation of printed book catalogs

Machines	Manufacturer
Flexowriter	Friden, Incorporated San Leandro, California
Listomatic Camera	Recordak Corporation 415 Madison Avenue New York 17, New York
Synchrotape Univac Solid State Computer 90	Remington Rand Division Sperry Rand Corporation 315 Park Avenue, South New York 10, New York
Keypunch Verifier Collator Sorter Tabulator Cardatype 704 Computer	International Business Machines Corporation 590 Madison Avenue New York 22, New York

Acknowledgements

The author is indebted to the following librarians who have provided valuable information through discussion, informal notes, and samples of systems used in their libraries:

1. Miss Dorothy Alvord
    King County Public Library
    1100 East Union
    Seattle 22, Washington

2. Miss Dorothy R. Cutler
    Columbia River Regional Library
    Wenatchee, Washington

3. Mr. Hillis Griffin
   Technical Library
   National Reactor Testing
   Station
   Phillips Petroleum Company
   Idaho Falls, Idaho

4. Mr. George Luckett
   U.S. Naval Postgraduate
   School
   Monterey, California

5. Mrs. Catherine MacQuarrie
   Mrs. Beryl Martin
   Los Angeles County Library
   322 South Broadway
   Los Angeles 53, California

6. Miss Anne McCann
   The Squibb Institute for Medi-
   cal Research
   New Brunswick, New Jersey

7. Mr. Richard H. Shoemaker
   Rutgers University Library
   New Brunswick, New Jersey

8. Mr. Charles A. Vertanes
   LILCO Library
   Long Island Lighting Company
   Hicksville, New York

9. Mr. William A. Wilkinson
   Organic Research Library
   Monsanto Chemical Company
   St. Louis 77, Missouri

Meeting The Challenge

The British Museum Reprints Its Catalogue*

By F. C. Francis

In January 1957, the Trustees of the British Museum announced a proposal to produce by means of photo-offset lithography,
a complete edition of the British Museum Catalogue as at the end
of 1955 in some 250-300 volumes in the very brief space of 5 or
6 years. The announcement of this vast project, carried through
at so phenomenal a pace, has not unnaturally aroused deep interest
in all parts of the world. Some 400 institutions in countries in
all parts of the world have already expressed their intention of
subscribing to the new edition. We expect still more will wish to
subscribe as soon as the volumes begin to be published.

The original announcement asked for indications of intention to
subscribe. One feature of the replies so far received which causes
me some concern is the poor response from the countries of the
Near and Far East, South America and Africa. It is in the libraries of countries which are now developing their cultural and
educational services that a universal catalogue of the character of
that of the British Musuem can be of the utmost value. It is a
guide to the literature of the Western World and a source of information on which collections of research material can be built up
by new and expanding libraries whether by the acquisition of actual

*<u>UNESCO Bulletin for Libraries</u>, 11;237-241, October 1957.

167

copies or by photocopies. Scholars in isolated libraries will, by
the use of the volumes of this catalogue, find their resources
greatly enriched.

I hope to discover the reason why libraries in these countries
have not been quick to indicate their interest and to encourage
them to make every effort to acquire a copy. It is important that
the extent of the likely demand should be known before printing
starts, as it will be very difficult to maintain any considerable
stock of so large a work.

History

It must be understood first of all that the catalogue is in
volume form, and not on cards as the vast majority of modern
catalogues are. By an ingenious system it is kept completely up
to date and thus may be said to combine the chief virtues of both
the volume and the card form of catalogue.

To explain how this is done it is necessary to glance for a
moment at the history of the catalogues of the British Museum.
They began in 1787 with a two-volume work entitled Librorum
impressorum qui in Museo Britannico adservantur catalogus. A
copy of this catalogue was interleaved and additional entries were
added in manuscript for the service of users of the library. In
1813-19 this was replaced by a catalogue with the same title in
seven volumes, which in turn was interleaved for the addition in
manuscript of new entries. This catalogue remained in use, en-
larged by the addition of new leaves for additions up to 1849. In
that year the plan of writing the entry for each book on a separate
slip, instead of on the blank leaves of the catalogue, was devised.

All the titles were written on separate slips and pasted into large
folio volumes of blank leaves. When it was put at the disposal
of readers in 1850 this catalogue filled 150 volumes. By 1880,
this catalogue of MS. entries had grown to nearly 2,500 volumes,
some of them very bulky. Besides being very expensive to maintain, this catalogue was very clumsy in use; consequently it was
decided to put the whole into print and at the same time to print
monthly lists of all the accessions. Printing was begun in 1881
and by a remarkable feat of organization was completed by 1900.
It contained nearly two and a quarter million entries. During the
period of the production of the catalogue entries for new books were
printed at regular intervals, but in 1900 all the entries which had
appeared during the period of the printing of the main catalogue
were cumulated and printed together as a supplement. This contained a further 325,000 entries; it was published during the years
1900 to 1905. Since then lists of Accessions have been printed at
regular intervals--from 1905 to 1915 every two weeks, from 1915
to date, monthly, except during the second world war when they
were published every two months.[1]

These publications, the original catalogue, the supplement,
and the accessions form the basic material from which the British
Museum General Catalogue as it is in use in the Reading Room is
made.

Present General Catalogue

The volumes of the 1880-1900 catalogue were cut up, column
by column, and mounted into large volumes of specially strong
blank paper, one column to a page or to a double-page opening.

Accessions entries are pasted into these volumes in their correct
alphabetical sequence, extra blank leaves being inserted in the catalogue as required to accommodate new entries.   The alphabetical
sequence for the accessions while it is independent of the alphabetical sequence of the original catalogue is closely linked to it.

The entries are mounted in the volumes in such a way that
those which fall within the alphabetical sequence indicated by the
first and last entries of each individual column are all entered
before the next column begins.   The user of the catalogue, therefore, if he is searching the catalogue under a particular author,
or set of authors, must first of all look in the 'column' and he
must then scan the accessions entries relating to that column.   An
illustration will perhaps make this clearer: in volume 43 of the letter F column 88 begins with FRANCIS (John) and ends with
FRANCIS (John Wakefield).   The four following leaves contain
accessions which fit into the alphabetical sequence between these
two names.   The next column begins with FRANCIS (Jonah) and
ends with FRANCIS (Lydia Mary), and this section is similarly
followed by the accessions relating to this section of the alphabet.
The strict alphabetical sequence in the accessions entries is maintained, and, if necessary, slips which have already been pasted
into the catalogue are transferred to another place to make room
for new insertions.   This is rendered possible by the method of
sticking down: each of the slips, which are 11 cm. long by about
2.5 cm. deep, is pasted at the top and bottom with a very thin
strip of binder's paste; this allows them to be removed easily by
the insertion of a thin paper knife. The General Catalogue, which

consists at present of some 1,250 volumes, is thus kept under continual revision; as I have indicated, new entries are added every month and corrections are made as required in manuscript. To ensure that these processes can be carried on without inconveniencing the users of the Reading Room, three identical copies of the catalogue are used. They are distinguished by the colour of their binding: dark blue (natural pigskin is gradually replacing this), red and green. The 'green' serves as the authoritative copy. This copy is used by an officer, called in the British Museum 'the incorporator', to indicate the correct position in which the new entries should be pasted and when the entries have been inserted in accordance with his instructions, this 'green' volume serves as the model by which the slips are pasted, in turn, into the red and blue copies--volumes of the 'red' copy of the catalogue are substituted for the 'blue' in the Reading Room to ensure that the copy of the catalogue in the Reading Room is complete, while the operation of 'incorporation' is proceeding.

By this process the British Museum has been able to maintain the volume form of the catalogue and to keep it up to date for over 75 years; and indeed, even before the catalogue was printed in 1880, the same system had been in operation with manuscript entries for some 30 years. Admittedly the process is an expensive one, but, by its use, the catalogue has rightly won international fame for ease of consultation and up-to-dateness. No one can doubt that for many purposes a card catalogue, because of its flexibility, is greatly superior to a catalogue in volume form. For a great general catalogue, however, used for scholarly, and

particularly historical, research, the volume form has much to
recommend it over the card form. A whole series of entries can
be scanned at the same time: note can be taken of various editions,
and relationships between various volumes can often be noted.

Second Edition

The British Museum Catalogue quickly went out of print, but
the demand for it continued, particularly in America,[2] where so
many new libraries were being established, and in the 1920's discussions took place which led to a decision to print the catalogue
as a whole a second time. It was expected that this operation
could be speedily carried out if alterations to the existing entries
were kept to a minimum. It was thought desirable to add in,
where necessary, the names of the publishers of English books
(which had been omitted in the original catalogue), and also the
pagination. By limiting the editorial corrections and additions in
this way it was hoped to be able to print the new edition, at the
rate of 12 to 15 volumes a year, in about 12 years. Publication
was begun in 1931, but from the start it was clear that, even with
the minimum of alteration, the proposed rate was quite beyond the
reach of the staff then available in the British Museum. Even
with an increase of staff which was accorded after a few years,
the labour of preparation and proof reading was greater than had
been anticipated, and it was found in addition that the amount of
revision undertaken by the editors of the catalogue showed a continued tendency to increase. This was quite natural, seeing that in
many cases the original entries had been kept very short, and
also that the bibliographical works of reference enabling authors,

editors, translators, revisers to be identified had increased enor-
mously since the original edition had been published. Furthermore
the quality of the librarians engaged on the work of editing the new
edition of the catalogue was such that scholarly revision was bound
to take place. In consequence the rate of production of the catalogue, even before the war, did not average more than three volumes
a year. With the impact of the war, production became even
slower, and it has been impossible since the war to increase the
rate of production to more than one and a half volumes per year.

This slow rate of progress really rendered the whole scheme
of publishing a revised edition of the catalogue impossible. It
would not have been completed in the foreseeable future, and the
method of production, by which each volume contained all material
available up to the time of its publication, rendered the catalogue
quite uneven in its coverage.

Production of New Edition by Photo-Offset Lithography

It is against this background that the present plan for a new
edition of the catalogue, based on an entirely new method of
compilation, has been put forward. The main considerations have
been: first, speed of production, so that the completed catalogue
can be in the hands of subscribers as soon as possible; second,
elimination of editorial work other than that of alphabetization--
this is necessary to avoid the slowing down of production such as
was experienced with the revised edition already referred to; and
third, the elimination of the expense of re-setting and proof-reading
matter which is already in print.

With these considerations in mind, the plan of producing the catalogue by photo-offset lithography was conceived. The idea is, of course, not a new one, since it has already been used with great effect by the Library of Congress in its author and subject catalogues. For the British Museum, however, with its own peculiar kind of catalogue, the proposition presents many new and unusual features. The problem of preparing copy for printing by offset lithography from material stuck down into bound volumes is both new and extremely complicated.

It was first proposed that the copy should be prepared by removing all the entries from the catalogue and re-mounting them in columns in a single alphabetical sequence. For this purpose it was proposed to commission a printer to employ a special staff who would be engaged entirely on the work of extracting and rearranging the entries. These would be photographed and lithographic plates made from the photographs. The main problems involved were those of securing sufficient skilled labour to carry out the work of mounting, and of making satisfactory negatives from copy in which the paper, having been printed at various times and having been in use in the catalogue for periods up to 75 years, was of varying degrees of colour, ranging from white to coffee.

These difficulties happily were not so formidable as was at first feared and a very satisfactory specimen was produced, which demonstrated conclusively that the proposition is entirely feasible. Further research however has revealed that it may be possible by employing a suitable camera to eliminate completely the tedious work of extracting and mounting the entries. Such a procedure would not only simplify the work of preparation, it would make it possible to overcome even more satisfactorily the problem of the different coloured paper. Experiments with this new possibility are still proceeding and we expect that they will be brought to a successful conclusion in the autumn. Once the negatives of the copy are prepared the remainder of the work will be a straight-forward printing job: lithographic plates will be prepared and copy printed off in the normal fashion.

Let me now describe the details of the operation. Volumes of one copy (the 'red') of the catalogue will be taken in turn--beginning of course at the point reached by the revised edition before it was abandoned, and the entries numbered in alphabetical order. This operation will require skilled knowledge of the catalogue, because all the entries from the original columns and from the accessions will have to be brought together in one sequence. In addition it will be necessary at this stage to ensure that any MS. corrections which appear in the catalogue are legible and so placed in relation to the entry to which they refer that they will reproduce satisfactorily. It is proposed to allot two or three members of the permanent cataloguing staff of the Museum to this work. The volumes of the catalogue marked up in this way will be sent at an agreed rate to the printer, who will either mount the copy in the order indicated by the numbers and photograph them, in columns, or will photograph the entries in the correct sequence. From the negatives thus produced, positives will be sent back to the Museum for checking--to see that no errors were made in the original numbering and to ensure that no entries have been lost or damaged. We intend to number the entries in such a way that the numbers will be reproduced in the positive used for checking, but will be cut off before the lithographic plates are made.

Once the copy is prepared and the plates made, the printing as I have already indicated is a straightforward, speedy operation. The slowest part of the work will be preparing the negatives. We have gone into the matter carefully, however, and have been able to suggest a rate of production of one volume of roughly 500 pages per week. In this way we shall be able to deliver the whole work in 5 or 6 years.

The price of the catalogue has not been finally fixed. I expect that it will be substantially below the Ŀ8 per volume quoted in our original announcement--probably about Ŀ6. By modern standards this is a cheap price for a book of 500 pages, roughly 35 cm x 25 cm., printed on good paper and strongly bound; it is only the speed of production which makes the cost seem high. Subscribers can be assured that it is not being produced at a profit and that the price is calculated at the lowest possible figure consistent with avoiding a loss. Production will begin in the autumn of 1957 and the first volumes are expected to be ready for dispatch in January 1958. Subscribers will be informed of the details of the arrangements for delivery in good time.

Comparison with Library of Congress Catalogue

The question has been asked: has not the need for the British Museum Catalogue been lessened by the appearance of the Library of Congress Catalogue. The answer is a decided no! A comparison of the coverage of the two catalogues produced some really striking results. A random sample covering some 250 authors

revealed that the overlap between the two was only 27 per cent
in the case of the authors, only 23 per cent in the case of works
mentioned and only 17 per cent in the case of the actual work.
The fact is that the two catalogues do not overlap to any significant
extent, they complement each other. Apart from English and A-
merican authors, which as might be expected, are more strongly
represented in the appropriate national catalogue, the British
Museum Catalogue is incomparably richer in books published
before 1800--19 out of 20 in the sample appeared only in the
British Museum Catalogue; it is also twice as rich in foreign books.

What of the Future?

The new edition of the catalogue will be complete up to the
end of 1955 and its publication will provide an opportunity for a
reconsideration of the method of publishing the accessions. The
most desirable course would be to produce these annually, cumulating at five and ten years. This must be combined, however, with
a method of production which allows new entries to be incorporated into the General Catalogue in the Reading Room every month as
at present. No definite plans have yet been made but I hope that
we may be able to produce our monthly accessions entries both in
a form which enables us to paste them into the catalogue, and
also on cards. The cards can then be used very simply for the
production of annual and five-yearly volumes, while the readers'
catalogue will be maintained as at present.

During the production of the new edition the General Catalogue
in use in the Reading Room will be replaced by the new volumes
as they appear and provision made for the pasting in of the acces-

sions entries into the new volumes. A separate catalogue, probably on cards, for all books acquired since 1955 will also be
maintained; it is expected however that this catalogue will gradually diminish in size as the new volumes become available. It
will in fact cover only that portion of the alphabet for which the
new volumes are not available.

Notes

1. For further details, see Francis, F. C., British Museum.
   The Catalogues of the Printed Books, 1952.
2. Indeed, so great is its usefulness that, despite the fact it
   was already some 50 years old, a commercial firm in the
   United States of America found it profitable to publish a reduced photographic facsimile in 1946.

The Book Catalog of the Los Angeles County Public
Library: How It Is Being Made*

By Catherine MacQuarrie
and Beryl L. Martin

Book Catalog versus Card Catalog

Los Angeles County Public Library has received a great many
inquiries concerning its IBM Book Catalog since the inception of
the catalog seven years ago. We have been honored by interested
visitors from nearly every state in the Union and from more than
twenty foreign countries. Much professional interest was also
shown in our exhibit at the ALA Annual Conference held in San
Francisco in July 1958, regarding which a University of California
Library news release stated: "Among the exhibition booths, undoubtedly the busiest were several non-commercial ones, particularly Los Angeles County Library's, with its examples of IBM card-
punched catalogs in book form." Because of this widespread interest on the part of librarians and the studies being made by the
American Library Association Inter-Divisional Committee on Book
Catalogs, we have been impelled to prepare this analysis of the
technical preparation and cost of the project.

Our Book Catalog is the basic tool with which we are striving
to render complete service to library patrons and expedite that
service on the branch library level. It is an integrated, annotated
listing of all adult and juvenile holdings--fiction, nonfiction, and

*Library Resources and Technical Services, 4: 208-227, Summer, 1960.

179

reference--available through regional and institutional branches. The story of its development has its origin in the postwar industria expansion of our County Library district, which is one of the larges in the country and one faced with many problems and opportunities resulting from the impact of soaring populations and large-scale changes in the constantly shifting patterns of civic and community life.

In 1952 we had 114 service outlets, only twenty-five of which were equipped with card catalogs. This meant that most of our branches were left without any key whatever to the entire holdings of the library system. The difficulty was intensified by the shifting of population from areas where cataloged branches were located to growing suburban communities in which new branches were rapidly becoming larger than the older ones equipped with card catalogs-- some of which had been installed as long ago as 1926. Because of the fluid nature of the County Library's collections, the books were in a continuous state of transfer from Central to branches. Branch collections differed accordingly, so that no single card catalog could be duplicated for, or used by, another branch. All this in- creased the need for a flexible tool providing branches with equal access to our entire book stock.

Library literature was then full of the plaints of library admin- istrators dealing with the high cost of cataloging and the library card catalog was generally considered to be the principal culprit in the matters of expense, space, and upkeep. We had long con- sidered the various cost-saving methods, such as shortening entries eliminating or using fewer subject headings, minimizing added entries, and analytics, and the setting up of mechanical processes used to produce cards. While such methods promised to reduce cataloging costs in some measure, it was decided that they would severely limit the usefulness of the card catalog, with the result that more time would be required for bibliographical searching. Since the extended use of printed bibliographies or reading lists likewise offered the reading public only partial coverage, the only effective way to reduce costs and still provide equal or better service appeared to be a change to a completely different type of catalog.

It was about this time that we heard of an experiment being made with book catalogs for branch libraries, prepared with International Business Machines equipment and suggesting the space-saving advantages we were already aware of in the Library of Congress printed book catalogs. The idea seemed feasible, and in August 1952, with the help of the local IBM office, we started ground work on our own book catalog. The plan provided for an annual children's catalog in author, title, and subject volumes, with cumulative bimonthly supplements, and an adult catalog to be issued annually in five sections. The adult catalog was to comprise an author catalog, a title catalog, and annotated subject lists for fiction and nonfiction, plus an auxiliary volume for books in foreign languages. The four principal adult parts were each to be made up of a group of volumes and were to include cumulative supplements designed to be issued monthly.

The Project under Way

Group meetings were held with Central Library and branch

personnel in the preliminary phases for the purpose of determining which items on the catalog cards were to be reproduced in the book catalogs in the event of the approval of the project. Following these meetings, questionnaires were sent to the branch librarians and their assistants. From the results of the meetings and the tabulations of questionnaire answers, we learned that many items on catalog cards long considered necessary by catalogers were either ignored or found to be confusing to the public. The filing arrangements in the branch card catalogs also met with considerable criticism.

After many conferences and a final library committee report--and in view of the fact that Los Angeles County Public Library is neither a research center nor a special library--we decided to include in the book catalogs only such information as was considered necessary by readers and branch librarians. Rather than scholarly or bibliographical aids, our intention was to make the catalogs quick-reference, alphabetic tools with logical and systematic arrangement of the various fields of knowledge.

The items considered necessary in the book catalogs were classification number, author (full name and all cross references), title, edition (other than the first), date of publication, volumes (when more than one), and a short annotation, with the reading level for children's books. The branch librarians requested many more subject headings and title references from partial titles than had customarily been made, and they generally disregarded joint authors or other added entries unless the publication in question was better known under an entry other than the author.

Interest was shown in editors and illustrators only for special titles and classics, or books featuring particular illustrations or famous illustrators. The only imprint item considered important was the copyright date, though we have since included the publisher. Collation was considered immaterial and descriptive notes were ignored except for contents and series, while bibliographical notes as such were regarded as being of occasional usefulness only. Branch librarians generally agreed that they wanted us to use present-day terminology and phraseology. They also asked that we develop and incorporate analytics, in order to expand and make the greatest use of the existing book collections. Still another useful suggestion that we received as a result of the group meetings was that the catalogs be divided, with adult catalogs separate from the juvenile, and with authors, titles, and subjects likewise listed separately.

In order to reduce operating costs, it was planned to perform the work on IBM machines used by other county departments, between their peak periods. Since the work was eventually to be done by four departments, the IBM staff also worked with the co-operating departments in order to acquaint them with the nature of our project. IBM designed our form for the key punch cards and wired the tabulator control panel, in addition to performing certain experimental work.

In the fall of 1952, Mr. Henderson, the County Librarian, requested the Chief Administrative Officer of the County to authorize a study of the book catalogs, as compared with conventional card catalogs, from the combined viewpoints of cost and public service. The CAO accordingly sent us two analysts who spent sixt

days studying the feasibility of the book catalogs to be prepared in

accordance with the proposal submitted by the IBM consultant, the

budgetary requirements, and the usability of the book catalogs for

both the public and the branch librarians.

On the basis of this exhaustive inquiry, the Chief Administra-

tive Officer approved the continuance of the project, with the added

recommendation that the Book Catalog should serve a multiple pur-

pose, namely:

1. Provide equal and complete access to the library's holdings for all County Library service outlets in the field.
2. Enable all library patrons to know that they have free
   access to these holdings--general collections, reference
   collections, special collections, and cataloged documents,
   pamphlets, and periodicals.
3. Describe and organize the holdings in such a manner that
   patrons may be more aware of their contents, importance,
   and usefulness.
4. Make foreign holdings available to patrons who wish to
   read in foreign languages.
5. Expand the use of the library's book collections through
   the use of analytics, cross references, partial titles,
   added entries, etc.
6. Give reading levels by age or grade in the annotations
   appearing in the Children's Catalog.

In order to expedite the project, the Branch Catalog Section

was organized within the Technical Services Division. A principal

librarian was to be in charge, whose responsibilities included neces

sary contacts with the IBM representative and the tabulating sec-

tions of the other county departments.

Children's Catalog

Since the library's holdings of children's books were smaller
and the entries shorter and simpler, and since the Children's
Division was willing to help with the annotating and grading, we
decided, for the sake of expediency, to start with the Children's
Catalog. Essentially a trial operation, the work was to a considerable extent a manual operation, such as the assigning of additional subject headings, the coding and filing, and the separating
of juvenile entries from the adult. Our card catalog included both
juvenile and adult entries, with Library of Congress subject headings and terminology.

Upon the completion of the first edition of the Children's
Catalog in 1952, the main question asked by parents, teachers, and
branch librarians was "Could we simplify the terminology used in
the subject headings?" In other words, why not use words and
subject headings children could readily understand, the kind used
in their school assignments? Accordingly, with the help of the
Children's Division and the County Superintendent of Schools, we
remade the Children's Subject Catalog entirely, changing to simple
and more popular terminology, as used in Eloise Rue's Subject
Headings for Children. We incorporated our own innovations and
adaptations, however, in order to follow the county school curriculum as closely as possible.

To date, we have issued seven juvenile editions, which now
comprise an author volume, a title volume, and three annotated
and graded subject volumes--five volumes in all. In the author
volume, we have indicated the order in which books in some of the

popular series are to be read, such as the "Betsy," "Little House,"
and "Moffatt" stories.   Many of the better-known publishers' series
are also indicated in the author entry for the particular title in the
series, with the complete list of titles appearing in the author
volume, under the name of the series, as in the case of the Land-
mark Books or the Makers of America series.

Adult Catalog

The preparation of the first edition of the Adult Catalog was
spread over a two-year period, 1953-1955.   Except for a few
temporary workers, we had but limited additional personnel on the
project, most of the work being performed by the regular cataloging staff as time and routine duties permitted.   Furthermore, only
part of the time spent on the project by catalogers was so charged
inasmuch as we completely revised our central union card catalog
in the preliminary phase of the work--weeding it, correlating subj
headings, eliminating unnecessarily detailed subject breakdowns, ar
changing over to up-to-date terminology.   For the first time in
thirty years our card catalog at the Central Library was complete.
revised and the subject and author authority files were brought up
to date.

The first edition of the Adult Catalog was completed in twenty
four volumes, each of which averaged 500 pages, 8.5" by 13" in
size, with 78 lines to the page.   Each of the approximately
161,000 titles required about ten punched cards (one line of print
to a card).

Copies of the first edition of the Children's Catalog were hand
bound in the Catalog Division, using pressboard covers, bookcloth

spines, and Chicago screws, so that labor costs constituted our biggest item.   Pressboard was also used for the Adult Catalog, but with commercially-assembled spiral bindings.

Annotations for the subject catalogs were adapted from those found in Book Review Digest, Standard Catalog for Public Libraries, A. L. A. Booklist, Wilson's Children's Catalog and Fiction Catalog, Baker's Best Fiction and other standard sources.   Subtitles were used as annotations whenever appropriate, as well as "contents" notes when not too long.

The IBM Method

The first step in the project was the designing of the tabulating card.   An electroplate was then cut to specification for the printing of the initial card order and for use on all reordering of cards. The same card layout form has been used for all types of entry.

Cards are 7.375 inches wide, 3.25 inches in height, and .0065 inches thick.   They are provided with different colored stripes along the top edge to indicate the particular catalog for which the card is to be used.   Greenstriped cards are used for authors, red for titles, plain manila for subjects, and yellow for subject headings and "see" and "see also" references.   Each contains eighty vertical columns and each column accommodates punched holes representing a single letter or number.   Columns are numbered 1 to 80, from left to right.   A single card makes one line of print for the book catalogs.   Upper left and right corner cuts assist in visual identification.

Transcribing of information from catalog card to tabulating card in the form of punched holes is accomplished by the use of

an IBM card punch, commonly referred to as a "key punch." The
data is punched into the cards in a key-driven operation similar to
typewriting. Verification of the punching may be done in several
ways, the most direct being a second key-driven machine operation.
Visual proofreading is an alternate means of verification.

Holes are punched in significant positions and are read and
identified by the "fingers" of the IBM machines as the cards feed
through the several machines--for machine responses are controlled
by what is read. The fingers of the IBM machines are wire
brushes which rest on the cards as they flow by and, when holes
come under them, reach through and complete an electrical circuit
with a contact beyond the card. In this way the IBM cards containing the data in the form of punched holes actuate the machines
into automatically performing the various operations needed in the
production of the book catalogs, i.e., the sorting and merging of
the cards and the reproducing of the card information on stencils
for multilithing of the catalog pages.

The tabulating card is further divided into six "fields." The
first field of 54 columns is used for the author, last name first,
followed by the title of the book, edition, copyright date, and any
necessary volume information; the second of 11 columns is for the
classification number, or serves to indicate "document" or "periodical;" the third is a free field of 6 columns and is used presently
for punching "9" in column 66 to indicate the year of acquisition;
the fourth of 7 columns is for the subject code; and the fifth and
sixth fields, comprising columns 79 and 80, are used for the card
sequence number.

In the preparation of the <u>Adult</u> <u>Catalog</u>, the preliminary work of the library catalogers included the checking of our subject authority files against the Central Card Catalog (780 Library Bureau trays). This meant verifying all subject headings and "see" and "see also" references, in order to be sure that they were in use and in suitable form. Due to machine limitations, certain Library of Congress subject heading forms had to be adapted to our special needs. For example, the curves were dispensed with, so that Composition (Art) became Composition in art; Cookery (American) became Cookery, American; Cookery (Honey) became Cookery-- Honey; Love (Theology) became Love, Theological; and Serpents (in religion, folklore, etc.) became Serpents in religion, folklore, etc. Other punctuation lacking on the county-leased machines were exclamation and question marks, colons, semicolons, and brackets. While some IBM machines with these marks were then available, those in use by the county departments concerned were not so equipped. The special type used on the no. 407 tabulator at the Registrar of Voters was similar to 8-point roman-gothic.

Subject headings and cross references were typed on blue cards, kept in alphabetical arrangement and sent for key punching to the tabulating departments in the offices of the County Registrar and Assessor. In order to use the machines, all filing had to be in straight alphabetical order, without regard to punctuation.

Machine Processes and Operation

Two types of tabulating card punches--types 24 and 26--or so-called "key punches," have been used in the production of our book catalogs. In the original phase of the work as performed for us by the aforenamed county departments, type 24 was used, but in the continued maintenance of the catalogs on our county-leased machines we used type 26. The two machines are essentially alike, however, the difference being principally in the printing mechanism. Cards punched on type 24 must be put through an "interpreter" in order to obtain the printing on the card. On type 26, punched characters are printed as they are punched. Each character prints on the line of the card above the punched column, thereby providing a full reading or interpretation of the card. When the punching on the card is printed on the face of the card itself, the printed translation is referred to as "interpretation." When punching on the card is printed on another form, the writing is termed "printing" or "listing."

The card-punch machine is relatively easy for a typist to operate. The program card, which is a basic part of the program unit, is prepared on a standard 80-column card for each punching operation and can be used repeatedly. It is mounted easily on the program drum, which is then inserted into the machine. Proper punching of the program card controls the automatic operations for the corresponding columns and allows for the skips and automatic duplication of part of the data from the master card and the key punching of the balance. The cards to be punched are placed face forward in the hopper, which holds approximately 500, and are automatically fed into position, front card first. A reading board provides ample space for the "control," or source, cards from which the IBM cards are punched.

The card punch has a combined alphabetic and numerical key-

board. By utilizing two punches in each column, alphabetic characters can be reproduced. For this purpose, each column is considered to contain two zones, the lower, consisting of positions 1
through 9, and the upper, comprising the 0, 11, and 12 positions.
A single punch in both the upper and lower zones is used to record
alphabetic characters. To form the letter "A," for instance, the
12 position and the 1 position are punched in a column, a combination
of the 12 and 2 positions producing a "B." Punctuation requires three
punches, and the 8 and a 3 in the lower zone and the 0 in the upper, in
order to produce a comma, and the 8, 3, and 12 for a period.

For the original setup, the most direct method of verifying the
keypunched information was used--the key-driven operation. This
was performed by a verifying machine operated in a manner practically identical with that of key punching. The verifying operator
reads the same information from the source card and depresses
keys in the same manner as in the original punching. Key depres-
sions are compared by the machine against the holes already in the
card and in the case of a discrepancy signals to the operator the
fact that the two recordings are unidentical and that an error has
been made--a robotian modus operandi. However, when using the
library-leased print punches, verification, or interpretation of the
punched holes, is accomplished by simply reading the printed record at the top of the card.

Sight-checking is another means of verification. When cards
in a given group contain identical data, they may be joggled into
alignment, so that light is visible through the common holes. Once
proofed and verified, the cards may, with normal care, be pro-

cessed many times. When changes are necessary, only the card affected needs to be repunched. While there is no particular need for proficiency, key punch operators and others working on the catalogs often find the ability to read punched cards a skill of considerable practical value.

Subject Headings

Subject headings and "see" references are punched on yellow-striped cards without the corner cut. The subject punching begins in column 12 and continues through column 54, the continuation cards beginning with column 15. There must be an X- or 11-punch in column 70 of the first cards for all subject headings and "see" references, in order to allow for the counting of headings and the control of spacing before and after the heading in the final tabulating operation of the subject catalog. Sequence numbers that are the same for subject headings and "see" references are punched in columns 79 and 80. The "see also" references are likewise punched on yellow-striped cards, beginning in column 15, with a different series of sequence numbers. "See also" references do not have an X- or 11-punch in column 70. The period is used to close all "see" and "see also" references, but subject headings are unclosed.

The subject headings and references were put through the electronic calculator and all the cards with the X-punch in column 70 were counted. The X-punch impulsed the counter control and, with the total count at hand, it was determined from the seven digits allowed on the IBM card for the subject code (columns 72-78), exactly how many numbers could be allowed between each code number, for future expansion. The calculator was set for punching the code numbers in progression, allowing for the predetermined expansion, or 240 units between subject headings. A second or duplicate set of cards was then reproduced for the master subject heading file. This reproducing is the operation by which the information punched in one set of cards is punched into another set. No verification is necessary, for the accuracy of the punching operation is verified simultaneously by the comparing feature of the machine.

The master set of subject headings was put through the no. 407 IBM accounting machine, commonly referred to as the tabulator, which printed 150 cards or lines per minute on continuous-form paper. The sheets were separated and numbered and bound in our own division, resulting in the first printing of our subject-heading code books. Additional headings, as required, are written in the subject code books in correct alphabetical order and a code number is assigned from the units allowed for expansion.

The clerical staff of the Technical Services Division copied from the Central Card Catalog, on waste stock, all main entries, author-name cross references, added entries, series, and analytics, including information in the body of the card previously agreed upon for use in the book catalogs. For nonfiction prior to 1940, we omitted all added entries, annotations, and partial titles. In accordance with the limitations of our IBM machines, curves were omitted (as in LC subject heading forms and the names of married women) and the dash was substituted for the colon, the comma for the semicolon, and the period for question and exclamation marks.

When lack of punctuation changed the meaning of the title, we made
a duplicate copy of the card for the "punctuation file," from which
the necessary punctuation was eventually added to the stencil by
typewriter.

All analytics and added entries were made in "see" reference
form.   For "see" and "see also" references there had to be an
X-punch in column 74 on the card following the "see" or "see also,"
or, in other words, the X-punch in column 74 had to be in the
second card in order to pick up the classification number in the
Dewey field.

Control Cards

The copied cards we referred to as "control cards." In the
upper left-hand corner of the 3 x 5 card appeared the classification
number, then the author's surname, full forenames, title of the
book, edition, the publisher's name in abbreviated form, and the
copyright date, followed by any necessary volume information. The
annotation on the card was given in note position, with the subject
tracing blocked below.   Cards were kept in alphabetical order.
The code number assigned from the subject heading code book
was then added in red in front of each heading.

Subject detail cards were then punched from the control cards.
These were the manilas, without a color stripe but with the upper
left-hand corner cut.   They included the author-title entry, plus the
annotation, and one complete set of the cards was punched for each
subject tracing or code number.   In punching the sets, the first
eight columns were always duplicated on the second and succeeding
overflow cards for the author-title, annotation, and title-author

entries, as a means of identifying and keeping the sets together.
The punching was identical for each set of cards, except for the
code number, the repetitive information being duplicated or punched
automatically. In the second and succeeding sets of cards, an X
was overpunched in column 72.

Upon the completion of the punching of the subject detail cards,
the entire group was put through an IBM no. 514 reproducer and one
set of green-striped cards was reproduced from the detail cards
without the X-punch in column 72. This gave us a set of green-
striped cards to make up the file of author entries for the Author
Catalog. The reproduced annotation cards were discarded later,
when it was decided that the Author Catalog would not be annotated.

Sorting

The subject entries were sorted numerically by subject code
and merged by an IBM collator behind the corresponding subject
heading cards. The collator is designed to interfile two groups of
cards arranged in correct sequence, an operation referred to as
"merging," in which the two sets of cards are merged according to
the subject code.

The yellow-striped subject heading cards are without corner
cuts, while the detail cards have a cut in the upper left-hand corner. This allows the subject headings to stand out in the file,
thereby exposing the cards for ready reference and setting up each
group of cards behind the subject heading as a separate unit.

Punching fields for the titles differ from those of other entries,
so that the titles must be punched separately. This is done on red-
striped cards. The first field of 54 columns is for the title, fol-

lowed by the word "by" and the initials and last name of the author.
The second field of 11 columns is for the classification. The third
field of 13 columns consists of the duplication of the 9th through the
21st space of the title, upon which the alphabetical sort of the IBM
sorter machine is used. Sequence numbers are punched in the
fourth field, columns 79 and 80.

The sorter reads one card column at a time and separates
the cards according to the punch holes they contain. To operate,
a group of cards is stacked face downward in the hopper. The
machine then slides a card from the bottom of the deck and feeds
it past the reading brush, which may be set to read any column.
Each card is read in the chosen column and is routed to one of the
thirteen stacking pockets. There is a single pocket for blank cards
or rejects and twelve pockets to receive cards containing any of
the twelve possible punches.

The sorter affords a speedy and accurate method of arranging
the title cards in complete alphabetical or numerical order. The
sorting operation is performed at the speed of 650 cards a minute
for each column sorted. Arranging the cards in an alphabetical
sequence requires double sorting of each column, since each letter
is recorded by two holes in a single column. Therefore, each
card goes through the sorter 44 times in order to alphabetize the
titles through the 22nd letter, which results in an almost complete
alphabetical arrangement. The sorting starts with the 22nd space
on the title card and works backward to the beginning of the title.

The Tabulator

The IBM accounting machine, or tabulator, prepares the proof sheets and stencils from the IBM cards. The machine prints information from 120 printwheels, which form a solid bank 12 inches wide. Each printwheel has 47 different characters, namely, all the letters of the alphabet, all the numerals, and special characters such as punctuation marks. Cards are read and printed by the tabulator at the rate of 150 per minute.

Automatic operation of the tabulator is performed through the control panel, the diagramming and wiring of which is exceedingly involved. Our original diagramming was done by the IBM office in order to incorporate all the requirements of the book catalogs; however, county tabulator operators made further changes for us as the project progressed. With careful programming and the use of alternate switches, the one control panel was used for the listing of the code books, for prooflisting, and for the final stencils for the Adult and Children's catalogs, without making changes in the wiring. The diagram was color-coded and wires in corresponding colors facilitated the wiring job.

The panel is wired through selector switches to allow for the proof-run showing the code numbers, the X-punches, and the acquisition and sequence numbers, since data punched in different fields on the cards may be shown by the class selectors in one run or be omitted in another, or be separated automatically in various positions on the printed form. An example of this is the classification number, which is punched in columns 55 through 65, and, by the use of selectors, appears on the left side of all printed forms. The panel is also wired through switches for six lines to the inch of printing in the Children's Catalog in order to allow for

ease in reading, and for eight lines to the inch in the **Adult Catalog.**
The double spacing allowed before and after the subject headings in
the catalogs is controlled by wiring in the panel through which
electrical impulses are "sensed" by the X-punch in column 70 of
the subject card.   The word "continued" is wired into the control
panel, to show on the stencil if a break is made in a "see also"
reference.

Forms are automatically positioned in the tabulator by the use
of the carriage, which is set up for operation by inserting the pre-
punched tape in the tape-controlled mechanism.   This control tape
is of narrow paper cut to correspond exactly to the length of the
form to be run.   It has 12 columnar positions, which are indicated
by vertical lines called channels.   The tape is first marked in the
channels in which the holes are to be punched, for which a small,
compact punch is provided.   The mark in the first channel is on
the horizontal line corresponding to the first printing line of the
form, the additional marks in the respective channels being for the
other skip stops and the overflow signal required for the form.
Of these tape channels, number 1 locates the first printing line,
i.e., the starting or "home" position; number 2 the first "body"
line, or opening line of text on the page; number 3 the predetermined total, or terminal line; and number 12, which is punched in
a position corresponding to the last printing line of the form, the
allowable overflow, or excess, line.

When subject entries carry over from one page to the next,
by "overflow skipping," the subject heading is printed at the top
of the second and succeeding pages.   When one stencil is filled to

the determined length, and the next stencil advances, the subject heading in use is printed at the top of the continued listing. This overflow skipping is caused by sensing a punch in a specific position of the tape.

Continuous-form paper for proofreading and continuous-form stencils for the multilithing of pages are used on the tabulator. The continuous forms carry marginal punches at half-inch intervals on each side. Pin-feed devices geared to the machine platen carry the forms into position for the printing.

For the original catalogs, cards were listed by the tabulator, and printed on the continuous-form paper for proofreading. The control panel was wired through selector switches to allow for the proof-run to show the code numbers, X-punches, and the duplication of the first eight columns on the author and detail cards. This was especially important, for incorrect punching in these fields would have become apparent in the finished catalogs. Proofreading was necessary in view of the two or three complete procedural cycles normally required for a punched-card job of this size to reach normal efficiency.

Upon the completion of the proofing and correcting of the original work, the cards for each section of the Adult Catalog-- Author, Title, Fiction and Nonfiction Subject volumes, and the Foreign Catalog--were then listed by section on continuous short-run stencils.

The stencils were proofed for typographical errors and correct pagination, and each heading in the subject sections of the catalogs was underlined by hand--our one entirely manual operation. The

underscoring was done with reproducing ink, in order to allow
subject headings to stand out on the page for ease in reading.
Stencils were duplicated on 8.5" x 13" book paper, using two no.
1250 multilith duplicators.   Two hundred copies were duplicated for
the Children's Catalog and 170 copies for the Adult Catalog.

Adult Author Catalog

Our Adult Author Catalog, presently in nine volumes, is a key
to the use of nearly a million and a half volumes.   It lists the
complete adult book holdings, both fiction and nonfiction, as well
as cataloged documents, pamphlets, and periodicals, available
through branches in the eight regional areas and the Central Library in downtown Los Angeles.   It is kept up to date with cumula
tive supplements listing new and other recently acquired publications, the supplements being eventually absorbed into the cumulative annual editions.

Entries in the Author Catalog are arranged in a single alphabe
generally by author and sometimes by issuing agency, as in the
case of a U.S. or California State government department, or an
association, such as the Brookings Institution.   To facilitate use
of the catalog, entries are made under real names and pseudonyms
with distinguishing dates for identical names.   References to the
accepted form of the author's name are made from variant spellings, women's married names, pseudonyms, and alternate forms
of organizational, or corporate, names.   Additional entries are
provided for names associated with given works, including those of
editors, sponsoring organizations, and occasionally translators and
illustrators, together with reference to main entries for fuller

bibliographical information.   A list of symbols is provided; also
the classification outline for nonfiction.   In the list of symbols is
the asterisk (*), which denotes titles of special interest to readers
of junior and senior high school age.

Also in the Author Catalog will be found, listed by author,
books written to be read in sequence.   Examples of these are
Allis: Field Family Saga, Galsworthy: Forsyte Saga, and De la
Roche: Jalna Saga.   Notations are made in the title for books that
have received special awards, in such manner as "Awarded the
Pulitzer Prize," followed by the year.   Cross references are made
from the Adult Catalog to the Children's Catalog and vice versa for
books appearing in both collections.   For two or more titles bound
as one, the note "Bound with" or "With this is bound" is included
in the entry.

In order to make the greatest use of our total book collection,
we have incorporated a number of special projects, including some
not brought out in the card catalogs.   Three hundred sixty-four
series have been traced to date, as, for example, the American
Lake Series, the Civilization of the American Indian Series, and
Rivers of America, with listings of the individual titles within the
series.   Many additional analytics have been worked out, as in the
cases of The Harvard Classics, Great Books of the Western World,
America in a World at War, the U.S. Bureau of American Ethnology publications, Reuben Gold Thwaites' Early Western Travels,
and the John Randolph Haynes and Dora Haynes Foundation monograph and pamphlet series.   Collective biography, innumerable
short story collections, and more than a hundred play anthologies

have also been analyzed.

Adult Title Catalog

The Title Catalog, in six volumes, is arranged alphabetically
by first word of the title without regard to "A," "An," or "The,"
first-word articles being given, hand-interfiled, only when meaning
necessitates.   No dates or editions are given, but more title
analytics and references from partial titles are made than customarily appear in card catalogs.   Following the generally accepted
cataloging rule, we have used distinctive titles only, since titles
commencing with such general terms as "Directory of" or "Complete
Book of" are excessive in number.   In the case of a title that is
the same, or similar to, the subject heading and obviously indicate
for the patron the subject under which the book may be found in
the subject catalog, we have omitted the title in question.   For
example, Hinckley's Directory of Antique Furniture is to be found
under the headings "Antiques" and "Furniture."

Cross references are made in the title volume for variant
spellings, such as "Handcraft" and "Handicraft."   For books available in the library under different titles but with the same text,
a notation is added to the title entry for each reading "Also available as."   The filing arrangement, due to the mechanical sorting,
differs from standard library filing.   By machine, the arrangement is period, dash, comma, phrase or sentence, and possessive
The hyphen is disregarded.

Adult Nonfiction Subject Catalog

The Nonfiction Subject Catalog, now in eighteen volumes, is
the largest of all the parts and combines practical features and

exhaustive coverage, with the needs of the reader foremost in mind. It is arranged alphabetically by subject, then alphabetically by author under subject. Complete entries are given, as in the Author Catalog, plus a descriptive note or annotation. If the library has several editions of a particular title, only the most recent appears in the subject listing, with the notation "For other editions, see Author Catalog." Used in the subject catalog are "see" references from the broad to the specific form, "see also" references to bordering subject fields, and explanatory references on the scope and reader interest of the subject.

Adult Fiction Subject Catalog

The four-volume Fiction Subject Catalog is a selective anno- tated list containing the classics and the best modern novels and short stories. Subject headings are arranged alphabetically and conform in general to those in Wilson's Fiction Catalog, but with many variations and additions. Entries under subject headings are alphabetical by the author's last name.

A special feature of this unique fiction catalog is the extensive subdividing of historical fiction by country and period. Gone With the Wind, for example, appears under Historical Fiction--U.S.-- 1861-1865, Civil War, and U.S.--1865-1898, Reconstruction Period, as well as under the separate headings Character and Characteriza- tion, Georgia, Love, Selfishness, and Slavery. Biographical fiction--in addition to being listed by various subjects in the Fic- tion Subject Catalog--is entered in the Nonfiction Subject Catalog under name of the biographee, as under Lincoln, Abraham, Pres., U.S., where biographees are not only to be found, but a list of novels about Lincoln under the subheading "Fiction."

Adult Foreign Language Catalog

The single-volume Foreign Catalog is arranged by language,
separated into nonfiction and fiction. Entries are by author's name
and in some instances they are annotated and give the title in
English. Thirty-five languages are represented in all. These entries also appear in the Author Catalog, in the Title Catalog and
in the Subject Catalog when appropriate.

Routines and Procedures

Most of the IBM procedures here described were used in the
original phases of the project, but all work subsequent to the first
editions of the catalogs has become maintenance. In view of the
quantity of new titles added each year, two punch card machines
have been required. Tabulating service by the other county departments is being continued; and the cards are sight-proofed and hand-
interfiled.

We have continued to issue the book catalogs on an annual
basis. In addition, the Adult Cumulative Supplement is published
monthly, in four sections--Author, Title, Fiction (by subject), and
Nonfiction (by subject). Cumulative children's supplements are
issued bimonthly.

The Classification and Catalog Section of the Technical Services
Division prepares the control cards representing the new titles
added to the library's collections and sends them daily to the
preparatory unit of the Branch Catalog Section. The annotations
appearing thereon are written by the book selectors, or "subject
specialists." All control cards are subject to editorial revision

before inclusion in the supplements or annual editions of the book catalogs, due to the necessity of adapting the annotations and entries to the IBM and book catalog requirements.

When a subject heading is new, a blue card for the heading is received with the entry, in the case of nonfiction, and a yellow card for fiction. The new subject heading is written into the subject heading code book, in correct alphabetical order, and a code number is assigned. The code number is then entered on the subject heading card, which, with the control card, is sent to the key punch operator for punching. All subject heading tracings appearing on the control cards carry assigned numbers.

On being received from the key punch operator, the punched cards are in four color groups for each entry--green for author, red for title, salmon for the regional assignment, and as many complete sets of manilas for the subject catalogs as there are subject tracings on the control card, each set having its individual code number. The salmon-striped cards indicate the regions in which the book is to be found, the regions being represented by the numbers 1 through 8 and the Central Library by the word "Central." The purpose of this liner, which appears only in the Author Catalog and its supplements, is simply to indicate for the patron the assignment of the particular title to his region, or whether it must be requested from another region or from Central. All cards are carefully revised against the control cards from which they were punched and are subsequently banded together in sets, separated into color groups, and filed into the supplement trays.

The yellow-striped cards for the new subject headings and

"see" and "see also" references are punched in duplicate.   After
being punched, one set is filed in the master file and the other in
the subject file for the annual edition.   The master file copy of
the subject heading is used in the monthly subject supplement and
for the running of the code books.   The duplicate heading is added
to the annual edition file as a new heading and remains without
detail cards until the cumulative supplement is interfiled in prepara
tion for the next annual edition.

Supplements are tabulated, stencils scanned, and the pages
multilithed in the same manner as are those for the annual catalogs.   However, they are printed on punched paper and placed in
loose-leaf binders, for temporary use in branches, along with the
bound editions.   Since supplements are cumulative, the superseded
numbers are discarded when new issues are received.

At the time each section of the annual edition of the Book
Catalog is to be published, the corresponding bank of cards representing the cumulative monthly supplement is interfiled with the
cards for the annual.   The revised annual edition of the Book Cata
log contains all the latest additions to the library's total book collection as of the time the catalog goes to print.

Substitutions, intended to change or correct established entries
are made regularly on receipt of notification from the Classificatio
and Catalog Section.   Substitute cards are punched in accordance
with the changes, additions, or corrections indicated, the original
punched cards withdrawn from the files, and the substituted cards
are filed as replacements.

Only the latest editions of titles are shown in the Subject

Catalog. When a new edition is received, the control card for the previous edition is corrected by marking out the subject tracings and pulling the punched cards from the subject catalog file. A set of cards is then punched for the new-edition entry and "For other editions, see Author Catalog" is added to the annotation, since all editions appear in the Author Catalog. The body of the original annotation is transferred to the card for the new edition, unless further change is necessary.

Punched cards are withdrawn from the files for all titles no longer in the library. For each title to be withdrawn, the Central Catalog main entry card is received by the Branch Catalog Section. The corresponding control card is then withdrawn, together with all related cards in the author, title, and subject files. Added entries referring to withdrawn entries are also canceled, so that all records pertaining to books no longer in the collection will be dropped from the next annual edition of the Book Catalog.

The punched cards are housed in full-extension metal suspension trays and are kept in taut position in order to avoid warping. Each file holds eleven double trays, with a total capacity for a working file of 66,000 cards. Trays are released by a push bar which disengages the compression lock. For the transporting of trays, a three-level metal truck equipped with two fixed and two swivel casters, makes maneuvering comparatively simple.

We now have in our files approximately 2,000,000 punched cards, with material under, the "see" references to, approximately 80,000 subject headings. During the fiscal year ending June 1959, 11,409 new entries were added to the Adult Catalog, necessitating

the punching of 119,517 cards. For the 4,051 adult substitutions
received from the Classification and Catalog Section, plus corrections, 59,833 punched cards were required. A total of 31,726
punched cards were withdrawn for titles no longer in collections
and for substitutions. During the year, more than 1,354,000 sheets
of multilith paper were processed for the catalogs and supplements.

In accordance with our continued practice, pages for the book
catalogs are assembled and collated by hand, each volume comprising about 200 sheets. The catalogs have been bound in various
ways--with Chicago screw-type bindings, wire spirals, and the
Cerlox plastic binding element, all with pressboard covers--but
they are now being stapled and bound by a commercial bindery,
which method has proved to be the most satisfactory.

Costs, Equipment, and Supplies

It is impossible to determine exact costs for the original set
of the book catalogs, since part of the work was done in cooperation with other county departments having the needed equipment.
As previously pointed out, International Business Machines gave us
much preliminary assistance with the layout for the tabulating
cards, the wiring of the control panel, and the setting up of the
tabulator for the various printing operations. Too, IBM spent
much time working with our cataloging staff and the other county
departments toward a mutual understanding of terminology and the
problems involved. The County Assessor's office is also to be
thanked for helping us to get started on the project.

Annual maintenance costs consist principally of two items,
the cumulative supplements and the new editions. Since the

number of new titles brought each year has increased from approximately 5,500 to 7,500 the result has been a corresponding increase in the number of cards punched and the size of the supplements, which ultimately increases the size and cost of the annual editions. Since last-copy discards have remained more or less constant, our net annual increase has been even more noticeably rapid.

A complete set of our Book Catalog, as of this writing, comprises 43 volumes and is contained in about four feet of shelving, as follows:

Adult Catalog (Third and Fourth editions, 1958-1959)

Author Catalog	9 vols.
Title Catalog	6 vols.
Nonfiction Subject Catalog	18 vols.
Fiction Subject Catalog	4 vols.
Foreign Catalog	1 vols.
Total	38 vols.

Children's Catalog (Seventh Edition, 1959)

Author Catalog	1 vol.
Title Catalog	1 vol.
Subject Catalog	3 vols.
Total	5 vols.

Equipment and Supplies

No. 026 Key Punch Machine
Electronic Calculator (original setup only)
No. 514 Reproducer (original setup only)
No. 77 Collator (original setup only)
No. 082 Sorter (original setup only)
No. 407 Accounting Machine (Tabulator)
No. 1250 Multilith Machine
Sorting Racks (made in Library Shop)
Electroplate for Tabulating Cards
Preprinted Tabulating Cards
Fanfold Proofsheet Paper
English Book Paper, 50 sub.
Continuous Short-Run Multilith Masters.

*Annual Maintenance Costs of the Book Catalog, 1958/59

Personnel (Salaries)	$80,637.46
Administrative Costs	14,618.53
Supplies	8,060.17
Rent of Building (1 floor)	6,542.40
Registrar of Voters Services (use of Tabulating Machine)	3,384.58
Binding Costs	2,969.74
Rented Equipment	1,440.00
Depreciation	1,214.41
Utilities	590.99
Maintenance	511.93

Total $119,970.21

Cost of annual maintenance of a set of the Book Catalogs, including Adult Catalog, Children's Catalog, and all Supplements $690.90

*Note: Costs for the original cataloging, the classifying, or the descriptive cataloging are not included in the analyses, since these apply equally to the card and the book catalogs. Processing of the books in the Technical Services Division has also been omitted.

A Word to the Wise

The economy of our Book Catalog is shown by the fact that a complete set of the volumes, overhead expenses included, costs only $690.90 to produce during 1958/59. However, during this period, we did not completely revise the catalog. The annual maintenance cost of our Central Card Catalog alone is in excess of $12,000, plus overhead. In other words, maintenance costs for the Card Catalog as compared to the Book Catalog are at least seventeen to one! In further consideration of the special features of the Book Catalog, such as annotations, increased subject headings and analytics, simplicity of filing arrangement, compactness, and ease in use--not to mention the importance of listing the entire holdings of the library for every branch--we feel that the advantages of the Book Catalog are more than considerable. In short, we are in total agreement with the eminent English librarian, Ernest A. Savage, whose opinion it is that every public library should have a printed book catalog in which to index its contents and at the same time publicize the existence of the library and its value throughout the service area.

Visiting librarians have felt that ours is a representative collection of the titles usually found in public libraries, and many have expressed the desire to buy copies of our Book Catalog or subscribe to it on an annual basis. Others have wanted us to make book catalogs for them by duplicating our tabulating cards whenever possible and by processing cards for their books not represented in our collection. So far, we have furnished partial sets of the catalog to most of the larger library schools, on request, and separate volumes as loans to interested libraries. Sample sets of the cards have been also supplied on request.

A book catalog installation does not spring full-grown. One of the major problems is that of converting from old methods to new—everything must be done at once, including the training of workers, the providing of adequate quarters, the designing of cards and forms, and the planning of operating time, not to mention supervision and the promoting of team work and high morale. Of vital importance to the success of this productive, highly mechanized library operation is a clear understanding of the purpose of the book catalogs, their acceptance, and the wholehearted cooperation and enthusiasm of the entire staff.

Comparative Costs of the Annual Maintenance of the Central Dictionary Card Catalog, 1958/59 (780 trays):

1. Personnel $11,267.96

                                              Salaries per week

   a. Preparation of Catalog Cards (Central and Regions)
       Prepare stencils for catalog cards
       5 Library Assistants 4/5 of their
       time at $1.66 per hr. $ 265.60
       Mimeograph stencils
       1 Typist Clerk at $1.41
       per hr.   56.40
       Type headings on cards and
       type small sets
       2 Typist Clerks at $1.41   112.80
       per hr.
       Revise work, supervise
       1/2 Intermediate Typist   33.20
       Clerk at $1.66 per hr.
       Overhead supervision
       1/8 Supervising Clerk at
       $1.74 per hr.   8.13

                               Per Week $476.13

       Cards for Central (40 per cent   190.45
       of the time)
       Cost for 52 weeks for preparation
       of cards for Central $9,903.48

   b. Interfiling of cards into the card catalog
       Weekly alphabetizing
       2 1/2 hrs. Library Assistant
       at $1.66 per hr.   4.15
       Interfiling into catalog weekly
       5 Library Assistants,
       2 hrs. each at $1.66
       per hr.   16.60
       Revising filing
       Librarian, 2 hrs. at $2.04
       per hr.   4.08
       Withdrawing 1 hr. a week
       Typist Clerk at $1.41 per
       hr.   1.41

                       Cost per week   26.24
            Cost of interfiling per year $1,364.48
2. Supplies   755.20
Cost of annual maintenance of one 780 tray
   card catalog $12,023.16

The Book Catalog of the Los Angeles County Public Library:
Its Function and Use*

By Theodore Hewitson

Eugene Field, a confirmed cubicularist, liked to read the catalog of the Oxford University Press in bed. While the forty-odd oversize volumes of our printed Book Catalog hardly constitute bedside reading, we at the Los Angeles County Public Library admit, like Eugene Field, to be smitten with "catalogitis" of the book variety--because of the desirability of the book catalog as a public library tool.

We feel that our Book Catalog offers many advantages over the conventional type of library card catalog, including logical arrangement, compactness, and a vastly greater number of cross references provided as aids to readers in matters of authorship, bibliographical information, and subject interrelationships, not to mention the features of speed and economy in preparation and upkeep. Its importance in the fields of child and adult education is heightened by the annotations and descriptive notes which appear throughout the subject volumes under a multitude of subject headings, for both fiction and nonfiction.

A library extension tool designed for use in all branches of the County Library System, the Book Catalog is under constant revision and expansion, together with regular supplements that are

* Library Resources and Technical Services, 4:228-232, Summer, 1960.

eventually absorbed into the annual cumulative editions. The
component catalogs are also kept up to date with monthly lists
which indicate changes in author entries, classification numbers,
and library holdings, as well as last-copy discards.

Under the regional plan, started in 1957 (by which the library
decentralized its service areas into eight regions), our remaining
card catalogs are used primarily by library personnel at the Central Library and at the regional headquarters. The main card
catalog is located in the Central Services Division and is important
as the definitive record of all books in the County Library system
and the subjects represented in its cataloged collections. Out of a
total of twenty-five in 1952, only three card catalogs are presently
maintained in the field--for three of the eight regional headquarter
branches--with the purpose of identifying and classifying all books
directly available within the particular region.

On the other hand, the cumulative book catalogs used in the
branch libraries, in author, title, and annotated subject volumes,
both juvenile and adult, include all titles represented in the
County Library's collections. They are indispensable tools of
value to patrons in requesting specific books or subject material
and to branch librarians in locating books in the branch and suggesting titles for use by patrons, in addition to their importance
to subject specialists and regional librarians in the areas of reference work, book selection, discarding, and assignment. All sections of the Book Catalog carry introductory pages and a list of
symbols and all branch libraries are equipped with a framed
placard entitled "How to Use the Book Catalog."

Since the Book Catalog is used in all our branches, book collections may be changed without the loss of countless hours devoted
to the shifting and filing of catalog cards, for which reason the
Book Catalog is a veritable timesaver. Each branch has its own
shelf list, so that it can be determined immediately whether or not
the requested book is in the branch collection. If the book is not
found in the local branch, an author-title request giving the necessary information is sent on to the regional headquarters or the
Central Library for special-loan service.

Our branch librarians and library patrons alike are enthusiastic about the Book Catalog. Since they are accustomed to using
dictionaries, encyclopedias, and telephone directories, the form
of the catalog appeals to them. They find the bound volumes
easier to use than cards and what is available on a given subject
can be seen at a glance; the separate volumes serve as indexes
and may be carried directly to the shelves, so that the material
on the subject already in the branch is used more effectively.*

The Children's Catalog, for instance, serves as a practical
guide to graded books for children and parents. They find the
separate listing of juvenile literature a distinct advantage, and the
branch librarians appreciate the fact that children do not mistaken-
ly ask for adult books listed in the card catalog, which are generally beyond juvenile reading levels. The division of the catalog into
author, title, and subject sections has also proved advantageous;
and the subject volumes have made it possible to dispense with ex-

*Original editor's note: In answer to a question, the author reports
that, so far, there have been no losses of the Catalogs; occasionally
a page is removed.

pensive juvenile readings lists.

In order that teachers and school curriculum advisers may know of the material available to pupils, copies of the Children's Catalog are supplied to the school districts throughout the county. This helps to eliminate the possibility of a teacher assigning a particular title for outside reading that may not be obtainable through our branches. As an additional service, subject headings and terminology have been specially adapted to children's reading levels and vocabulary, and changes are frequently made in order to conform to subject headings used in school assignments. "Norse men," for instance, has recently been changed to "Vikings," with a cross reference from the former term.

The use of the Book Catalog is becoming increasingly important in book selection, for it reveals library holdings on a subject basis clearly on an open page. Publication dates take on new significance, and scanty holdings in important fields are more noticeable. While the card catalog must still be consulted for special bibliographic data, this necessity is offset by the copious annotations in the subject volumes, a tested feature that appeals to both library patron and branch librarian and the point at which the card catalog becomes of little or no service. Before the annual re-run of the nonfiction subject volumes, the book selectors indicate titles in the margin for deletion and discarding consideration a technique that keeps the material timely and at the same time helps the specialist to keep in touch with the titles in his particular field.

Considerable use of the Book Catalog is also made by cata-

logers and library searchers, especially in the determining of suitable subject headings and in establishing author entries on a "no-
conflict" basis. However, we shall always need an author card catalog at Central as a control. We need the tracings and the occasional bibliographical notes, particularly for new editions and for
series, periodicals, and other open entries. The tracings are also
necessary in order to complete procedures when the last copy of
a title is withdrawn from the collection and removed from the
Book Catalog. Nevertheless, established notes, annotations, and
classifications appearing in the Book Catalog are often helpful in
resolving cataloging and withdrawal problems.

Among the adult sections, the Fiction Subject Catalog is being
currently emphasized. Subject headings are undergoing careful revision and expansion, new annotations are being supplied and old
ones corrected or rewritten, and entries in general are being
worked over on a thoroughly selective basis. Our approach to the
work is by way of elevating the reading of novels over mere enter-
tainment, into the realism of the informative and the inspirational,
through emphasis on historical fiction, biographical narratives,
classics, young adult reading, and the outstanding novels of the
year. Special projects recently under way have included the ana-
lyzing of short story collections and the expansion of subject coverage in the important field of historical fiction.

Mention needs also to be made of our composite Foreign Catalog, a single volume without subject headings, which is a ready
source of information for the reader who wants material in a particular foreign language but may be uncertain about the author or

title.   As described in the preceeding article, it is separated
into nonfiction and fiction and covers thirty-five languages in all,
with many of the titles carrying annotations in English.

The Book Catalog of the Los Angeles County Public Library
is an integrated key to the use of nearly two million volumes of
fiction, nonfiction, and reference (197,000 adult titles and 12,500
juvenile) available through the branches in our regional service
areas and from the Central Library in downtown Los Angeles. Its
maintenance and continued improvement are part of a decentralize
long-range regional program.   There are restrictions on what we
can accomplish, as determined by the limitations of the printed
page and IBM mechanical operation, as well as staff and organiza
tional problems.   But it is a live and fluid project; we are condu
ing experiments and working out new ideas for bindings, format,
annotations, subject headings, and special features such as the
locating of regional copies in the Adult Author Catalog.

Our Book Catalog, started in the spring of 1952, is definitely
pioneer product and no one can say for sure just what is ahead.
IBM machines, information retrieval, audio-visual refinements,
book catalogs--these are yet new and potential tools in public library service.   Following Emerson's advice, we have hitched ou
wagon to a star.   Below is presented the introduction to the auth
catalog.

Introduction to the Author Catalog

This Author Catalog is an essential part of the Los Angeles
County Public Library's integrated book catalog.   It lists the
complete adult book holdings, both fiction and non-fiction, as wel

as cataloged documents, pamphlets, and periodicals, available
through branch libraries located in the regional areas of the County
Library system.

The related book catalogs are the Title Catalog, the one-volume
Foreign Catalog, and the extensive Non-Fiction Subject Catalog and
Fiction Subject Catalog, both of which contain annotations describing the books listed therein. Books for children are listed in a
separate catalog kept in the Children's Section.

Catalogs are kept up to date by cumulative monthly supplements.
These supplements list recently acquired and new publications and
are eventually absorbed into the cumulative annual editions.

Entries in the Author Catalog are arranged in a single alphabet,
generally by author, but occasionally by title and sometimes by
issuing agency, as in the case of a U. S. or California State
government department, or an association, such as the Brookings
Institution. To facilitate use of the catalog, cross references are
made to variant and pseudonymous names of authors and alternate
forms of organizational, or corporate, names.

Additional entries are provided for names associated with given
works, including those of editors, translators, illustrators, and
sponsoring organizations, with references to the main entry for fuller bibliographical information. Books in important series are
also listed under the series title or name of the issuing body.

For a list of symbols and the classification outline for nonfiction, see the two following pages in this Author Catalog. Included in the list of symbols is the asterisk (*), which denotes
titles of special interest to readers of junior and senior high school
age, such books being marked with a crosshatch (#) on the spine.

Location of books on the shelves is indicated for non-fiction,
by the classification number to the left of each entry. In the case
of fiction, which is unclassified, arrangement is by author's name.

Books listed in this catalog but not included in the Branch Library collection may be requested for home use through the Branch
Librarian. Exceptions are reference books and Californiana, which

may be used by patrons within the branch or at Regional Headquarters.

The National Library of Medicine Index Mechanization Project*
by Seymour Taine

Increasing pressure on the Current List to do more and to do it better and faster helped to bring about a report to the National Library of Medicine Board of Regents in November 1957 on progress, problems, and possibilities in indexing. Discussion of the report led to the suggestion that funds be sought wherewith to investigate the feasibility of mechanization. There was prepared in January, submitted in February, and approved in April, 1958, an Outline of Proposal to the Council on Library Resources, Inc., with the

"Specific aims [of] develop [ing] and demonstrat[ing] in the field of medicine improved methods for the rapid and efficient publication of comprehensive indexes to the literature of broad scientific fields with simultaneous provision for meeting the requirements of specialties within these field, making use of hitherto unutilized mechanical applications."

The Council on Library Resources agreed to make the sum of $73,800 available to the National Library of Medicine over a period of two years (July 1958-June 1960) for undertaking this project, and the Department of Health, Education and Welfare officially accepted the grant in June 1958.

The assets and resources of the National Library of Medicine at that point were several and significant. First, there was index-

*Bulletin of the Medical Library Association, 49:5-7; 13-19, January, 1961. Pages 5-7 are the "Introduction and History," and Pages 13-19 are the section on "Photographic Equipment and Processing."

ing experience, 80 uninterrupted years of it, with considerable
variety in procedures and products to its credit.   The Library staff
was steeped in the theory and practice of subject headings, ephemeral and "permanent," in classified and alphabetical arrangement,
in card catalog and published index, and accustomed to the complexities of great size and the point of view of both librarianship
and medicine.

Second, the Library had the largest collection of medical
periodicals in the world to work with.   It knew what there was and
what was asked for.   Its acquisition policies were subject to continual testing by the demands made on its reference services.   All
material could be evaluated at first hand.

Third, NLM had learned how to work with large quantities
of material, keeping it moving and keeping track of it as it moved.
There are certain problems that do not arise until large quantities
of material are dealt with.   It would be hard to overestimate, for
instance, the value of what Current List experience had taught
in how to adjust the order of processes, so that backlogs may be
kept close to the ideal zero at all stations, without causing any
station to run out of work.

Next, the staff was qualified not only by education and training
in library work, but also by an unusually broad working knowledge
of foreign languages.   The staff had also acquired familiarity with
typographical design and problems of the printing industry, and
knew what was involved in composition, proofreading, assembly,
and in meeting production deadlines.

Less important, perhaps, but still worthy of mention, was the

Library's experience and repeated success in taking reorganization in stride. The Current List alone had in the course of eight years made three complete physical moves from one building to another without interruption of its schedule.

So much for the resources. The lacks and limitations included (1) restrictions inherent in the government framework, (2) lack of mechanical training, (3) the limited number of personnel available to work on the project, especially during the first 18 months when the Current List was still continuing, and (4) limitations of the physical plant.

Under rigid government rules, grant funds are handled in the same way as appropriated funds. Every expense has to be justified. Every investigation has to be "worth while." Some of the project activities to which government regulations proved too restrictive might have proceeded more smoothly if they had been farmed out under contract. The hiring of new personnel likewise had to be done according to Civil Service procedure.

The project officially began with the acceptance by U.S. Department of Health, Education, and Welfare of the grant from the Council on Library Resources in June 1958. This was short notice for the acquisition of major mechanical equipment, most of which requires at least three or four months for delivery. Work with machines calls for considerable knowledge of machine design and capacity in addition to operating skills. At the start of the project no trained machine operators were on hand. There were available two consultants on mechanical matters; one of them had formerly been on the Library staff, and the other on the staff of an earlier research project.

The physical plant consisted of about 3,500 square feet of a third floor, 59 steps up from ground level, with no elevator. Partial sound proofing and air conditioning had recently been installed. The atmosphere was, however, not sufficiently clean to permit processing of photographic film on home ground.

These were the resources and limitations with which NLM set out to attain the following objectives:

1. To cover more journals, up to nearly twice as many articles as were currently being covered.

2. To improve currency still further.

3. To eliminate tedious composition, filing, and proofreading procedures.

4. To improve legibility.

5. To eliminate the shuttling back and forth from index to register that the Current List required of the user.

6. To discover and implement multiple and derivative uses of the prepared material; and permit such by-products as the Bibliography of Medical Reviews, or special subject bibliographies, to be prepared without completely recasting the entries.

7. To provide a demonstration of methods that might aid scientific indexes in general, and assist in similar enterprises in other fields.

8. To distinguish among index imperfections which might be cured by money, which by technological advances, which by education, arbitration, and convention, and which cures might be mutually incompatible.

By the end of June 1958 considerable work had been done on project design. Slowly, by study, investigation, and conference, the general outlines of how to go about the project had been evolved. Development of machines was not part of the plans. Machines and equipment were to be chosen from what was already available in other lines of work; they were to be adapted and combined rather than to be specially designed. At one stage, development of a special type face was contemplated, but this was abandoned. With the exception of a single box made for stripping film into page format, all the equipment was standard and generally available, though not always ideally suited to the particular requirements of the job. The work was done on the premises and by augmented staff of the NLM Index Division, aided by consultants, rather than through hiring a specialist to take charge or by farming the work out under subcontract. The Index Division declared no moratorium in its other business, but throughout the project carried on the work of seeing the Current List through the final December 1959 issue.

Photographic Equipment and Processing

The camera, as the machine which promised to reduce end time in the monthly schedule of producing the Index Medicus, became the dominant piece of equipment in the mechanical scheme. It did away with the burden of shingling (and the burden of transporting huge boxes of heavy twenty by twenty-four-inch page boards to the printer) without sacrificing the advantage offered by shingling. This advantage consisted in flexible, time-saving, cold-type composition on the typewriter, piece, by piece and final proofreading at an early stage, piecemeal if convenient, with all entries remaining manipulatable until the last-minute check of alphabetical order. This is in contrast to the backlog problem inherent in hot-type composition of manuscript that cannot go to the printer one section

at a time, but must wait for ordered arrangement of the whole to
be completed after the cut-off date for additions, before printing,
not to mention proofreading, can begin.

The principal photographic devices studied were the Varityper
Corporation's Foto-List, Eastman Kodak's Listomatic and Lithoid's
Composo-List camera.   Only the first two were available at the
beginning of the project.

The Listomatic and Foto-List both require the use of standard
tabulating equipment punched cards as the vehicle for the introduction and manipulation of data in the system; the Composo-List is
not tied to a card of a set dimension.   In the first two systems
the entry is typed onto an area at the top of a punched card and
later fed into the camera which photographs the text on the cards
in various desired reductions down to 50 per cent; the Composo-
List system permits the text to be placed in any location for which
the camera aperture has been permanently adjusted.   The Foto-
List handles a single line of text on the card at a speed of 120
cards (lines) per minute;   the Composo-List will photograph the
entire text previously imprinted on the card at the same rate of
speed.   The Listomatic can photograph entries ranging from one to
three lines intermixed at a speed of 230 cards (up to 690 lines)
per minute.

The advantage of the Foto-List revolves around the excellent
quality of the finished negative and the greater ease and flexibility
of accurately positioning the text on the card.   The Composo-
List's chief virtue resides in the availability of a larger area of
the card for text.   The Listomatic, though considerably faster than

the Foto-List one line system, could conceivably photograph fewer lines per minute than the Composo-List set for an aperture accommodation of seven or more lines. The paramount attribute of the Listomatic, which it alone possesses, is its ability to change the size of the camera aperture to accommodate texts of varying numbers of lines from one card to the next.

The soundest justification for the use of any of these expensive pieces of equipment (all are in the $10,000 to $20,000 price range) is its application to procedures that, as a basic requirement, involve the handling of relatively huge quantities of text comprising an aggregate of very short unit items; furthermore, there should be a need for one or more later generation publications, either by the updating of existing material or the provision of cumulated editions. For the smaller one-shot publication the existing traditional composition techniques such as shingling and continuous typing for photo-offset reproduction should not be ignored.

The Listomatic camera was chosen by the National Library of Medicine because it was the only one able to intermix citations of one or more lines with reasonable facility. To allow routinely three lines' worth of space for one-line or two-line entries would waste an enormous amount of page space and would result in a spotty and unattractive appearance. To settle on a fixed one-line entry, on the other hand, and to try to handle all longer entries by strings of run-over cards would soon make files excessively bulky and difficult to handle.

Once the choice of camera has been made, all other elements of the system must be brought into line. The first requirement is

the utilization of a standard tabulating punched card. The space
available for the imprinting of text material which is subsequently
to be photographed is contained within the area shown in the following illustration:

LISTOMATIC IMPRINTING AREA

The remainder of the card, not used for text imprinting, may be
used for punching purposes, except that punched codes in Column
52, corresponding to the number of lines of text imprinted on the
card, must be used to trigger the appropriate opening of the
camera aperture. Within the camera field entries of one, two,
or three lines can be imprinted, providing the proper type size,
spacing and photographic reductions are selected.

Roll film for the camera is available in three different widths,
8, 4, and 2.67 inches, and each requires a special kit to accommodate it in the camera. The cost is approximately $120.00,
$60.00, and $45.00, respectively, per four hundred foot roll of
Listomatic film, which is panchromatic rather than the more commonly used orthochromatic film. The Listomatic design "package,"

consisting of the desired type size and style, the degree of reduction required, the linear length of the line, the number of lines per vertical inch, and the typewriter ratchet size, must be carefully devised for many reasons, not the least of which is the considerable cost differential resulting from the use of one of the wider film sizes where a narrower one would suffice.

These elements can be combined in a variety of ways, after the form of entry and format are determined. The top eleven-sixteenths of an inch of the punched card, excluding a border fifteen-hundredths of an inch at the top edge, is available for imprinting of text which will photograph. The entire field, however, need not be used for imprinting. Portions of the card may be consumed by punches which are needed to meet a machine sorting or collating requirement; the lateral sections of the card may not be used for text imprinting simply because the final length of line desired after reduction by the camera does not permit it. It should be noted that the camera functions symmetrically from an approximate mid-line on the punched card, photographing material equidistant on both sides. The text must, therefore, be placed precisely within the Listomatic imprinting area both vertically and horizontally. The camera reacts to any failure in meeting this rigid specification by ruthlessly chopping off the portions of text that fall outside the prescribed area.

At this point it should be explained that the size of the type selected will play a key role. The original size can be reduced by the Listomatic camera down to 45 per cent (from 1:1 down to 2.2:1, in 0.1 steps) by making the proper manual settings which can be done very easily and quickly. In order to obtain the desired reduction, it is also necessary to make special provision for synchronizing the advance of the film with the optical mechanism of the camera. This is accomplished by the use of film advance kits, which are available in sizes ranging from 6 to 14 lines per inch. The final vertical spacing after reduction is, consequently, limited to these whole numbers of lines to the inch. In the determination of the vertical length of the column to be accommodated on the page of the final printed product this information is essential. In the case of the Index Medicus the No. 10 Film Advance Kit is used to provide for 10 lines of text to the vertical inch.

These are the rudiments of the process of devising the various essential components of the Listomatic design package. For every different job, one or more of these elements will probably have to be changed. The interchange and resetting of parts in the camera is fairly rapidly accomplished, and the necessary kits and parts are not excessively costly.

The speed of the camera is more than ample for the NLM operation. Speed, however, must be coupled with reliability of function; the gain accruing from rapid operation is lost if the job must be run more than a single time. In this regard, the camera has not yet proved itself. This vital ability to perform routinely without significant dysfunction and subsequent rerunning has not been demonstrated by the NLM Listomatic camera to date; experience with Listomatic cameras elsewhere would, of course, be impossible for NLM to document. At the time this report was written, eight regular monthly issues of the Index Medicus had been filmed. Out of this number only the last issue was completed in a relatively trouble-free manner, and only after a crack team of engineers and maintenance personnel had performed an all-out investigation and overhaul prior to its run. Significantly, most of the camera's difficulties are related to the part of the mechanism governing the variable opening of the aperture, which seems to be its most vulnerable aspect. When the camera aperture is set for the exclusive filming of one line entries, similar to the Foto-List camera, there appears to be less difficulty encountered in its operation.

During the camera's operation there is no way of determining the efficacy of its performance. There are no gauges or other instruments on the camera to alert the operator to any malfunction; this will come to light only after the film has been processed. Paper proof copy (either positive or negative), however, can be run through the camera and used to some extent as a test, but the possibility of a change in performance by the camera between the time the paper copy is filmed and the final film running should not be excluded. Ozalid copies may also be generated from the processed film, but this method has grave weaknesses as a proofreading procedure, since any errors or deficiencies brought to light in this manner would require a second consumption of film. Film is about three times as costly as paper. In the NLM operation, the original plan called for the use of paper proof copy only through the initial shakedown stages, but the erratic performance of the camera has caused this phase to be stretched beyond the first few issues.

The reliable operation of the camera must be combined with a level of film processing that will consistently yield a satisfactory product. Obviously, a poor processing job can undo perfect performance of the camera. At present, the best piece of equipment for this purpose appears to be the Oscar Fischer continuous proce sor, which costs around $4,500. After investigation of the proble the decision was made to rely on the Recordak organization for film processing rather than to do it on the NLM premises. At the time, long before the first issue of the Index Medicus was ready for processing, the Oscar Fischer tank closest to the Library was located in New York. Assurance was given that one would be installed in Washington shortly, but this has still not materialized. Consequently, each month it has been necessary to ship the expose film to and from New York for processing, causing a delay in the production schedule. In addition, the quality of the processing has been uneven as evidenced by a variation in the background density of the film, despite any absence of alteration in the camera setting

This situation illustrates one of the fundamental desiderata of a Listomatic system, namely, centralized control over a maximum number of the individual, separate operations. The exception to this rule seems to be the use of the Listomatic camera for a serv ice-bureau type of operation, receiving for processing from other organizations material already composed and ordered on cards which are then put through the photographing operation. NLM has successfully performed several "outside" jobs of this kind. What this probably means, more precisely, is that card preparation operations should be centralized, and film processing operations should be centralized, but that the two groups of operations are separable.

Following processing, the finished film, in the form of rolls up to 400 feet in length, must be cut into column segments and assembled into page arrangement necessary for the further photo-lithographic processing. There are a number of methods available for this purpose, illustrating three general approaches; the use of "goldenrod" paper as a backing material, the use of photographic masks similarly, and direct connection of columns of film without the use of any backing material. There are advantages and dis-advantages in each method. All three have been tried, and al-though the photographic mask method is being used for the entire first year of the Index Medicus, in the second year it is planned to switch to the direct method which dispenses with backing material of any kind. Instead, special light boxes are being built. In the meth-ods based on the use of a backing material, the columns of film are inserted and adhered within "windows" that are cut out of the backing material to allow for the insertion of the film. By the use of the spe-cially designed light box, the film strips are positioned precisely, with little effort, on a perforated plastic box, and held securely in place by a vacuum created with the box itself. Adhesive tape (Paklon) is then placed simultaneously on the contiguous edges of each pair of film strips until the page is completed; the finished page is then removed from the box by momentarily switching off the source of suction. After a minimum of opaquing, the stripped pages which comprise the issue are shipped to the printer

AML52-1969

DITTRICH, Frans, 1888-
30 Jahre nationaler und sozialer Kampf in der oetmärkischen Apothekerschaft und die Verteidigung einer nationalen und sozialen Zielsetzung, Bewriafführung durch eine Aktien- und Aufsatzsammlung. Wien, 1941?, 75 p.
1. Pharmacy - Austria
QV704 D617d   AFML53-4466

DITTRICH, G
Das Lachtheilverfahren und seine Anwendung ... Berlin, Steinitz 1901, 84 p.   WB300 D617L
AML52-1504

DITTRICH, Paul, ed.
Festschrift Herrn Hofrat Prof. Dr. Hans Chiari aus Anlass seines 25 jährigen Professuren-Jubiläums gewidmet von seinen Schülern. Wien, Braumüller, 1908. 421 p. illus., port.
1. Chiari, Hans
Title: Festschrift Hans Chiari aus Anlass seines 25 jährigen Professoren-Jubiläums gewidmet
QZ200 D483f   AFML53-7107

DITTRICH, Paul
Lehrbuch der gerichtlichen Medizin für Ärzte und Juristen. 2. verm. und vollständig umgearb. Aufl. Leipzig, Haase, 1921.
iv, 300 p. illus.
W700 D617L   AFML53-943

DITTRICH, Paul, ed.
see HANDBUCH der ärztlichen Sachverständigen-Tätigkeit, unter Mitwirkung der Herren Gabriel Anton, Karl Bayer et al., Hrsg. von Paul Dittrich. Wien, Braumüller, 1908-   v. 1, 1908,
WB100 H2385   AML51-4749

DIURETIC review. v. 1-
May 1952-
New York, Lakeside Laboratories.
v. illus.
1. Diuretics & diuresis 2. Urology - Period.   I. Lakeside Laboratories, inc.
WI IB887   AFML52-7749

DÜVAL, M
see DUVAL, Mathias Marie, 1844-1907
AFML X54-1684

... p. ... (...)
1. First aid
WA292 D618r   AML51-13589

DIWOK, Wilhelm
Richtig helfen, bei Unfällen und plötzlichen Erkrankungen, ein Ratgeber für die erste Hilfeleistung bis zum Eingreifen des Arztes. 16. Aufl. Hamburg, Fröhlich, 1952.
100 p. illus. (Fröhlich Höcher)
1. First aid
WA292 D618r   AFML52-9466

DIX, Dorothea Lynde, 1802-1887
A collection of miscellaneous bio-bibliographical material on this person, together with abstracts, résumés, etc. of his works, may be found on the shelves under the above call number.
WZ100 qD619   AML51-1201

DIXON, Andrew Francis, 1868-1936
Manual of human osteology. London, Oxford Univ. Press, 1912.
xii, 318 p. illus.
WE200 D621m   AFML53-11152

DIXON, Andrew Francis, 1868-1936
Manual of human osteology. rev. by E. B. Jamieson. 3d ed. London, Oxford Univ. Press, 1937.
ix, 485 p. illus. (Oxford medical publications)
1. Osteology   I. Jamieson, Edward Bald, ed.
WE200 D621m   AML50-6321

DIXON, C   W
The diagnosis of smallpox. Leeds, Lumby, 1951,
12 p. illus.   W6 P3
Cover title.
1. Smallpox
AMI52-3092

DIXON, Claude Frank
The effect of sodium chlorid on certain disturbances in the motor mechanism of the upper intestinal tract. Minneapolis, 1925.
31 f. illus.
Thesis (M. S. in Surgery) - Univ. of Minnesota.
Typewritten copy.
1. Sodium chloride
W4A D6195e   AMI51-8720

for photo offset reproduction and binding.

A four hundred foot roll of film, representing some 135 three-column pages produced from about 21,000 cards, can be exposed, granting perfect operation of the camera, in 1.5 hours. It requir three full rolls of film to produce the average issue of the Index Medicus (450 pages). To cut and strip the 450 pages requires the use of three men for about two and a half days (seven and one half man-days).

References

Billings, John Shaw. "Our Medical Literature," Transactions Inter national Medical Congress (7th). London, 1881. p. 54-71.

Larkey, Sanford V. "The Army Medical Library Research Projec at the Welch Medical Library," Bulletin of the Medical Librar Association. 37:121-4. April 1949.

Rogers, Frank B., and Adams, Scott. "The Army Medical Library's Publication Program," Texas Reports on Biological

Medicine 8: 271-300, 1950.

Larkey, Sanford V. "The Welch Medical Library Indexing Project," Bulletin of the Medical Library Association 41:32-40, January 1953.

Brodman, Estelle. The Development of Medical Bibliography. Medical Library Association, 1954. (especially Chapter 5)

Medical Library Association. Handbook of Medical Library Practice. 2d ed. Chicago, American Library Association, 1956. (especially p. 358-365)

Brodman, Estelle and Taine, Seymour I. "Current Medical Literature: A Quantitative Survey of Articles and Journals," Proceedings of the International Conference on Scientific Information (Washington, 1958), v. 1, p. 435-447.

The MEDLARS Story At The National Library of Medicine*

Introduction

The National Library of Medicine dates back to 1836, when its predecessor, the Library of the Surgeon General's Office, was established. The first large-scale indexing of current medical-journal literature using institutional team-approach methods had its start in 1879 with the publication, by this Library, of the first volume of the first work to use the title Index Medicus. This was followed in 1880 by the first volume of the first series of the Index Catalogue of the Library of the Surgeon General's Office.

In 1916 the American Medical Association started the publication of a Quarterly Cumulative Index to Current Medical Literature. In 1927 this material was merged with that of Index Medicus to form the Quarterly Cumulative Index Medicus. In succeeding years, circumstances brought about other changes, with the result that two indexes are currently produced: the monthly Index Medicus, published by the National Library of Medicine, and the annual Cumulated Index Medicus, accumulated by the National Library of Medicine and published by the American Medical Association.

The preparation of the basic publication, the monthly Index Medicus, is a monumental task. In 1961 the publication averaged

*This section comprises the introductory part to The MEDLARS Story at the National Library of Medicine. Washington: U.S. Department of Health, Education, and Welfare, Public Health Service, 1963. pp. 1-6. The full report was prepared by the General Electric Information Systems Operation.

450 pages in length and contained references to more than 10,000 articles per average issue. The annual total of items indexed has increased from 120,000 in the first annual volume (1960) to 140,000 in 1961, and it will reach an estimated 250,000 in 1969. A total of 14,000 journal issues were indexed in 1961, and this figure is expected to reach 25,000 by 1969.

In addition to Index Medicus, the Library regularly publishes one special recurring bibliography, the Bibliography of Medical Reviews, and services assorted non-recurring requests for bibliographies of various complexities. It is expected to expand the list of regularly-published bibliographies to a total of 50 by 1964. The non-recurring "demand" bibliographies will reach an estimated total of 2,500 in 1964 and 22,500 in 1969.

With the installation of MEDLARS, the Library expects to add monographs to its list of source material to be indexed, and a total of some 5,000 English-language monographs is foreseen for 1964. These will be combined eventually with foreign monographs, and total of both should reach 13,000 by 1969. The grand total of articles and monographs indexed is expected to reach 160,000 by 1964 and 250,000 by 1969.

The predecessor publication of the monthly Index Medicus was the Current List of Medical Literature. Its preparation was a manual operation which increased in difficulty as the publication grew in physical size and scope. In 1950, a shingling technique, a method of manually arranging the publication's entries in sequence for photographing, was adopted as the first step in the printing process. Shingling gradually became a bottleneck, preventing

future expansion. In 1960 a new mechanized system was adopted
for the publication of the Index Medicus.

The mechanized system - which is the existing system - involves the use of tabulating cards, upon which the citations are
imprinted. The cards are also punched with machine-readable sorting information. After machine sorting and matching, the cards,
suitably arranged, are automatically photographed with a Listomatic
camera upon rolls of film which are then cut and assembled into
page arrangement for printing.

Although the existing mechanized system offers distinct advantages over the older technique, it is limited solely to a publication
system. It cannot satisfactorily meet growing demands for rapid
retrieval of complex requests specified according to multiple subject axes. Some way had to be found to accomplish more, to do
it better, to take less time, to operate more efficiently, and generally to provide a greater all-round versatility.

This was the situation that led to the initiation of the
MEDLARS Project. That system is described in the following pages
in order that the reader be allowed a comprehensive knowledge of
MEDLARS he is introduced to the system as a whole, then by obser-
ing it at work, and then is given the technical particulars of its
individual components.

What MEDLARS Will Do

MEDLARS is designed for use by the National Library of Medicine to perform various functions of literature analysis and retrieval.
It will involve the use of a digital computer and special composing
equipment capable of providing excellent typographic quality. Knowl-

edge of the specific objectives of the system is basic to an appre-
ciation of what MEDLARS is designed to do and how it will be
done. Accordingly, this chapter begins by first outlining the
objectives of the system. This is followed by a description of how
these objectives are to be met. In the description, a brief overview of the entire system precedes a somewhat detailed examination of the system's component parts.

MEDLARS' Objectives

The objectives of MEDLARS may be summarized as follows:

Improve the quality of and enlarge Index Medicus and
at the same time reduce the time required to prepare
the monthly edition for printing from 22 to 5 working
days.

Make possible the production of other compilations
similar to Index Medicus in form and content.

Make possible for Index Medicus and other compilations the inclusion of citations derived from other
sources, as well as from journal articles.

Make possible the prompt (a maximum of two days)
and efficient servicing of requests for special bibliographies, on both a demand and a recurring basis,
regularly searching up to five years of stored computer files.

Increase the average depth of indexing per article by
a factor of five, i.e., 10 headings versus 2.

Nearly double the number of articles that may be
handled annually - from 140,000 now to 250,000 in
1969.

Reduce the need for duplicative total literature screening operations.

Keep statistics and perform analyses of its own operations, to provide the information needed to monitor

and improve system effectiveness.

Permit future expansion to incorporate new and as
yet not completely defined - and hence secondary-
objectives.

An idea of the anticipated capacity and capability of MEDLARS
over the present system may be gained from Table 1.

Table 1

Comparison of Capacity of Existing System and MEDLARS

Item	Existing System Current	MEDLARS 1964	1969
Journal issues indexed	14,000	16,000	25,000
American monographs indexed	-	5,000	-
American and foreign monographs indexed	-	-	13,000
Articles and monographs indexed	140,000	160,000	250,000
Recurring bibliographical requests filled*	-	50	50
Demand (non-recurring) bibliographical requests filled	-	2,500	22,500

*The bibliographies produced will be prepared at an average rate
of three or four issues per day; they will recur with periodicities
ranging from one week to six months.

Overview

Under MEDLARS, the regularly published products will continue to be, for the foreseeable future, the monthly issues of Index
Medicus, the annual Cumulated Index Medicus, annual printings of
Medical Subject Headings and List of Journals Indexed, and such
recurring bibliographies as Bibliography of Medical Reviews. The
typography for these will be of a quality comparable to the currently published issues of Index Medicus, through use of the specially-
designed Graphic Arts Composing Equipment (GRACE). GRACE will
compose finished copy on film suitable for offset printing. In

addition, demand (non-recurring) bibliographies will be produced to meet specific requests as they are received by the Library. Most demand bibliographies and all statistical information prepared by the system will be printed by a standard computer printer.

The various operations required to produce these publications may be logically separated into three subsystems.

1. Input and Conversion Subsystem

   In this subsystem, journals, monographs, and other documents are received and indexed or cataloged; a "unit record," consisting of a citation and its associated headings, is prepared for each article, book, and serial title; search requests are received and prepared; and unit records and search requests are transformed into machine-readable form with punched paper tape as the primary medium.

2. Manipulation Subsystem

   The heart of this subsystem is a high-speed, digital computer. It accepts the unit records on paper tape, checks them for the presence and correctness of those elements for which such checks are possible, does some pre-processing to facilitate and speed the subsequent processing, and stores the unit records on magnetic tape. In response to search requests, it searches its cumulation of unit records for those that qualify for retrieval and edits and composes them for output on magnetic tape.

3. Output Subsystem

   This subsystem transforms the magnetic-tape output of the Manipulation Subsystem into exposed film from which publications may be printed. When high-quality typography is not required, the standard output of the computer's mechanical printer is utilized.

The way in which the three subsystems, or groups of operations, will relate to each other may be visualized in a capsule description of the operations of the system as a whole: Journals received by the Library will be distributed to a staff of indexers for the selection of articles to be indexed, the translation of foreign article titles, and the indexing of article citations with appropriate subject headings and other tags.   Documents such as monographs will be distributed to a staff of catalogers who will perform some-what similar functions.   A unit record will be prepared for each article indexed and for each document cataloged.   The unit records will be punched on paper tape in a form suitable for computer in-put.   The paper tape will be read into the computer, which will accept the information, process it, compress it, and store it on magnetic tape.   The unit records will be ordered in chronological sequence and will be stored for at least a five-year period.

Once a month, for the publication of Index Medicus, the unit records placed into storage over the past month will be expanded, sorted, edited, and rewritten in final form on magnetic tape. Once a year the material will be merged for the Cumulated Index Medicus.

The magnetic tape output of the computer will be used by the Graphic Arts Composing Equipment, which will compose each cita-tion, properly arranged, on photographic film. This film will be developed, inspected, and transmitted to the printer. It will be used to make the offset plates from which the pages of Index Medicus will be printed.   Film will also be prepared for printing the annual Cumulated Index Medicus and recurring bibliographies.

Recurring bibliographies may cover one or more clinical or re-search areas which are responsive to the bibliographic needs of specialized consumer groups.   Periodically, the subject-heading parameters and output format requirements will be prepared by search specialists and entered into the computer on punched parameter cards. An increased depth of indexing, as well as the combining of the subject headings and other search tags (such as relate to journals, authors, and year of publication), will be possible. The magnetic tape output from the computer will be handled in the same way as the tape produced for Index Medicus. The printed format of recurring bibliographies will be flexible and can be similar to that of Index Medicus.

Requests for demand (non-recurring) bibliographies will be processed by a staff of bibliographic searchers and be converted to machine-readable form on punched paper tape. The tape will be read into the computer, which will then search its files for the citations that meet the request requirements. These retrieved citations will be properly arranged by the computer and then printed by means of the computer printer. In some instances, the Graphic Arts Composing Equipment will be used for printing demand bibliographies.

All of these operations, plus storing information and preparing statistics necessary to monitor and improve system effectiveness, will be performed speedily. The monthly issues of Index Medicus will require five working days for completion; both recurring and demand bibliographies will be processed in one or two days, with priority demand requests being given same-day service. Broadly outlined, these are MEDLARS' operations.

Recataloging*

By M. Ruth MacDonald

Growth is an essential element of libraries just as it is an essential element of nature. Growth means change. Growth does
not always mean an increase in size; it may represent a change in
composition or in pattern. The growth of a library is usually
determined by either or both of two elements: its acquisitions
and its services. These elements, in turn, are governed by the
library's purpose or purposes.

The purposes for which a library is established and maintained
are bound to change. The change may be deliberate, planned
and directed by the library itself. They may be the result of a
slow evolutionary process. On the other hand they may be sudden
and compulsory, caused by developments and demands outside the
library. In any event changes in purposes and services do occur
and as they are recognized there usually is an accompanying
recognition of related changes needed in the library's collections
and their records. Such changes are encompassed in the term "recataloging" a word of low esteem in the library world.

It is interesting to speculate on the reasons for this unfavorable attitude toward recataloging, which is, after all, a part of
library growth and development. Possibly the unfavorable attitude
can be understood and accepted more easily when comparable situa-

*Bulletin of the Medical Library Association, 49: 426-433; July, 1961.

tions in other areas are considered. For instance, anyone prefers to spend his time and money on new things, rather than on maintaining or renewing old things. This is as true in relation to the librarian's house as to his library's catalog. Whereas it is a pleasant task to determine the type of electrical wiring and the outlets needed in his new house, the rewiring required to modernize his old home (or to meet fire regulations) is apt to register as a nuisance and an expense. Another quite obvious reason for the general dislike of recataloging is closely akin to the common reaction to major change; it upsets the status quo. Although the end result of the change is greatly desired and will be much appreciated and admired, its accomplishment is disliked for the inconvenience it causes and the habits it disrupts. This is as true for rewiring a house as for revising a library catalog.

Recataloging is the result of some library change or development, not the cause. Therefore an integral part of any recataloging discussion is the cause or reason for it. Until the question 'Why is recataloging needed?" is thoughtfully answered there can be no good answer to the question 'What recataloging is needed?"

The subject 'Recataloging" is particularly pertinent at this time because of the proposed revision of the ALA Rules for Author and Title Entries, 2d ed., 1949. The revision, which may become another Anglo-American code or even an international code, will, if accepted, force librarians to make some drastic cataloging decisions. In this paper I shall discuss some of the effects the new cataloging rules may have on the form and content of library catalogs, with emphasis on the catalogs of large libraries.

For the past seventy-five years the dictionary card catalog has been the form adopted by most American libraries. The term "dictionary card catalog" identifies the type of library catalog which presents all varieties of catalog entries in a single alphabet. The reasons given for its adoption include the flexibility of the card form, the convenience of the single alphabet, and the current completeness of the cataloging record. Its claims of inclusiveness and self-sufficiency have been greatly stressed and lauded by the chief users of the catalog--the library staff.

What is the current judgment on the dictionary card catalog? While it remains an effective tool for a small library, it is no longer an effective tool for a large library. The dictionary catalog can be an effective tool in a small library just because it is small. Its very size is an indication of the number of entries included, which number in turn places a limitation on the complications that can enter into its arrangement and alphabeting. Immediately there arises a question as to the size of a small library. From the standpoint of the dictionary catalog, it is suggested that problems of size begin to be troublesome when a catalog contains card records for about 30,000 titles. Therefore, in terms of this discussion, a library ceases to be a small library at some point between 30,000 and 50,000 titles, the exact point of change being determined by the combination of the number of titles cataloged, the subject concentration of the collection, and the age of the catalog.

The dictionary catalog is not an effective tool for a large library because it is no longer flexible, its arrangement requires many alphabets and some classified sections, and it cannot hope to achieve the goal of "current completeness." While efforts made to achieve the goals of inclusiveness and self-sufficiency have not been successful, they have resulted in gigantism that aggravates all the card catalog's imperfections: lack of uniformity in entries: inadequate cross reference structure; subject heading problems; misfilings, and other errors of omission or commission.

The size, age, and complexities of the dictionary catalog have forced it to become a conventional tool that cannot be responsive to new situations. It has grown so big as the result of continuing accumulations that it lacks the ability to be a modern catalog or to serve specialized needs. On the other hand it has taught its users a method for selecting new materials by searching for clean catalog cards--a method that sometimes tricks the users. Because of its size, maintenance is expensive and apt to be kept at a minimum by the pressure of needed new work. The difficulties the catalog users encounter and the cost to the library in housing the catalog present an urgent problem which cries out for solution.

Recataloging in the past has usually consisted of efforts to correct and improve the library's cataloging record. In only a relatively few instances has recataloging constituted a complete renewal of the catalog. In the future it is doubtful that any large library will undertake to recatalog its collections on the scale undertaken by the National Library of Medicine in 1946. Today, even the cataloging refinements of the past are becoming increasingly difficult and costly because of the catalog's accumulations and complexities. The result is a further weakening of its quality and reliability.

For at least two decades the pressures of increased acquisitions and ever-expanding subject fields have stimulated catalogers to study and revise their tools and to devise new procedures. Unfortunately, a part of this effort has been wasted because there has been no comparable pressure in public service areas. The time is near, however, when this situation may well change as libraries begin to feel the increased demands that are expected to result from population increases.

Actually the proposed changes in cataloging rules are only one part of the whole pattern of change facing libraries today. Some librarians who are still active can recall supervisors who bemoaned inadequate library school courses that did not include instruction in library hand-writing, long after typewriters became commonplace. It took a whole generation to complete that change. Now, librarians must be ready to meet and cope with changes that come almost overnight. All this would seem to indicate that the time has come to discard the traditional and conservative concepts of the dictionary catalog and of recataloging in large libraries, for mere refinements are no longer sufficient. Furthermore, the proposed new cataloging rules present a challenge to librarians to shape new service patterns along with the new cataloging patterns that will free current catalogs and cataloging from the burden of the past.

The discussion of the new cataloging rules within any library or group of libraries should include representation of all work areas. Such joint efforts are mutually educational; they insure understanding, even though they may not insure acceptance by all members of the group. They also provide a means for safeguarding the needs of all work areas. For instance, library-wide participation will guard the information the staff must have to insure correct title searching, although the searchers may be required to use printed lists or other sources to supplement or in part replace the card catalog. Another reason for a joint approach to the new rules and the changes they imply is the importance of the personal element in recataloging. Probably the best way to avoid unnecessary changes and to insure essential changes is a full and free discussion of the whole situation. No amount of recataloging can by itself accomplish the major changes needed; it must be supplemented by similar changes in work habits and attitudes.

Instead of the old piecemeal approach to recataloging, a modern approach would be to study the whole catalog in the light of current and foreseeable needs, keeping in mind the advances in technology that are rapidly coming closer to meeting library requirements. Such an approach to the dictionary catalog will necessarily include a study of its subject headings and subject cross references neither of which is directly related to the proposed revision of the cataloging rules. Although a catalog study limited to the entries related to the revised rules would constitute a task of considerable magnitude, it is still suggested that the proposed rules provide a timely incentive to study the whole catalog.

What are some of the catalog changes which will result from the proposed revised rules? (It should be noted here that the changes will vary somewhat in different libraries because it is expected that alternate rules will be provided for small and popular libraries.) Three of the proposed major changes are:

1. The literary unit rather than the bibliographical unit will become the basis for cataloging (i.e., all editions of a work will be cataloged under the original title). This principle has already been accepted and used in cataloging the work of voluminous and classic authors through the device of the "standard title." Even though this change may be adopted by agencies that sell printed catalog cards, the cards could easily be converted to old style cards (by drawing a line through the original title which will appear as the "standard title" following the author entry) and thus be useful to libraries preferring that form.

2. The entry for an institution or a society will be made under the direct form of the name (i.e., University of Washington, rather than Washington (State) University). This principle has previously been accepted for certain types of organizations with distinctive names, such as Washington University, St. Louis. This proposed change raises a question about Cutter numbers that have represented place or government unit. There is no one answer to this question. A library may decide to retain the old Cutter numbers for new publications because this would keep all the publications together in the shelf list and thereby provide a geographical approach. Should a library decide to adopt the Cutter number for the new form of entry the old and new publications may be tied together in the shelf list and on the shelves by the simple expedient of direction cards and shelf dummies.

3. A corporate name that has changed will be used in the

form current at the time the item being cataloged was published. This is a complete break with the traditional plan to enter all publications under the latest form of the name. Some libraries have already adopted this rule for changed corporate names, notably the National Library of Medicine, which has applied the rule since 1946. This change is a very desirable one for it will free current cataloging from the increasing burden of changing entries for old publications and will preserve the integrity of bibliographical citations based on information in the publications.

Any desire to revise present catalog entries to conform to these principles using traditional procedures would be too time-consuming and too expensive to be taken literally. The amount of recataloging involved would make chaos out of the dictionary catalog and at the same time curtail the cataloging of new material.

Recataloging can be achieved through an almost infinite variety of procedures of different levels and degrees. It can be accomplished, or avoided, by a sorting and rearrangement or a weeding of records, or both. It can be a mechanical procedure or a highly intellectual one. It might be effected by a decision to let past records remain as they are and to concentrate time and efforts on future records. How then, can the proposed changes in cataloging rules be implemented without causing an immediate and gigantic upheaval?

It seems reasonable to suggest that in attempting to deal with the problem of the large dictionary catalog and the proposed changes in cataloging rules, the old edict "divide and conquer" presents the best approach. Even the application of this edict offers a wide variety of choices. Because cataloging consists of choices determined on the basis of a code of rules, choices determined on the form of the instrument to present the results of cataloging are an inseparable part of the whole process. For example, on the date set for the application of the new rules a new catalog could be started. The date could be arbitrarily set as the cataloging date or could be a more flexible combination of publishing and cataloging dates. The new catalog could be in dictionary form or it could break the traditional pattern and be a divided catalog. A new dictionary catalog could be more truly alphabetical dispensing with all possible subalphabets and classified sections. A new divided catalog offers many choices of form, inclusions, and arrangement.

In considering whether the new catalog should be a dictionary catalog or a divided catalog, a very homely comparison can be studied: the telephone directory. The directory is issued in two separate parts, the alphabetical name section and the classified section. Either part may be reissued without affecting the other. The two sections are equally available, yet there is little problem as to which should be used for a particular question. And some-times one section is used to supplement the other. In their di-vided form they are quite simple in form and easy to use. If the two sections were combined into a single alphabet the resulting directory would be clumsy in size and complicated in arrangement. In other words, a combined telephone directory would present some of the problems of the dictionary catalog.

This is a good place to insert a brief statement on the di-vided catalog which is a good form of catalog for both large and small libraries. Any card catalog that occupies, or will occupy, more than one catalog drawer may be a candidate for divided catalog status. There is one paramount consideration in planning for a divided catalog: the basis on which the division will be made. This decision is of paramount importance to the makers and the users of the divided catalog because there are so many possible ways to divide the three major categories of catalog cards and their related cards. Any division and combination of the cards that fits the local library's needs can be adopted. Whatever plan is adopted must, however, be strictly adhered to by the catalog makers and be well publicized so that it will be understood by the catalog users.

The two-part divided catalog in the National Library of Medicine may be cited as an example of one type of division. The Name Catalog contains all "name" entry cards (i.e., authors, editors, series, titles, and names used as subjects). The Subject Catalog is strictly a "subject headings" catalog. In each drawer of the two catalogs there is a printed guide card on colored stock which defines the scope and arrangement of the file.

An important decision in planning a new catalog is to leave the old catalog "as is" for the time being. Some exceptions will be expected, such as a decision to transfer cards for certain types of books or for publications of certain dates to the new catalog. Another exception will be the insertion of printed direction cards designed to bridge the changes in forms of entries used in the old and new files. It may be desirable to compress the old catalog cards into fewer trays to provide space to house the new catalog.

Or it may be desirable to expand the old catalog into additional drawers in order to permit cards in corresponding sections of the alphabet of the old and new catalogs to be placed in the same drawer. Such exceptions are minor, however, and need not confuse the overall decision to leave the old catalog intact for the present.

The postponement of decisions relative to the revision, reorganization, or replacement of the old catalog should have salutary effects on the catalog makers and users. Preserved in its present form it will supply the same help as always. It will probably be preferred by its users until the new catalog is of a size that wins them away. When that time comes they will more readily participate in making plans for the disposal of the old catalog. Another reason for postponement is to give the new catalog and cataloging rules time to become established so that the catalogers will be better able to cope with the old file. A pertinent reason for delay is the development of technological devices which will surely produce the means to help librarians dispose of the old files in ways that will insure their future satisfactory use. And, last but not least, the delay will afford time to re-evaluate library collections and time to plan any needed weeding of superseded editions, out-of-scope and duplicate copies. Such re-evaluation might even be done regionally and cooperatively rather than on a strictly individual basis.

When the time comes to deal with the old catalog the primary task should be to identify the part of the file that is essential for the future use of the library's materials. This part, which will probably include the main entries, titles, secondary entries, and series cards, may be preserved as a separate card file until it can be economically reproduced in book form or in some other more modern form. The remaining old catalog cards can then be studied in the light of their age, condition, frequency of use, and duplication of information elsewhere available. After discarding as many as possible, the remaining cards can be retained pending their reproduction in some economical and usable form. The disposal of the old catalog will set the pattern for periodically converting the new card catalog or catalogs to another form while still another "new" catalog is begun.

Putting the library's basic tool into a compact form will do more than solve the problems of dictionary catalog size and complexity. The method will provide better access to catalog information through multiple copies and will take care of the demand for catalog information in outside locations and new branches.

Furthermore, the practice of periodically retiring the card catalog will lead to a compartmentalization of the catalog and the collections by date. By this means the record of each period will be preserved in the form and language of the period and thus the need for large-scale recataloging will be eliminated.

The big problems that can be foreseen are those of personnel and work habits. The staff has prided itself on supplying rapid replies to questions of the sorts the traditional catalog has answered, and thereby has created an expectation for immediate service. The curtailment of the card catalog's coverage and the need to supplement it by earlier catalogs and bibliographies will often

cause the staff to use more than one record and therefore require
more time to answer "catalog questions." Even though a library's
several catalogs, indexes, and bibliographies may differ in form
and arrangement and may be uneven in the consistency and depend-
ability of their records, they can serve adequately to indicate location of materials. It must be admitted that poor records, whether
due to incompleteness or inaccuracy, serve poorly for replies to
bibliographical questions. The old records in whatever form will
remain as good as, and no better than, they were in the old catalog. In spite of such practical problems the staff will adjust to the
changes if the need for them and the advantages they offer are
understood.

The decision to have a new catalog cannot be lightly made because it is a decision that will be costly in time, equipment, and
service. It is a decision which can be encouraged on the basis
that it would be less costly than the wholesale recataloging required
to renovate an old catalog, which would still contain all of its former problems of size, age, and complexity.

Librarians can approach the future in either of two ways. One
way is to cling to the traditional patterns and accept only the
changes that are essential. The other way is to welcome the
opportunity to modernize their collections as well as their catalogs
and to educate catalog users to understand and accept the moderni-
zation. If the big changes are accepted, it is possible that the
term "recataloging" in the future may be more acceptable as it
will come to mean the ordinary day-by-day adjustments required to
fit new acquisitions into the collection and the catalog. The word

"compartmentalization" will designate a new and affirmative approach to the overhaul jobs which the term "recataloging" once implied.

References

Lubetzky, Seymour. Cataloging Rules and Principles: a Critique of the ALA Rules for Entry and a Proposed Design for Their Revision. Washington. Library of Congress. 1953. 65p.

Institute on Cataloging Code Revision, Stanford University, 1958. Working Papers. 1958.

------. Summary of Proceedings. 1958. 62p.

Verona, Eva. "Literary unit versus bibliographical unit." Libri 9:79-104, 1959.

Code of Cataloging Rules: Author and Title Entry. An Unfinished Draft by Seymour Lubetzky. With an Explanatory Comment by Paul Dunkin. American Library Association. Mar. 1960. xv, 85p.

Institute on Catalog Code Revision. McGill University, 1960. Working Papers. Chicago. 1960.

------. Summary of Proceedings. American Library Association, 1960, 93 p.

A Short Title Catalog Made With IBM Tabulating Equipment*
By Phyllis A. Richmond

The Problem

Recently the University of Rochester established several departmental libraries in science and engineering in answer to a need for better library facilities to support its academic expansion. Each of these libraries is an entity, with its own standard card catalog. While these catalogs were being made, the faculty and students had to use a temporary file arranged by author and a serial list posted on a convenient stack.

The lack of a catalog was a severe handicap to the librarians. The faculty and students survived fairly well, probably because neither group really knows how to make effective use of a catalog. In fact, the faculty in each library were so used to getting along without a catalog that when one was finally completed, they did not use it.

This was apparent from a steady stream of orders for books already in the library. In addition, books which the library had never owned were frequently assigned for reserve reading, to the distress of student and librarian alike. Since the faculty did not come to the catalog, it seemed logical to devise some way of taking the catalog to the faculty.

*Library Resources & Technical Services, 7: 81-90, Winter, 1963.

The Remedy

The problems arising from ineffectual use of the card catalog became quite expensive. By the time a duplicate order was caught, for example, a considerable proportion of the acquisition procedure might have taken place. In some cases, duplication was not discovered in time to cancel the order. The waste in expensive personnel time also was taken into account. To choke off duplicate orders at their source, it was decided to make a short title printed catalog from standard 80 column IBM cards and give a copy to each faculty member to keep in his office. The punched card form was chosen because, in the long run, this could be more readily updated.

As time went on, another practical reason for having some arrangement other than a standard card catalog for listing library holdings became apparent. The students and faculty, and particularly the library committee chairmen involved in book selection, wanted to know what was in other departmental libraries without traveling to the Main Library to use the union catalog. In particular, faculty, students, and the local industrial research laboratories all wanted to know which library subscribed to what periodicals. Putting short title printed catalogs in each departmental library and sending copies to the industrial research libraries would not only be convenient on campus, but would cut out the "Do you have - ?" step in local interlibrary loans, saving time for the Main Library's Circulation Department, which handles such calls.

Steps to Create a Printed Catalog

The University of Rochester has both a Computing Center and

a Tabulating Center. Consultation with the staffs of these centers determined that a short title catalog on IBM cards was a tabulating job. This was a financial relief because the IBM 407 tabulator time could be rented by the Library for $7.50 an hour, whereas the IBM 707 computer costs at least $100 an hour.

The first catalog to be put on punched cards was that of the Engineering Library. The problems involved in getting desired results were discussed thoroughly with the Assistant Director of the Tabulating Center, who then drew up diagrams for wiring the plug boards and explained general machine procedures. It was informative to a librarian to see how much could be done easily with machines.

Keypunching was begun, using a student assistant for two hours each week. The first catalog took almost ten months to punch, partly because considerable experimentation was done before satisfactory patterns of operation were established. The second catalog, for the Physics Library, took only three months at the same rate. If one has access to a keypunch full time, it should be possible to punch the cards for a 6,000 title library in about two weeks.

The final running of the Engineering catalog was quite exciting. It took some experimentation and rewiring before the desired results were obtained. It should be emphasized that short title catalogs via IBM equipment cannot be made without the help of those experienced in working with the machines.

The copy from the tabulator was sent to the Print Shop to be reduced, reproduced and bound. The cost of printing made it necessary to eliminate the subject listing as originally planned, but several copies were made on the tabulator, and put in pamphlet binders to serve anyone who needed them. As it turned out, the demand has not been great enough to justify the cost of printing. On the other hand, a separate periodical listing, which was also omitted as an economy, is in great demand and will be included in the next edition. The first catalog covered the contents of the Engineering Library to January 1, 1962. It was run off, printed, bound and distributed within a month of the cut-off date. Part of a sample page is shown below:

```
INT NICKEL CO          NICKEL ALLOY STEELS ED.2                        MC TA0479
INT NICKFL CO          RAPID IDENTIFICATION OF SOME MFTALS & ALLOYS    40 QD0098
INT PWDR METALL CONF   POWDER METALLURGY                              61 TN0695
INT SYM HIGH TEMP      PROCEFDINGS                                     59 QC0276
INT SYM NUCLEAR FUEL   NUCLEAR FUEL ELEMENTS                           59 TK9360
INT SYM STR WAVE PROP  INTERNATIONAL SYM STRESS WAVE PROP IN MAT       60 QC0191
INT UNION P&A CHEM     EXPERIMENTAL THERMOCHEMISTRY                    56 QD0511
IOFFE ABRAM F          PHYSICS OF SEMICONDUCTORS                       60 QC0612
                       IRON AGE V. 171- 1954-                             TS0300
ISBIN H       S        TWO-PHASE PRESSURE DROPS                        54 QA0911
ITALY                  SPECIAL NUMBER ON PILOT PLANT TECHNIQUES        54 TP0517
JACKMAN LLOYD M        APPLICATIONS NUCLFAR MAGN RESON SPECTROSCOPY    59 QD0476
JACKSON ALBERT S       ANALOG COMPUTATION                              60 QA0076.4
JACKSON JACOB          COOLING TOWERS                                  51 TP0159.C6
JACKSON WILLIS         COMMUNICATION THEORY                            53 Q 0360
JAHNKE EUGEN           TABLES FUNCTIONS FORMULAE & CURVES REV. ED.     43 QA0047
JAHNKE EUGEN           TABLES OF HIGHER FUNCTIONS ED6                  60 QA0047
JAKOB MAX              ELEMENTS OF HEAT TRANSFER & INSULATION ED. 2    50 QC0320
JAKOB MAX              ELEMENTS OF HEAT TRANSFER ED. 3                 57 QC0320
JAKOB MAX              HEAT TRANSFFR                                   49 QC0320
JAKOB MAX              HEAT TRANSFER                                   57 QC0320
JAMES THOMAS HOWARD    FUNDAMENTALS OF PHOTOGRAPHIC THEORY             48 TR0200
JAMES F. LINCOLN FNDN  ARC WELDING IN DFSIGN                           39 TK4660
JAMES F. LINCOLN FNDN  DESIGN FOR WELDING                              48 TK4660
JAMES F. LINCOLN FNDN  STUDIES IN ARC WELDING                         45 TK4660
JAMES F LINCOLN FNDN   WELDED DECK HIGHWAY BRIDGES                     50 TG0380
JAMES F LINCOLN FNDN   WELDED HIGHWAY BRIDGE DESIGN                    52 TG0425
JANZ GEORGE J          ESTIMATION THERMO PROPERTIES ORGANIC COMPOUNDS  58 QD0501
```

Procedure

The physical arrangement of the form of entry used in the short title catalog is a modification of that devised by Dr. Charles Vertanes for the printed catalog of the Long Island Lighting Company Library.[1] Eleven spaces are allowed for the classification number, twenty-one for the name of the author, forty-six for the title, and two for the date. In the case of current periodical subscriptions, the holdings are indicated in the title section, i.e., v.1- 1945- , and columns 79 and 80 are purposely left blank so

that a periodical listing can be compiled at any time by sorting for
cards with blank columns 79 and 80.

The master cards were keypunched directly from the shelf list,
which at the University of Rochester Library is composed of Library of Congress catalog cards or equivalent, with call numbers
and accession numbers added in the left margin. The master
punched cards were then run off on the IBM 407 tabulator for proof
reading against the shelf list. After corrections were made, three
permanent decks of color-coded punched cards for author, title
and classification were reproduced, and one special deck for
periodicals. These were printed in the interpreter in such a way
that the author's name came first in the deck arranged by author,
title first in the deck arrangement by title, and call number first
for both deck arrangements by subject and the periodical listing.
Each of these decks was sorted and filed. When it was time to
make the catalog, the decks were taken from the drawers, headings
and blank spacer cards inserted, and the packs fed into the hopper
of the tabulator. Since there were about 4, 000 titles, running off
took an hour for each deck except the periodical listing, which
was much shorter. The decks were then returned to their drawers
and were ready to run again after updating with new accessions
added since the last printing.

The one-line, 80-column entry affords great economy in listing
and is easy to read. The call number consists solely of the
classification number. The book number is omitted because the
classification number will get the reader to the correct shelf and
he can find his book there in alphabetical order. The system is

very successful with Library of Congress classification numbers since almost all such numbers can be expressed within ten columns, always reserving column 7 for the decimal which divides classification symbols from book number. In the rare cases of a decimal number with a subdivision, i.e., TK7872.5.A23, the subdivision was omitted. In actual practice, all classification numbers were completed in ten columns and the programmer used column 11 for control in the final running.

The names of most authors fitted into the twenty-one column allotment without difficulty. Corporate entries, however, had to be abbreviated and a special list of abbreviations was included, as some of the abbreviations, especially conferences and symposia, were not immediately self-evident. A general list of abbreviations was also included and these will be kept uniform in all the science library catalogs. All subheadings of corporate bodies were omitted unless the related title was completely non-distinctive. Thus, all publications of the United States government have been entered under U.S. Surprisingly, only one title has been ambiguous so far. This was something of a shock, but the small size of the libraries probably accounts for it.

Most titles fitted easily into the forty-six column allotment. Longer ones were easily shortened into something recognizable. Dissertations were not always satisfactory in this respect, but fortunately there were not many of them.

The date of publication is an important aid in identifying the book. In some rare cases, this was the only difference between identical titles. Few 19th century books are found in most scientific libraries; therefore only 20th century book dates were distinguished.   Books published prior to 1900 (code date 00) were given the code number HS; books with no date received ND, and monographic continuations still in the process of being published, MC.   Monographic continuations which had been completed were given the earliest publication date.   Where different editions of a monograph were in process of publication, the number of the edition was given in the title section, as with any single-volume monograph.

In the process of keypunching, several cataloging decisions had to be made.   The imprint date was chosen in preference to the copyright date when there were both.   The publication dates of the proceedings of a conference, symposium or other meeting were used in preference to the date of the meetings.   In cases where the date was given as "1961, i.e., 1960", the corrected date was chosen.   Initial articles were omitted in titles, both to save space and to avoid filing difficulties.

Abbreviations had to be standardized.   The first word in a title was never abbreviated.   The first word in an abbreviated form of a corporate entry always had to be identical with the first word in the Library of Congress entry so that the item could be retrievable in a standard card catalog, even though in some instances a different abbreviation would have made it easier to recognize the organization.   Great care was taken to ensure that the printed catalog mirrored the form of entry in and organization of the card catalog, since there was no intention of divorcing the two.

Special Conditions: Filing

Machine filing and library filing are sufficiently different to create special problems in sorting the punched cards. Standard library practice is to file first by primary entry, which is the author or the title if there is no author, or the subject heading or the added entry. After that one files by secondary entry, which is title in the case of an author entry, and author in a title or added entry. In teaching new personnel to file, one points out the physical position of the various entries on a unit card and indicates filing order among them. Then there are a whole collection of special conditions: certain words are ignored, numbers are treated as if spelled out in the vernacular, initialisms are filed before words in a letter class, etc., etc. The sorter sorts from right to left to produce the final result in reading order which is left to right. Blank columns file before columns which are punched because one picks the cards from the pockets from right to left. This means that title entries come before author entries. Numbers file before letters because they require only one pass through the machine, whereas letters take two. Initialisms file exactly as they are spelled: the Mac's are separated from the Mc's and Ire comes between Iraz and Irea. Abbreviations are filed exactly as spelled and not necessarily interfiled with the words they represent. One thinks filing is largely letter-by-letter until one uses a sorting machine, which actually sorts letter-by-letter.

The sorter will normally get words into good alphabetical listing by sorting only 4 or 5 columns of the author or title fields. It is not necessary or desirable to sort all the columns. In order to file any IBM card with two fields, such as author and title, one must sort for the secondary field first.   One could file by hand, as with ordinary catalog cards, but IBM cards are delicate and if nicked or dented will jam the machines.   Therefore they should not be handled any more than is necessary.   When one has made a machine sort by secondary and then by primary field, the whole must be printed out, examined and handsorted in those areas where library and machine filing do not agree.   One bonus reaped from the printed copy at this stage is that it also shows up lack of uniformity in entry, a factor which does not appear until the cards are sorted.

The following two pages, show samples of unrevised MACHINE sorting.   The author listing, page 267, was sorted for columns 12-16.   A double sort in the column order 33-37, 12-16 would still require handsorting under the letters G, R and T to make a perfect library-style file.   The title listing, page 268, was sorted for columns 33-37.   This then has to be handsorted to produce library-style filing.   The cards in both cases were originally in shelf list order, since they were keypunched directly from the shelf list.

Results

The immediate results of the short title printed catalog are now apparent.   The ordering of books already in the library has practically ceased.   Books not in the library are rarely assigned for reserve reading.   The faculty in the libraries which do not yet have printed catalogs are asking when they will have them.   Interlibrary loans to the industrial research libraries have increased.   There is a widespread demand for a list of scientific periodicals in

the whole library system, which can be satisfied, complete with holdings for each library, when the project of making short title catalogs is finished. A temporary, indicative list is being made in the interim.

Equipment and Costs

The machines used to make the short title printed catalog were:

Keypunch	IBM 026
Reproducer	IBM 519
Interpreter	IBM 557
Sorter	IBM 082
Tabulator	IBM 407

The cost of the Engineering Library catalog was:

Tabulating Center charges

Rental:	keypunch	$ 77.25
	interpreter	9.00
	reproducer	9.00
	sorter	23.25
	tabulator	27.75
Card stock		8.40
Paper		2.00
Advice and assistance		50.00
		$ 206.65

Library

Labor costs, student and staff   252.10

Print Shop

Printing and publishing 100 copies   279.00

Total $ 737.75

References

1. Vertanes, Charles A. "Automation raps at the door of the library catalog," Special Libraries, 52:237-42, 1961. Dr. Vertanes' LILCO catalog may be borrowed from the Special Libraries Association Loan Collection, School of Library Science, Western Reserve University, Cleveland 6, Ohio.

Research Problems in Book Catalogs*

By Maurice F. Tauber

Research in any aspect of librarianship requires the presence of interested personnel, availability of precious time, and sufficient support. Librarianship as a whole in the past has been characterized as a field in which there has been a minimum of interested and qualified personnel, a lack of specific correlated programs that are designed to overcome difficulties in particular areas, and the availability of funds. Moreover, it has been observed that lack of coordination in such library studies as have been made has resulted in a slowness in providing solutions to practical and pressing problems, and in not adding significantly to our knowledge of principles or guide lines for future procedures. Indeed, all of these criticisms may hold true, but even after admitting this, it is clear that if there is to be any progress in the profession, systematic research of important problems must be fostered and supported.

The development of research programs in more library schools, especially on the doctoral level, the availability of research funds from governmental and foundation sources, and the growing interest on the part of more persons in research, suggests that perhaps

* Some parts of this statement have been rephrased from Maurice F. Tauber, Cataloging and Classification (in The State of the Library Art, ed. by Ralph R. Shaw, vol. 1, pt. 1). New Brunswick: Graduate School of Library Service, Rutgers University, 1960, pp. 239-250.

more studies will be pursued in the future in the area of catalogs,
both card and book, and bibliography in general.   As the bibliography to this compilation of papers shows, there has been consideration given to several aspects of the book catalog, but the research
has been uncoordinated and sporadic. [1]

The literature reveals that there have been some studies in the
history, structure, costs, and uses of catalogs.   Some of these are
contained in this compilation, and others are referred to in the
bibliography at the close of the volume.   However, reference may
be made to two studies that show depth analyses that are not often
found in the literature.   James Ranz, in his History of the Printed
Book Catalog in the United States (Ph. D. dissertation, University of
Illinois, 1960), studies the early development of book catalogs in
America; and Fred Heinritz, in his Book versus Card Catalog Costs
(Ph. D. dissertation, Rutgers University, 1963) examines the question of whether the book or card form of the catalog was the
cheaper to produce, distribute, and use.

In general, it appears that there is a great need for a detailed study of the large card catalog in American libraries in order
to define its present problems, to describe the conditions it presents to efficient administration and users, and to point up the possibilities for the future records, particularly in respect to book
catalogs.   Ordinarily, it would appear that studies in the field of
book catalogs might be concerned with the following areas:

1.   Analysis of library materials:
    a. The present practices in recording materials received by
       libraries (the nature of bibliographical controls, e.g.,

(1) card catalogs, (2) book catalogs, and (3) other
records.)

b. An exhaustive study of printed book catalogs, including
those (1) developed for particular libraries, (2) developed
for particular collections, and (3) developed for special
fields.

c. An analysis of the structure of such catalogs in terms of
cataloging procedure and classification.

d. A study of foreign catalogs in terms of scope and coverage.

e. Analysis of card catalogs in relation to printed book catalogs.

2. Recording of the analysis:

a. The relation of the dictionary card catalog to the printed
book catalog as an intermediate step.

b. The problem of supplements to the book catalog (regional
or branch library systems, large research libraries with
departmental and professional school libraries).

3. Administrative matters:

a. The practicality of converting card catalogs, or sections
of them, to book catalogs, on an individual library basis
(large research libraries) or as joint operations (libraries
of a particular region).

b. The relation of the practicality of maintenance of the card
catalog in its various parts (e.g., author entries, subject
entries, and other entries) to generally available bibliographical tools, such as The National Union Catalog.

c. The consideration of the card catalog in respect to major
problems of physical maintenance, e.g. editing, revising,
and rehabilitation.

4. Cataloging and classification procedures:

a. A full-scale synthesis of the operations of centralized and
cooperative cataloging, with the consideration of the emer-
gence of book catalogs generally or in special areas.

b. The relation of international cataloging rules to the estab-

lishment of national bibliographies on a standard or uniform basis, leading to easier correlation of entries in
book catalogs.

    c. The relationship of book catalogs to union catalogs.

Undoubtedly, the new attention to book catalogs has represented
the turning of a circle in American library thought in respect to
the recording of materials in libraries. Some libraries, such as
that of the British Museum, has continued over a long period of
time with the book catalog as the basic instrument for revealing
holdings. The examination of questions related to the book catalog
would undoubtedly provide the type of guidance that librarians need
today in their search for making contents of their collections easily
and quickly, as well as economically, available to their users.

Perhaps a fruitful approach would be for major libraries in cooperation with graduate library schools to support needed investiga-
tions. A step in this direction is currently under investigation between The New York Public Library and the Columbia University
School of Library Service.

References

1. Maurice F. Tauber. Cataloging and Classification (in The
    State of the Library Art, ed. by Ralph R. Shaw, vol. 1, pt. 1)
    pp. 7-11. Reference is made to several studies of historical
    aspects of book catalogs, e.g., those by Dorothy M. Norris,
    Ruth F. Strout, Julia Pettee, Beverley Ruffin, Ruth Schley, and
    Sarah R. Corcoran.

Selected Bibliography

Note: Items reprinted or published for the first time in this volume are not included in the bibliography. The bibliography is not intended to be exhaustive, and does not include all items contained in the "References" at the ends of papers.

Alvord, Dorothy. "King County Public Library Does it with IBM."
Pacific Northwest Library Association Quarterly, 16:123-32,
Apr. 1952.

Andersen, S. B. "En god katalog." Bogens verden, 33:406-7, Nov.,
1951.

Besterman, Theodore. "Library of Congress and the Future of its
Catalogue." Journal of Documentation, 1:194-205, Mar., 1946.

"British Museum Catalog in Photolithographic Edition." Library
Journal, 86:68, Jan. 1, 1961.

Coney, Donald. "Librarian and the Catalog." ALA Bulletin, 29:
593-7, Sept., 1935.

Cutler, Dorothy. "The Columbia River Regional Library Demonstration." Library Resources and Technical Services, 2:181-2,
Summer, 1958.

David, C. W. "Proposed Expansion of the Library of Congress
Catalog--Books: Authors, into a Current National Union Catalog.
A Symposium." College and Research Libraries, 17:24-80,
Jan., 1956.

---- "The Reproduction of the National Union Catalog." College
and Research Libraries, 15:20-26, Jan., 1954.

Dewey, Harry. "Punched Card Catalogs: Theory and Technique."
American Documentation, 10:36-50, Jan., 1959.

"Duopage Process Converts Card Catalogs to Book Form." Library
Journal, 86:3761, Nov. 1, 1961.

Egger, Eugen. "Gesamtkataloge; Aufbau und Organisation eines
Gesamtkataloges im hinblick auf die Benutzung." Libri 6, no.

2:97-107, 1956.

Francis, F.C. "The British Museum Catalogue." Library Review, no. 121:18-21, Spring, 1957.

---- "The New Catalogue of the British Museum." Wilson Library Bulletin, 32:44, 46, Sept., 1957.

Griffin, Marjorie. "Printed Book Catalogs." Special Libraries, 51:496-9, Nov., 1960.

Gull, C.D. "The Cumulative Catalog Technique at the Library of Congress." American Documentation, 2:131-41, Aug., 1951.

---- "Substitutes for the Card Catalog." In Taube, Mortimer. Studies in Coordinate Indexing. Washington, Documentation, Inc., 1953. p. 77-95.

Also appeared in: Library Trends, 2:318-29, Oct., 1953.

Heinritz, Fred. Book versus Card Catalog (Ph.D. dissertation, Rutgers University, 1963).

Henkle, H.H. and others. "Symposium on the 'Library of Congress and the Future of Its Catalogue.'" Journal of Documentation, 2:245-54, Mar., 1947.

Hjartøy, H.J. "Bibliotekkataloger og bibliografier." Bok og biblio tek, 15:156-61, June, 1948.

Ho, W. "Card Catalog and the Book Catalog." In Chinese. In: Kiangsu sheng-li Soochow t'u-shu-kuan nien-k'an. (Annual of the Provincial Kiangsu Library of Soochow), 1936. p. 1-16.

Jackson, J.B. "Loose-leaf Printed Catalogue." Library Association Record, 57:470-3, Dec., 1955.

MacDonald, M.R. "The Army Medical Library Author Catalog, 1950." Bulletin of the Medical Library Association, 39:102-4, Apr., 1951.

McNiff, P.J. "Lamont Catalogue; Catalogue of the Lamont Library, Harvard College." I.L.A. Record; Journal of the Illinois Library Association, 7:56-9, Jan., 1954.

MacQuarrie, Catherine. "IBM Book Catalog." Library Journal, 82:630-4, Mar. 1, 1957.

Metcalf, K.D., and Osborn, A.D. "Proposal for Publishing the National Union Catalog." College and Research Libraries, 17:36-40, Jan., 1956.

Muller, R. H. "Lamont Catalogue; Implications of the Lamont Library Catalogue for College Libraries." I. L. A. Record; Journal of the Illinois Library Association, 7:59-62, Jan., 1954.

"New Book Catalogue in the National Library, Paris." UNESCO Bulletin for Libraries, 15:169-70, May, 1961.

Philip, A. J. The Production of the Printed Catalogue. London, Atkinson, 1910.

Pierrot, R. "Le nouveau supplement au catalogue général des livres imprimés de la Bibliothèque nationale." Association des Bibliothécaires Français, Bulletin d'informations, 34:7-9, Mar., 1961.

Rafikov, A. Kh. "Printed Catalogues and Bibliographical Indexes of China's Libraries." LLU Translations Bulletin, Dept. of Scientific & Industrial Research, London, p. 1-4, Aug., 1959.

Ranz, James. History of the Printed Book Catalog in the United States. Thesis, (Ph. D. dissertation, University of Illinois, 1960), 326 p.

Rider, Fremont. "Alternatives for the Present Dictionary Card Catalog." In: Randall, W. M., ed. Acquisition and Cataloging of Books. Chicago, University of Chicago press, 1940. p. 133-62.

---- "Possibility of Discarding the Card Catalog." Library Quarterly, 8:329-45, June, 1938.

Rogers, F. B. "Army Medical Library Catalog, 1951." Journal of Cataloging and Classification, 8:150-2, Dec., 1952.

Schwegmann, G. A., Jr. "The Rationale, Planning and Technique of the Published National Union Catalog." American Documentation, 8:296-9, Oct., 1959.

Spitzer, E. F. "Printed Subject Catalog for an Industrial Research Library." Special Libraries, 32:261-3, Sept., 1941.

Tauber, Maurice F., and Associates. Technical Services in Libraries. New York, Columbia University Press, 1957. p. 109-10; 118.

Taylor, Archer. Book Catalogues; Their Varieties and Uses. Chicago, The Newberry Library, 1957. 284 p.

Teague, S. J. "Printed Catalogues." Library Association Record,

53:92, Mar., 1951.

Vertanes, C. A. "Automation raps at the door of the library catalog." Special Libraries, 52:237-42, May, 1961.

Vollans, R. F. The Published Booklist and the Exploitation of Stock. I. Printed catalogues. Bibliography and Book Stock, London and Home Counties Branch of the Library Association. London, 1954. p. 25-33.

Wilson, Angus. "New Catalogue for British Museum Library." Canadian Library, 17:182-3, Jan., 1961.

Wood, A. F. "Large Dictionary Catalog Faces Der Tag." ALA Cataloging and Classification Yearbook, 8:39-42. Chicago, American Library Association, 1939. Abridged in: ALA Bulletin, 33:104-5, Oct. 15, 1939.

Appendix A

California State Library

Union Catalog Workshop

Held in Sacramento
February 13-14, 1963

Summary or Proceedings

Recorder: Mrs. Elizabeth Bruno
Editor, California State
Library Union Catalog

Revised June 1963

Sacramento, California
1963

California State Library
Union Catalog Workshop

February 13, 1963   Room 166, Dept. of Education Building

1:00 P.M.   Welcome to the Union Catalog Workshop
            Mrs. Carma R. Leigh, California State Librarian.

            Mrs. Phyllis I. Dalton, Presiding

            Conversion of Card Catalogs to Book Form
1:10 P.M.   Conversion of State Library Union Catalog to book
            form--how this project would vitally affect the develop-
            ment of library cooperation in California.
            Mrs. Bertha Hellum

1:40 P.M.   Description of Union Catalog in relation to conversion.
            Mel Oathout

2:00 P.M.   Methods of making the conversion.
            Mrs. Catherine MacQuarrie

2:30 P.M.   A discussion of how three libraries might adapt to a
            book catalog.   Panel: Fred Wemmer, Margaret Fulmer
            and Eleanor Wilson. Mrs. Phyllis Dalton, Moderator.

3:15 P.M.   Discussion of the conversion problem.   Resource Panel:
            Mr. Patrinostro, Mrs. MacQuarrie, Mrs. Hellum.

            Centralized Cataloging and Cooperative Use of Machine Records
4:00 P.M.   Initiation and use of centralized cataloging by the
            Econolist Company to furnish individual and Union book
            catalogs.
            Mrs. Catherine MacQuarrie

4:30 P.M. -
5:00 P.M.   Steps MVT is prepared to take to initiate centralized
            cataloging.
            Mr. John Shaw, President MVT Industries

            Dinner (Restaurant list available)

                    * * * * * * * * * *

7:00 P. M.   Discussion of the Econolist system for conversion of
              present records to book form on individual cooperative
              basis; and the use of Econolist records in a central-
              ized cataloging system.
                   Mr. Frank Patrinostro

7:45 P. M.   Open discussion on the Econolist system and central-
              ized cataloging.   Resource panel: Mr. Patrinostro,
              Mrs. MacQuarrie, Mrs. Hellum

8:30 P. M. -
 9:00 P. M.   Inventory of interest

State Library Union Catalog Workshop
Summary of Proceedings

Present: The Administration of the State Library, contributors
to the California Union Catalog, some observers from
other libraries, Miss Dorothy Doyle of Washington
State Library, Mrs. Brigitte Kenney of Mississippi,
and from the Econolist Division of MVT, Los Angeles,
Frank Patrinostro, General Manager; Robert Sage,
Production Manager; John Shaw, President of MVT In-
dustries; Cleet Ganning, Data Processing Specialist,
and James Hardy, Data Processing Specialist.

Seventy-eight people were in attendance.

The workshop met in the Department of Education Building on
Wednesday, and a smaller group in the State Library on Thursday.

Wednesday, February 13.

In her opening speech, Mrs. Carma Leigh, State Librarian, gave
four arguments for book catalogs as opposed to card catalogs:

Patrons and librarians find the books easier to work with.
The sweep of entries one after another, visible on the
printed page, gives a more instantaneous idea of the contents of the catalog.

Books can be carried to convenient work areas.

In Book Selection, the subject index is a valuable aid to

282

point up strengths and weaknesses, and catalogs can be used in conjunction with reviewing media.

Mrs. Phyllis Dalton, Assistant State Librarian, took the chair and introduced the speakers.

A. Conversion of Union Catalog to Book Format; Use of Los Angeles County Cards for Basis of This Conversion and That of Individual California Libraries' Catalogs.

1. Conversion of the State Library Union Catalog to book format - how this project would vitally affect the development of library cooperation in California. Mrs. Bertha Hellum, County Librarian, Contra Costa County.

Mrs. Hellum listed the following eight advantages:

a. Multiple copies of a book catalog are more flexible to use than a card catalog as more than one searcher can be working in the same area at the same time.

b. Readers' Services will be improved. Several sets of book catalogs could be placed at the circulation desk and other service points where needed.

c. Patrons will know what is available in other libraries and in the State Library. Speeding up the borrowing process will satisfy borrowers who now are no longer interested by the time a book arrives - this is about 50% of them.

d. Each library will have a record of all the titles in the system, instead of only those in its own stock.

e. The book selection committee, with a subject catalog in front of them, can better judge the areas that need strengthening.

f. Personnel time in technical services will be cut down. A time-cost study needs to be made. At least one year of parallel cataloging will have to be done, so that if book cataloging does not prove economical, the card catalog will be there to continue its function.

g. The possibility of spreading the knowledge of the contents of the catalog is great. Complaints have been received from such persons as the Executive Director of the Taxpayers' Association that the library does not give back in terms of service what taxpayers put into it in terms of money. Book catalogs would help prevent such criticism.

h. Teachers making school assignments can consult a copy of their local county library catalog placed in their school library, before deciding on subjects to assign.

2. Description of the Union Catalog in relation to conversion. Mr. Mel Oathout, Chief, Technical Services Division, State Library.

Mr. Oathout described the physical set-up of the Union Catalog and enumerated the operations necessary to get the file in order; namely, complete consolidation of duplicates onto master cards, supplying of necessary added entries, and checking of present indicated locations of the titles against holdings of member libraries to correct inaccuracies.

This last operation could be carried out in conjunction with the conversion of the Union Catalog by Econolist. The firm could distribute proofsheets of a preliminary edition, showing no locations, to member libraries, who would check against

284

their holdings, and return the proofsheets together with cards for titles they hold but which are not listed. These returns could be amalgamated and a correct bank of machine cards compiled, from which the first conversion of the Union Catalog would be printed. This first master bank could also be used by member libraries or others to have catalogs for their own stock retrieved and printed separately.

3. Methods of making the conversion. Mrs. Catherine MacQuarrie, Chief, Technical Services Division, Los Angeles County Library.

Mrs. MacQuarrie's proposals for the conversion of the present Union Catalog into a book catalog are essentially the same as those of Mr. Oathout. The copy run off by Econolist would have Author, title, edition, publisher, date, and for classics, editor and perhaps illustrator (enough to identify each title). The first run would be in proofsheet form or in the cheapest form possible. Copy would be prepared for each participant or member of the Union Catalog, and perhaps for other libraries who asked to become members, and sent to them letter by letter for checking against their holdings. The conversion of the card catalogs of individual libraries or groups of libraries to book format could be done in any of five ways:

a. Share the work Los Angeles County Library has already done in the development of book catalogs. Each library could check its catalog against the author catalog of Los Angeles County; prepare control cards (A control card is

285

essentially the same as a main entry card except for a
slight rearrangement of the information.) for entries that
are not in the Los Angeles County collection; and send the
new control cards to Econolist for inclusion. When the
library had the same books as Los Angeles County but
cataloged differently, the library could either revise its
cataloging to conform to the Los Angeles practice or make
a note that in this library the entry is classed in _____;
or the book is entered under _____ (author), and make
a cross-reference from the entry used in that library.

b. An individual library that preferred its own practices could
make its control cards from its card catalog; revise and
check them for correctness and consistency; make code
cards for subject headings; proof and make all corrections
needed. In other words, make a catalog for that library
from start to finish. It would be more costly than to share
and cooperate with other libraries.

c. Some libraries may prefer to start with a partial conversion to book catalogs, leaving the card catalog as it is,
making no additions to it from a specific date on starting
with printed book supplements as of that date and having
the firm do all the cataloging, etc., from then on. After
5 years or so, withdrawals having been done as usual, the
original card catalog would have shrunk enough to make its
conversion economical as presumably by this time, the
books still listed in the card catalog are the important ones
that will always be retained in the library.

d. Conversion for a large library with a central research collection. There are several possible variations of book and card catalogs that could be developed.

   1. Retain a complete card catalog for the central collection and use book catalogs in the branches.

   2. Have a complete union book catalog of all holdings at central with the book catalogs for the branches including only titles found in branch collections. Some subject bibliographies made from the complete holdings could also be used.

   3. Library with subject departments - prepare book catalogs of the books in each specific subject field according to the departmental specializations, with complete union catalogs for the branches.

   4. Complete union catalog for both branches and for central.

e. If groups of libraries wanted to use the Los Angeles County master deck, they could check Los Angeles County's Author Catalog against their holdings, each library entering its symbol in front of the titles held. The marked titles would be sorted out and a union catalog made. If each library in the group wanted an individual author catalog, this could be done from cards in their union catalog, sorting by the code number for that library.

The point to be emphasized is that Book Catalogs are flexible and can be made to fit the needs of the library.

4. A panel discussion of how three libraries might adapt to a book catalog. Three libraries, Sacramento County, Kern

County and Whittier Public, have had copies of Los Angeles County's most recent author supplements, adult and juvenile, and based their observations on a comparison of these with their card catalogs.

Mr. Fred Wemmer, County Librarian, Sacramento County, said the major advantage of book catalogs was that each outlet would have a copy or copies of the holdings of the whole system. A single card at headquarters would act as master, shelf list, etc. Mr. Wemmer was so eager to get the project under way that he has already budgeted $60,000 for it.

Miss Eleanor Wilson, County Librarian, Kern County, found a sufficiently large discrepancy between class numbers assigned by Los Angeles County, and their own, to raise a problem. If the Los Angeles County numbers were used, many books would have to have their class numbers changed. Also, subject headings were different. The obstacles were not insurmountable, and Miss Wilson thought Econolist catalogs would be a great help, especially in equalizing service. (Later on in the discussion we were informed that a library that used Los Angeles County Econolist cards could have a line of information added to follow any of the Los Angeles cards, which would contain the class number on the author entry used in that library if it differed from the Los Angeles entry. There would be very little extra cost for this.)

Mr. Eric Teel, Chief, Technical Services Division of Whittier Public Library, said that cataloging was the most expensive part of technical services; technical services staff at Whittier was in favor of change, Readers' services not so enthusiastic. All wanted the State Union Catalog in book form.

During the discussion period Mrs. Alice Reilly, County Librarian of Fresno, pointed out another advantage of Econolist subject catalogs, namely that subject bibliographies could be run off or Xerox'd for patrons. Also, the full cataloging of the book catalogs would enable assistants even at the smallest outlets to verify requests and get them bibliographically correct. Mrs. Kent pointed out that branch collections of county systems should not make catalogs with locations within the system, as locations changed continually. Headquarters should have a record of the location of each title, and closed-circuit teletype provide rapid information.

Mr. Cleet Ganning of Econolist described the technical aspects of programming and coding. A master deck of cards consists of IBM cards, each with only one line of information in the form of print on it. * Other information is coded into the cards, such as subject interest, location, class number, serial number within the deck, and all cards with the same information can be retrieved in one operation, and printed up. Then the information can be transferred to magnetic tape. This tape can communicate with the typed cards, and pick out the specific symbol or number of any specific library or group of libraries, from the typed card. The tape can rearrange material and decide on the number of printed pages

* Cards with 2 or even three lines of print can be used.

needed to print up the material it has selected. It can scan the whole collection of cards, and then proceed to draw up lists, as instructed. The more cards there are in the decks the more information can be retrieved. Therefore, as the decks of cards are built up and more libraries join the system all members can share the information that they have in common. Thus, each library will have to have fewer cards made for it individually and its costs will correspondingly be less per unit. One master deck made from the Union Catalog will theoretically contain every title held by every participating library. If any of these libraries want catalogs of their own collections, the master cards are already coded for these libraries, and the only cost for preparing individual catalogs would be the cost of retrieval, printing and binding.

B. Centralized Cataloging and Co-Operative Use of Machine Records.

1. Initiation and use of centralized cataloging by the Econolist Company to furnish individual union book catalogs. Mrs. Mac-Quarrie. If several libraries decide to start book catalogs, they can also start co-operative cataloging of all new titles added to their collection. The Econolist Company proposes to do the professional cataloging if enough libraries are interested. Each library placing an order for a new title would send a copy of the order to Econolist, which would, by return mail, (if the title is already in the Econolist deck) send back one catalog control card complete with classification number and tracings for each title ordered. When the library's copies of the ordered titles arrived, the library would process

the books from the information on the control card. Each library could continue to process its books according to its own system - a clerical job. If any of the titles ordered were not yet in the Econolist deck, Econolist would catalog the copy which they would receive from a Greenaway plan program. For titles not received through subscription, Econolist could request that the library send one copy to them for cataloging. These would be mainly local items and specialized or foreign books. A flat charge would be made per title, and would depend on the number of participants. As all titles new to the library, new books, rare items, municipal and county publications and local items would be cataloged by Econolist, which would catalog in depth and detail, the result would be a unified, finished product that would be used both for the individual library's catalogs and for the Union Catalog.

2. Steps Econolist Company is prepared to take to initiate centralized cataloging. <u>Mr. John Shaw, of Econolist.</u>

Mr. Shaw described setting up a Department of Cataloging, with 4-5 professional catalogers, and dwelt especially on the speed with which they would be able to supply catalog cards and book catalogs. With Los Angeles County, they supply the supplements complete (adult author, title, subject, and fiction and children's author, title, subject) eleven days following the end of the period covered by each supplement. Mr. Shaw also pointed out how much libraries could economize on their professional staff with this system.

3. Discussion of the Econolist system for conversion of present

291

records to book form on individual basis and on a co-operative basis; and the use of Econolist records in centralized cataloging.   Mr. Frank Patrinostro of Econolist.

The proposal is to convert the State Union Catalog to bound book volumes in the form of an Authors' Index.   Each entry would indicate the exact location or locations of the listed title among the libraries contributing to the Union Catalog.   Once the master deck of machine cards had been created, the cards for titles held by any particular library could be readily sorted out by data processing equipment to effect a bound Authors' Index for that library.

For those titles in the Union Catalog which are also held by the Los Angeles County system, the machine cards could be retrieved to convert individual catalogs for Subject, Title, Fiction and Juvenile indexes from the master files already composed for the Los Angeles System.

Another major proposal is the adding of current titles to the Union Catalog in book form through centralized cataloging by an Econolist Division of the current volumes received by member libraries.

Since the most feasible and economical application of the Econolist system to bound book catalogs is a uniformity in classification, annotations, subject headings, etc., Econolist proposes to set up a Cataloging Division which would consist of recognized and highly skilled catalogers whose cataloging procedures would be determined by a coordinating committee of libraries participating.   (The coordinating committee - Catalog

292

Advisory Committee - has been appointed and is working on standards.)

The Los Angeles County deck could be used as a basis for current work, if Los Angeles County authorities give their permission, which they have not granted so far because it has not yet been cleared through the County Counsel as to its legality. By joint exercise of power other county libraries might make contracts with them.

It was pointed out finally that co-operation and the abandoning of individual preferences in cataloging practices were pre-requisites for centralized cooperative cataloging as a project. If the firm did the cataloging for participating libraries as of a certain date, there would be uniformity with resultant lower costs for all material acquired after that date; older material can then be brought in gradually. The newer material would have classification numbers, the older not. The Union Book Catalog made from State Union Catalog would have holding location symbols only, as its major use would be for inter-library loan.

C. Inventory of Interest by Member Libraries.

Members present were then asked, were they interested in having the State Union Catalog converted to book form, and, were they interested in centralized cataloging.

Library	Conversion of UC	Centralized cataloging
Alameda Co.	yes	yes
Butte	curious	Proc Center
Berkeley	interested	
Contra Costa	yes	yes
El Dorado	yes	yes
Fresno	yes	yes
Inyo	yes	yes
Kern	yes	yes
Lassen	yes	yes
Los Angeles County	yes	yes
Los Angeles Public	yes - 10-25 copies	no
Mississippi River (visitor)	yes	
Marin	yes	NBC
Mill Valley	yes	NBC
Monterey	yes	yes
Orange	yes	curious
Placer	yes	yes
Plumas	yes	Proc Center
Porterville	yes	yes
Napa	yes	NBC
Richmond	yes	don't know
San Bernardino	yes	no ?
San Diego	yes	needs further study
San Francisco	can't say	curious
San Luis Obispo	yes	yes, conditionally
San Mateo	yes	yes, conditionally
Solano	yes	NBC
Sonoma	yes	NBC
Stanislaus	yes	don't know
Sutter	yes	Proc Center
Tehama	yes	yes, conditionally
Ventura	yes	yes
Yolo	yes	yes, conditionally

Agenda

A. Conversion of existing catalogs to Book Format.
 1. Methods used by Econolist to effect the conversion of card catalogs to book form. Bob Sage, Production Manager of Econolist.

 2. Planning and preparatory work needed by each library that is converting. Mrs. MacQuarrie.

 3. Cost analysis of conversion by the Econolist system. Mr. Patrinostro.

 4. Cost analysis from the library point of view. Bill Davis, Budget Analyst of the Chief Administrative office. Discussion by other budget officers present.

B. Centralized Cataloging
 1. Cooperative cataloging possibilities as a cost saving in connection with these projects.

 2. Possible time table for the development of these projects. Mr. Patrinostro.

 3. Summing up of action to be taken.

The meeting on the 14th was limited to libraries actively interested in the book catalog project.

A. Conversion of Existing Catalogs to Book Format.

 1. Methods used by Econolist to effect the conversion of card catalogs to book form. Mr. Robert Sage, Production Manager of Econolist.

 Mr. Sage described the mechanical process used by his firm. There are eight steps:

 1. Lay-out and plotting: determining what the page will look like, the types to be used, length of line, etc.

 2. Receipt of information. The library control cards are received; they are just like ordinary 5 x 3 catalog cards, only the information is arranged slightly differently.

3. Proofreading. The cards are processed through a camera to make a proof. (Sample given.) Content and quality are checked. Errors are corrected and incorrect cards pulled from the deck. Correct cards substituted.

4. Data processing stage. Each card gets sequence numbers. This is for automatic filing, retrieval, abc'ing, pulling of information.

5. Check for completeness is made and cards are arranged in pages. Special counting machines arrange cards so that no entry overruns a column. Page number cards are inserted, and this separates the one group of cards into smaller groups, as many as there will be pages in the book.

6. Econolist card sequence camera now used and a strip negative for each page results. This negative is used for printing.

7. The strip is cut in two and spliced to make a two-column page.

8. Type is set off the negative, the pages are printed, picked up, bound and dispatched. Printing is done on a two-sided platen that takes 16 pages on each side, so that 32 pages are printed simultaneously.

The making of a supplement. Once the master deck has been made, a supplementary deck builds up for the supplements; at the end of the cumulating period, the supplement deck is interfiled with the master deck. At this point withdrawals and other corrections are made. If the Union Catalog is cumulated

296

once every four years only, it will be necessary to publish a separate withdrawals list periodically.

The master films are kept in a fireproof vault, so that if the master deck is accidentally destroyed, it can be built up again. This is covered by insurance. All libraries who wish can have one control card, 5 x 3, sent for each title, and so maintain one file, to be used as master file or shelf list.

2. Planning and preparatory work needed by each library that is converting. Mrs. MacQuarrie.

The contributors to the Union had to make some basic decisions.

a. Should all titles and all of the contributions of the present Union Catalog be included in the project (juvenile titles, contributions of the University of California only)?

b. What should be the frequency of publication and cumulation? Format?

Annual supplements with 5 years cumulations?

c. Degree of bibliographic data - finding list versus complete information useful to scholars?

d. Should the finished product be available to contributors only? or, should other libraries be allowed to participate, or could copies be sold on a subscription basis? Public libraries only?

Many school and college libraries make heavy use of Inter-library loan through the present Union Catalog.

The meeting was in favor of University of California (and presumably, Harvard, Michigan, Chicago and Wesleyan) holdings being excluded from the printed Union Catalog. Cataloging should be in depth, very thorough, more so than present Library of Congress cataloging. This saves staff time later. Frequency should be four-yearly; that is, a basic set will be issued, then three annual cumulations, each cumulating the previous annual or annuals, and in the fifth year, a new cumulated basic set. The physical format should be quarto, thick, case bound.

Mrs. MacQuarrie repeated the process through which present Union Catalog holdings could be checked by member libraries, as described the previous day, and pointed out that added entries should be added to the catalog when the collation of members' returns is completed and before the first set is printed.

A feasibility study of the maximum number of locations to be given for any one entry, should be made.

When the master deck was completed and coded for member libraries, the machine could extract cards for the holdings of any of the members (or for additional libraries that joined and marked their holdings on the preliminary copy of the catalog) and print up catalogs for these libraries, of their own holdings only, without Union Catalog location listings. An added line could give an individual library's call number.

Financing was a difficult subject. If the State Aid Bill passes CLA and SL would request all the 210 public libraries in the state to apply for a portion of the aid to finance their participation in the conversion of the Union Catalog and then each library could get book catalogs for their own collections. The question of the purchase of the Juvenile Catalog of Los Angeles County in book form was raised by participants of the meeting. Mr. Shaw said that if Los Angeles County was willing, Econolist would estimate the price of various quantities desired and send the estimates to the libraries.

The following libraries indicated a desire to purchase the Los Angeles County Juvenile Catalog in book form: Ventura County, Kern County, Contra Costa, Fresno County, Stanislaus, and Sacramento County. The number of copies varied but 100 was a common figure. The libraries also indicated to Mr. Shaw when they would require the estimates of cost in order to put the amounts in their budgets. He agreed to meet these deadlines.

3. Cost analysis of conversion by the Econolist system. <u>Mr. Patrinostro.</u>

The following is a summary of figures quoted. Mr. Patrinostro made it clear that these figures should in no wise be thought of as final.

<u>The Union Catalog.</u> Five year costs: If the present Catalog is converted and updated annually, it would cost $1,055,995. If it is converted and updated every four years, with three annual cumulations, the basic set with three annual cumulations, would cost $646,024.

The pattern would be as follows:

1963	14 thick quarto volumes, case bound	$ 327,995
1964	1-volume supplement	19,316
1965	2-volume supplement	36,300
1966	3-volume supplement	48,513
1967	19 thick quarto volumes	213,900

These figures are based on 800,000 titles (i.e. excluding the University titles), author listing only.

Individual catalogs.   A library of 50,000 titles, retrieving from the above master file, which contains everything it has, would pay $9,500 for basic volume plus monthly supplements made of new receipts. If lines of information are added, the cost would be $10,500.   In reply to a question, Mr. Patrinostro said that he could not say what the costs would be for such libraries if they were allowed to use the Los Angeles County deck.   On Wednesday he had given some figures, but now he would rather work it out for individual libraries, as differences were too great to generalize.   At this point a count was asked, of how many libraries would want to use Los Angeles County's cards, if they were made available:

	Size of library	
Stanislaus County	60,000 titles	90% held in common with Los Angeles County
Fresno County	100,000	50
Ventura County	60,000	75
Contra Costa	90,000	50
Kern	90,000	50
Sacramento	50,000	50 (not sure)

The libraries estimated they held about 90% the same titles.

4. Cost analysis from the library point of view. Bill Davis, Budget Analyst of the Chief Administrative Office, Los Angeles County.

Mrs. MacQuarrie read Mr. Davis' paper.

Los Angeles County changed over to IBM book catalogs in 1952, and now has its entire holdings on IBM cards. There were card catalogs in 28 of its 115 branches. At the 1952 level it cost the County $78,611 annually to maintain these 28 card catalogs. If all branches were to be provided with card catalogs, it would cost $400,000 plus. (1952 cost figures.) Comparing the card and book forms, the Administrative Office found the book catalog better because it provided equal and complete records to all users of the library system, enabled patrons to know to what kind of materials they had free access, described these materials in a more understandable form than card catalogs do, made foreign holdings available to foreign language reading patrons, expanded the use of the collection through enlargement of use of added entries, gave reading levels by age and grade in the annotations in the children's catalog.

Although the expense of changing from IBM to Econolist was high, the Administrative Office sanctioned it in view of future advances (progressively cheaper work over IBM product) and the advantage that IBM print consisting of capitals only is very trying to read, and Econolist used variable sizes and fonts of print. The saving in space was also substantial. At question time Mrs. MacQuarrie told of a further economy: if Econolist takes over all their cataloging, they would free 14 positions in the Catalog Division. There was no further discussion of Mr. Davis' paper.

B. Centralized Cataloging

1. Co-operative cataloging possibilities as a cost saving in connection with these projects. Direct savings were those of the
   salaries of the personnel of cataloging sections in libraries
   participating. Indirect savings were:

   1. Reference and Branch research time is saved, as catalog-
      ing will always be at a high level in the new catalog.

   2. Catalogers who do nothing but this type of cataloging do a
      far better job.

   3. Space, time and equipment are saved.

   4. There is no backlog of cataloging.

   5. The ordinary and extraordinary cataloging of each library
      will be included, because if libraries close down their own
      cataloging sections, gifts, rare items, etc. will be sent to
      the firm to catalog.

   For ordinary cataloging libraries will send Econolist copies of
   their order slips as mailed, or cumulated weekly or monthly.
   If there is a master card in Econolist files, as was described
   earlier, a copy will go to the library immediately, and its
   name coded onto the master card. Otherwise the firm would
   do a special job of cataloging each new title.

   The Catalog Advisory Committee to be appointed would set the
   Standards and would ensure that Econolist Cataloging met
   these Standards. Mr. Shaw pointed out that they would have
   to make a cost analysis study and get much more information
   before they could start giving final cost figures for cataloging.
   He mentioned $2.00 per title as a possible starting cost if 7

302

or more libraries participated.

2. A possible time table for the development of these projects.

   <u>Mr. Patrinostro.</u>

   Econolist would need six months to complete the initial conversion of the present Union Card Catalog, once their organization was set up. It would not be entirely possible to have the whole Union Catalog available for consultation at all times during this period, as boxes of cards would constantly be traveling between Sacramento and Los Angeles.

   It was pointed out to the firm that checking of proofslips by member libraries was going to take more time than they perhaps realized, and could not be looked upon as a short term project.

   If the State Aid Bill passes, money for the conversion might be available by January 1. If not, steps to secure the permission of the Los Angeles County to use their deck of cards would be initiated.

3. Summing up of action to be taken.

   The meeting felt that it could not sum up action to be taken, and appointed a four-man committee to go into the details of planning.

<u>The Committee*</u>

      Mrs. C. MacQuarrie of Los Angeles County, Chairman
      Mrs. C. Chadwick of Ventura County
      Mrs. A. Reilly of Fresno County
      Miss E. Wilson of Kern County

The Workshop closed at 4 o'clock.

* Mr. Oathout was later added to the committee as an ex-officio member.

Subsequent Action

Committee to Plan for the Preparation of the State Union Catalog
in Book Form

The Committee met at Ventura and again at Fresno to discuss:

1. Extending the Union Catalog to include all public libraries
   in California that are interested in becoming members.
   Now limited to 64 members. There are approximately
   220 public libraries.

2. Limiting the coverage to holdings of public libraries.

3. Excluding federal and state documents as they are adequately indexed and can readily be obtained from the
   State Library.

4. Including local documents that are cataloged.

5. Including juvenile titles. This is a point that is not decided as this type of material, except rare books or
   classics, is seldom requested for interlibrary loan.

The Committee also obtained cost figures for the production of
such catalogs.

Committee members have also consented to give talks when requested to groups of librarians in the state discussing the State
Union Catalog Project and familiarizing librarians with it so that
when funds become available we will have the backing of the interested libraries.

A second follow-up committee was appointed to act as a Catalog Advisory Committee to work with the firm that is to do the centralized cataloging for libraries participating in book catalog projects.
The membership of this committee is:

Chairman and consultant - Catherine MacQuarrie

Catalogers
    Chief, Technical Services, Ventura County - Elizabeth Hurt-
        chison
    Chief, Technical Services, State Library - Mel Oathout
    Chief, Technical Services, Whittier Public Library - Eric
        Teel

304

Reference Librarians
    Senior Reference Librarian,   L. A. County - Rose Salem
    Reference Librarian, Contra Costa County - John Thayer

Library Administrator
    Monterey County - Lois Koolwyk

The Committee met at U. C. L. A. at the Southern District Meeting,
CLA.   The purposes and functions of the Committee are:

    To prepare Standards for cataloging, based on those used in
    Los Angeles County Public Library.   The Standards are
    mainly for public libraries in California for use by Econolist,
    who is to do Centralized Cataloging for the cooperating group;

    To maintain the above Standards by reviewing the Econolist
    Cataloging;

    To act as the intermediary between the participating libraries
    and Econolist to keep the cataloging responsive to the needs
    of the user libraries;

    To keep informed of future developments in cataloging and to
    incorporate those that are applicable into the above Standards.

The California State Aid bill, A. 590, has passed one house and is
now being studied in the Senate.

Appendix B

Book Catalogs and the Free Library of Philadelphia*

In Volume I, Part I, of the State of the Library Art, Maurice F. Tauber lists, as a suggested research project for the future, a "study of the practicality of converting card catalogs, or sections of them, to book catalogs, on an individual library basis."

For many years the card catalog has been accepted in this country as the most efficient and satisfactory means of displaying the holdings of a library. However, two developments of the comparatively recent past -- one in the library world and one in the printing industry -- have caused librarians to reconsider the merits of the book catalog.

One such development is the changing concept of library service and the growing recognition that this service must be supplied on a regional, rather than a local basis. The card catalog that is satisfactory for a single library proves awkward in format and expensive to maintain when (1) the holdings of a system of libraries, rather than a single library, are to be shown, and (2) the information regarding holdings must be made available over a wide geographical area.

In the printing industry revolutionary technological changes have made financially possible book catalogs which, only a short time ago, would have been prohibitive in cost.

*Supplement to D.A.C. Bulletin, dated August 17, 1962.

Today a number of library catalogs are being produced in book form. Probably the best known and most important book catalog, since the book catalog was rediscovered, is A Catalog of Books Represented by Library of Congress Printed Cards, which ultimately became The National Union Catalog. Among the public libraries which have adopted the book catalog the most notable are the King County Public Library in the State of Washington and the Los Angeles County Public Library.

Various kinds of equipment have been used in the preparation of book catalogs. I. B. M. equipment is used by some libraries including the Los Angeles County Public Library. In addition to a detailed report of Los Angeles County's experience, which appeared in the Summer 1960 issue of Library Resources and Technical Services, there is also a published account of the National Library of Medicine's index mechanization project using the Eastman-Kodak Listomatic camera.

In view of the unsolved problems in the Free Library and an important new development - the new regional library - it seemed advisable to study the book catalog at its present stage of development. For this reason, in June of 1961 a visit was made to the Los Angeles County Public Library and the I. B. M. Advanced Systems and Research Library in San Jose, California. Three thousand miles away and several weeks later it was concluded that the I. B. M. method was too cumbersome for the Free Library's purposes and that, if a better system was not at hand, it would be well to wait until it came along.

Los Angeles County's problems and those of the Free Library

are not identical. Since it is expected that, for the time being, a card catalog will be retained for the collections in the Central Library, a method of producing a book catalog from 3 x 5 cards seems desirable. The equipment mentioned above cannot accept 3 x 5 cards. Also, hand arranging of cards preparatory to photographing is an expensive step which, it is thought, should be done mechanically.

It now seems possible to demonstrate that there is equipment on the market which meets these requirements, although the equipment has, to date, not been used to produce a book catalog. To finance such a demonstration requires a budget and support for continuance.

The type of book catalog presently being considered is a catalog listing titles acquired after a given date by agencies of the Extension Division. It would be a dictionary catalog and would be in two alphabets, one for adult and young adult titles and one for children's books. The latter would be kept up to date with bi-monthly cumulative supplements and the former with monthly supplements. It is proposed that the present card catalog for the Northeast Regional Library form the basis of the initial book catalog.

The reader using such a catalog would, of course, find references to books other than those in the branch he is using. A reader's primary interest is in what is available. If a book he wishes to borrow is not on the shelf he is not concerned with whether a given branch owns it or not. He merely wishes to obtain the book. As at present, the reader would be asked to leave a reserve, and it would be the branch assistant who would determine whether the branch's own copy could be used to fill the reserve or whether a copy would have to be borrowed from another agency. That there would be an increase in this type of request seems indisputable but, on the other hand, the reader will be made aware of the larger resources at his disposal.

The book catalog is not viewed by anyone as a panacea. Its use would create problems as well as solve some. However, it is felt that the catalog in book form would encourage the use of catalog records by the public and perhaps enable the reader to help himself. It is frequently maintained that the general reader finds the card catalog a formidable obstacle in his search for books and that a book catalog, to quote Dean Shera, "looks good like a bibliography should." Also, at very little additional cost, copies of a book catalog could be deposited in offices and other locations remote from the card catalog, whether in the Free Library or in other organizations and institutions. Numerous other advantages relate to the reduction in the cost of housing, filing and editing some 83 catalogs throughout the Free Library System.

It is hoped that the Free Library will be given an opportunity to participate in this important new development, which has particular pertinency today when regional library service is being encouraged in Philadelphia and Pennsylvania and when the accessibility of all library materials has never been more important.

Margaret C. Brown

Free Library of Philadelphia

Extension Division

Catalog, May, 1963

Introduction

Card catalogs have long been standard equipment in all branch
libraries in the Free Library of Philadelphia. These catalogs
served adequately in the past, but, for several reasons, some of
which have only recently become apparent, they serve less well today.

First of all, the increase today in the use of all library materials means that information regarding the availability of material
in a library system, or in a metropolitan area, or even in a state
is frequently more important than knowledge of the contents of a
single, rather small collection.

Secondly, as Pennsylvania's program under the new Library
Code develops, the Free Library will be serving citizens of the
Commonwealth who reside outside the City of Philadelphia and who
have no convenient means of consulting the card catalogs in the Free
Library.

For these reasons the Free Library is planning to make available in book form catalog records previously furnished to branch
librarians in card form only.

Scope. This catalog contains a listing of those books which
were added to the collections of the Extension Division during the

month of May 1963. The Extension Division of the Free Library includes all branches, bookmobiles and deposit libraries. This catalog is not an index to the research materials in the special collections of the Central Library.

All books listed have been purchased for at least one agency of the Free Library's Extension Division. In some instances a copy or copies of a title will be found in every agency of the Extension Division; in other cases a copy of a title may be available in only one branch library. All titles listed, but not necessarily the identical editions, are also available in the Central Library.

Location of copies. To learn whether or not a given agency owns a specific title, refer to the card catalog of that agency. To learn which agencies in a given section of the city own a book, consult your Librarian.

Arrangement. This catalog is in two parts. Books added to the adult and young adult collections compose one part; books added to the children's collections make up the second part. Books are listed here under author and, when appropriate, under subject, title, editor and translator.

Works of fiction, except those in the children's catalog, are not listed under subject. A book is listed under title when there is no author or when the title is distinctive. For example, a book with the title Stranger in the House would be listed under title as well as under author; but a book whose title is Poems would not be listed under title in this catalog.

All authors, subjects, titles, etc. are arranged in a single alphabet. If there are several books on the same subject, these are arranged alphabetically by author under the subject. If there are several books by the same author, these are arranged alphabetically by title under the author's name.

Future Issues. It is expected that, in the future, monthly cumulative lists of adult and young adult books newly added to the collections will be published, as will also bi-monthly cumulative lists of additions to the children's collections. A new edition will be published annually.

Appendix C

Selected List of Recent and Announced Book Catalogs

American Numismatic Society. Dictionary and Auction Catalogues of the Library of the American Numismatic Society.

Bangor. Public Library. Bibliography of the State of Maine.

Boston. University. Catalog of African Government Documents and African Area Index.

California. University, Berkeley. Library. Author-Title Catalog.

California. University, Los Angeles. Library. Author-Title-Subject Catalog.

Columbia University. Catalog of the Avery Memorial Architectural Library.

---- Dictionary Catalog of the Library of the School of Library Service.

Columbia River Regional Library. Catalog.

Harvard University. Author and Subject Catalogues of the Library of the Peabody Museum of Archaeology and Ethnology.

---- Catalogue of the Lamont Library.

Hawaii. University. Dictionary Catalog of the Hawaiian Collection.

Hebrew Union College-Jewish Institute of Religion. Klau Library. Dictionary Catalog of the Cincinnati Library.

Hispanic Society of America. Catalogue of the Library.

Howard University. Catalogue of the African Collection in the Moorland Foundation.

IBM. Advanced Systems and Research Library. Catalog.

Insurance Society of New York. Life Insurance Catalog.

King County Public Library. Catalog.

Lake County Public Library. Catalog.

Library of Congress. See pages 13-18 of this volume.

London. University. Catalogue of the School of Oriental and African Studies.

---- Library Catalog of the Warburg Institute.

Long Island Lighting Co., Hicksville, Long Island. Catalog.

Los Angeles County Public Library. Fiction Subject Catalog (Adult).

---- Foreign Language Catalog (Adult).

---- Nonfiction Subject Catalog (Adult).

---- Title Catalog (Adult).

---- Children's Catalog.

Massachusetts Horticultural Society. Dictionary Catalog of the Library.

Metropolitan Museum of Art. Dictionary Catalog of the Library.

Monsanto Chemical Co. Library. Union Catalog.

National Academy of Sciences. Medical Sciences Division. Cardiovascular Literature Project.

National Library of Medicine. Catalog.

National Reactor Testing Station. Catalog.

National Union Catalog.

New York Public Library. Dictionary Catalog of the History of the Americas Collection.

---- Dictionary Catalog of the Jewish Collection.

---- Dictionary Catalog of the Oriental Collection.

---- Dictionary Catalog of the Schomburg Collection of Negro Literature and History.

---- Dictionary Catalog of the Slavonic Collection.

---- Subject Catalog of the World War I Collection.

New York (State). Library. Checklist of Books and Pamphlets in the Social Sciences.

Newberry Library. Dictionary Catalog of the Edward E. Ayer Collection of Americana and American Indians.

---- Dictionary Catalogue of the History of Printing from the John M. Wing Foundation.

Northwestern University. Catalog of the African Collection.

Pennsylvania. University. Catalog of the E. F. Smith Memorial Collection in the History of Chemistry.

Philadelphia. Free Library. Catalog of the Carson Law Collection.

Rochester. University. Engineering Library Catalog.

U.S. Department of Agriculture. Botany Subject Index.

Yale University. Dictionary Catalogue of the Yale Forestry Library.

---- Catalog of the Yale Collection of Western Americana.

Index

Bishop, William Warner, 13.

Bonk, Wallace J., 135-136, 143.

Book catalogs. Advantages and disadvantages, iv-v, 40-41, 43-44, 56-59, 149-151, 283-284. Functions, 213-220. Libraries using, 164-165. List of recent and announced book catalogs, 315-317. Multiple copies of, 78. Origins and relations to card catalogs, 1-29, 50, 55-68, 69-79. Standards, 45-51, 129-143. Twentieth century, 13-29. Union book catalogs, 49-50, 63-64, 279-303. Use, 1-12, 213-220.

Boston Athenaeum, iii.

Bowers, Fredson, 134-135, 143. Quoted, 134.

Bowker, R.R. Co., 108, 121.

Branscomb, Harvie, 13.

British Museum catalogs, 3, 50, 135-136, 167-178, 275.

Brodman, Estelle, 235.

Brown, Margaret C. "Book Catalogs and the Free Library of Philadelphia," 307-310. "Is the Card Catalog Obsolete?" 80-87.

Bruno, Elizabeth, 279-302.

California. State Library. Union Catalog Workshop, 279-305.

California. University. Libraries. Printed catalogs, 85, 88-91. Use of L.C. Subject Catalog, 63-64.

Cameras. See Compos-O-Line; Econolist; Foto-List; Listomatic camera; Sequential cameras.

Card catalogs. Advantages, 80-81. And book catalogs, iv, 69-79. Importance of, 38. Migration to book, 93-99. Numerical, 75-76. Origin and problems, 1-29.

Cardiovascular Literature Project, 9, 32, 35, 154-155.

Cards. Die form cutter, 34. Locating information on, 95. Re-designing unit cards, 97. Stock and dimensions, 93-95.

Carter, Mary D., 135-136, 143.

Casey, R.A., 163.

Catalog code revision, effects of, 249-251.

Cataloging-in-source experiment, 75.

Catalogs. In state of flux, 95-96. See also Author arrangement in book catalogs; Book catalogs; Card catalogs; Dictionary catalogs; Divided catalogs. Subject arrangement in book catalogs; and

Dubester, H.J., 163.

Eastman Kodak Co., 110.

Econolist, 285-302.

Egger, Eugen, 275.

Electrical line finder, 33.

Fichero Bibliográfico Hispanoamericano, 94.

Filing, 265-266. Rules, 97-98, 146.

Fischer Continuous Processor, 232.

Flexowriter, 7, 152-156.

Form of name, latest, 251.

Foto-List, 110-111a, 116, 226-227.

Francis, F.C., 276. "Meeting the Challenge; The British Museum Reprints Its Catalogue," 167-178.

Fruton, Joseph, 5, 12.
Ganning, Cleet, 289-290.

Gesamtkatalog, 3.

Gosnell, Charles, 21-23.

GRACE (Graphic Arts Composing Equipment), 240-243.

Graphic Arts Composing Equipment. See GRACE.

Griffin, Hillis L., 28, 166.

Griffin, Marjorie, 10, 276. "Printed Book Catalogs," 149-166.

Guiding catalogs, 96.

Gull, C.D., 36, 68, 121-122, 276.

Hall, G.K. & Co., 31-32, 43, 102. "A New Shaw List," 116-117, 121.

Hamilton, William B., 5, 12.

Handbook of Medical Library Practice, 235.

Hannigan, Jean, v.

Harmon, Marian, 137, 143. Quoted, 137-138.

Harrer, G.A., 75.

Harvard College. Library. See Harvard University. Libraries.

Harvard University. Libraries, iii. Cooperation in card catalogs, 39, 49. Kilgour Collection of Russian Belles Lettres, 67. Lamont Library, 8. Lamont Library Catalog, 8, 20, 35, 114-115

Hayden, Horace E., 53.

Heinritz, Fred, 272, 276.

Hellum, Bertha, 284-285.

Lake County Public Library, Munster, Ind., 10.

Lamont Library. See Harvard University Libraries.

Larkey, Sanford, 234-235.

Leading, 94.

Lebow, Irving, 121.

Leigh, Carma, 282-284.

Libraries using printed book catalogs (address list), 164-165.

Library Binding Institute, "Minimum Specifications for Class A Library Bindings," 141.

Library of Congress, 37. Cards, 14, 124. Cataloging, use of, 74-75. Catalogs, card and book, iv, 67. Classification numbers, 263. Cyrillic Union Catalog, 46, 138. Depository Catalog, 13-14, 56. Filing Rules for the Dictionary Catalogs of the Library of Congress, 141. National Union Catalog, See National Union Catalog. Printed Catalogs, 1, 8, 12-15, 42, 60-61, 63-64, 101-104, 116, 121-122, 124, 137, 176-177. Public Catalog, 131. Rules for Descriptive Cataloging in the Library of Congress, 140. Subject Headings Used in the Dictionary Catalogs of the Library of Congress, 142.

Listomatic camera, 9, 32-34, 111-111a, 119-122, 134, 154-155, 226-228, 232.

London University. School of Oriental and African Studies, 47.

Long Island Lighting Co., Hicksville, Long Island, New York. Catalog, 9, 156, 158, 261.

Los Angeles County Public Library, 182. General discussion of the whole catalog, 8, 24-27, 29, 35, 57, 85, 125, 153. Costs, equipment and supplies, 208-210. Functions and use, 213-220. Physical format, 51. Procedures, 179-212. General discussion of the Adult Catalog, 186-187, 198, 200-201, 218-220. Fiction Subject Catalog (Adult), 203-204, 217. Foreign Language Catalog (Adult), 204, 217. Nonfiction Subject Catalog (Adult), 202-203. Title Catalog (Adult), 202. General discussion of the Children's Catalog, 112, 185-186, 197, 200-201, 215-216.

Louisiana State Union Catalog, 57, 139.

Lubetzky, Seymour, 163, 257.

Luckett, G.R., 164, 166.

al for a," 75.

National Institute of Health, 32.

National Library of Medicine, 221-235. Catalog, 9, 17, 253. MEDLARS story, 236-243. Recataloging at, 244-257.

National Reactor Testing Station, Phillips Petroleum Co., 10, 27-30, 35, 155.

National Union Catalog, 124, 127, 130, 133, 140-142, 273.

New Serial Titles, 8-9, 17-18, 55, 125, 137.

New York Public Library, 274. Arents Tobacco Collection Catalog, 124. Cooperation in card catalogs, 39, 49. French Revolutionary Pamphlet Collection, 44. List of Subject Headings, 31, 35. Oriental Catalog, 46, 47. Slavonic Catalog, 35, 46, 67, 102, 105-106. Talleyrand Collection, 42.

New York State Library. Checklist of Books and Pamphlets in the Social Sciences, 20-24, 35, 57, 112, 120, 154-155.

Norris, Dorothy, 2, 272. On origin of card catalog, 2.

"Number System for Current Publications, A Proposal for a National Code," 75.

Numerical card catalogs, 75-76.

Oathout, Mel, 285-286, 324-325.

O'Connor, Mildred C., 53.

Originals, limitations of, in reproduction, 95.

Osborn, A.D., 276. "Crisis in Cataloging," 42.

Ozalid copies, 231.

Paklon (Adhesive tape), 233.

Paper tape, 151-152.

Patrinostro, Frank, 293-294, 320-321, 324.

Peabody Institute, iii.

Pennsylvania Regional Library Resource Centers, 82.

Pennsylvania State Library Code, 81, 87.

Pennsylvania. University. Library, iii.

Pettee, Julia, 272.

Philadelphia. Free Library. Projected book catalog, 307-313.

Philadelphia Union Library Catalogue of the Metropolitan Area, 83-84.

Philip, A.J., 277.

Phillips Petroleum Co. See National Reactor Testing Station.

Photographic reproduction, 85. Equipment, 225. See also
Cameras; and entries under Reproductions.

Photo-offset, 11, 100. And British Museum Catalog, 173-176.

Pierrot, R., 277.

Piternick, George, 45, 53. "Shelf List as Union Catalog," 88-91.
"Techniques of the Modern Printed Catalog and Its Supplements,"
123-128.

Pitney Bowes Tickometer, 111.

Plant Science Catalog; Botany Subject Index, 124.

Pollard, A.W., 49.

Princeton University Library, iii, 2, 21. Alphabetical Finding
List, 61. Card and book catalogs, 67.

Production methods, book catalogs, 8-36, 100-122, 149-212, 258-
269.

Publications. "A Proposal for a National Code Number System for
Current Publications," 75.

Publishers, cooperation of, 77.

Punched cards, 11, 37, 196-201, 258-269. Printout equipment,
125. See also entries beginning with IBM.

Rafikov, A. Kh., 277.

Ranz, James, 272, 277.

Recataloging, 244-257. And book catalogs, 254-255.

Redgrave, G.R., 49.

Reilly, Alice, 290, 324.

Remington Rand Division of Sperry Rand Corp. Flexoprint, 109.
Synchrotape, 162.

Reproductions. Equipment, 11, 100, 231. Of cards, by whole
cards, 100, 101-106. Of cards, by parts of cards, 100, 106-
112. Originals, limitations of originals for, 95.

Research, needed, 271-274.

Richardson, E.C., 21, 42, 132, 143. Quoted, 133.

Richmond, Phyllis A. "A Short Title Catalog made with IBM Tabulating Equipment," 258-269.

Rider, Fremont, 277.

Rochester. University. Engineering Library. Catalog, 258-269.

Rogers, Frank B., 234, 277.

Ruffin, Beverley, 272.

Ruggles, Melville J., 54.

Sage, Robert, 296-318.

Salen, Rose, 305.

Schley, Ruth, 272.

Schwegmann, George A., Jr., 35, 277.

Science Press, Inc., 34.

Sears, Minnie E., 42.

Seaton, J.R., 164.

Sequential cameras, 111a, 119-120, 122. See also Compos-O-Line;
Foto-List; Listomatic camera.

Shaw, Charles B. A List of Books for College Libraries, 113-114.
"Shaw List, A New," 100-122.

Shaw, John, 292, 320, 323-324.

Shelf list, 76, 88-91. And master cards, 262.

Shera, Jesse H. "The Book Catalog and the Scholar," 1-12.

Shingling of cards, 118-119, 125.

Shoemaker, Richard, 45, 53. "Some American Twentieth Century
Book Catalogs: Their Purposes, Format and Production Techniques," 13-36; cited, 122, 123, 129, 166.

Singer, T.E.R., 164.

Slocum, Robert, 138, 143.

Snell, Edgar W., Jr., v.

Sorting of cards, 265-266.

Southern Illinois University. Library, 10.

Spence, A.N., 121.

Spitzer, E.F., 277.

Squibb Institute for Medical Research, 10.

Standard Registry Co., 33.

Standards. General, 144-145. Bibliographical, 129-143, 146-147.
Cataloging, 129-143. Physical, 147-148.

Stanford University. Card Catalog, 48.

Stevens, Robert D., 53. On location of printed catalogs in Library
of Congress, 60-61. "Bibliographic and Cataloging Standards for
Book Catalogs," 129-143.

Strout, Ruth, 272.

Subject arrangement of printed catalogs, 90.

Subject headings, Los Angeles County Public Library catalogs, 192-194.

Supplements, 48, 97, 126-128.

Surgeon-General's Library Catalog. See Index-Catalogue of the Library of the Surgeon-General's Office.

Synchrotape (Remington Rand), 162.

Tabulators (IBM), 196-201, 258-269.

Taine, Seymour. "The National Library of Medicine Index Mechanization Project," 221-235.

Tapes. Paklon adhesive, 233. Paper, 151-152. Synchrotape (Remington Rand), 162.

Tauber, Maurice F., 277. "Research problems in Book Catalogs," 271-274.

Taubes, Ernest, 111a.

Taylor, Archer, 277.

Teague, S.J., 277.

Technical Journals at the National Reactor Testing Station, 28.

Teel, Eric, 289, 325.

Thayer, John, 305.

Tickometer (Pitney Bowes), 111.

Transliteration, 97-98, 141, 146.

Twentieth century book catalogs, 13-29.

Type size, 94.

Tysse, Agnes, 54. "Card Catalogs versus Printed Book Catalogs and the Catalog Users," 55-68. Relations among book and card catalogs, 52.

Union catalogs, 279-326. Shelf lists as, 88-91. See also names of specific union catalogs.

Union List of Serials, 17, 49, 83.

U.S. Atomic Energy Commission, 27.

U.S. Department of Agriculture, 124.

U.S. Library of Congress. See Library of Congress.

U.S. National Library of Medicine. See National Library of Medicine.

U.S. Naval Postgraduate School, Monterey, Cal., 153.